THE COLORADO NO-TRAP TOURIST GUIDE

How to Leave the Beaten Path and See the REAL COLORADO. Discover Hundreds of New and Interesting Adventures, and Most at Little or No Cost. This Book Tells it ALL!

Tamara Faye Hedley Kunz

V.H. Hedley Publishing Co.
P.O. Box 291270
Davie, Florida 33329

First printing 1987

Library of Congress Cataloging-in-Publication Data

Kunz, Tamara Faye Hedley, 1963-
The Colorado no-trap tourist guide.

"Discover hundreds of new and interesting adventures, and most at little or no cost. This book tells it all!"—
Includes index.
1. Colorado — Description and travel — 1981-
Guide-books. I. Title.
F774.3.K86 1987 917.88'0433 87-8373
ISBN O-942125-00-2

$12.95

THE ROAD NOT TAKEN

Two roads diverged in a yellow wood,
And sorry I could not travel both
And be one traveler, long I stood
And looked down one as far as I could
To where it bent in the undergrowth;

Then took the other, as just as fair,
And having perhaps the better claim,
Because it was grassy and wanted wear;
Though as for that the passing there
Had worn them really about the same,

And both that morning equally lay
In leaves no step had trodden black.
Oh, I kept the first for another day!
Yet knowing how why leads on to way,
I doubted if I should ever come back.

I shall be telling this with a sigh
Somewhere ages and ages hence:
Two roads diverged in a wood, and I—
I took the one less traveled by,
And that has made all the difference.

by ROBERT FROST

GENERAL INFORMATION

1. Letter from Editor 1
2. How to Use This Book 2
3. Bed & Breakfast Inns 3
4. Rockhounding 4
5. Ghost Towns & Souvenirs 6
6. National Forests & Parks 9
7. Camping & Skiing 14
8. Hunting & Fishing 15
9. Colorfest 16

AREA ONE

1. Aspen 19
2. Carbondale 21
3. Craig 22
4. Dinosaur 25
5. Eagle 26
6. Fruita 28
7. Glenwood Springs 29
8. Grand Junction 30
9. Grand Mesa National Forest 33
10. Maybell 34
11. Meeker 35
12. Palisade 37
13. Rifle 38
14. Steamboat Springs 40
15. White River National Forest 41

AREA TWO

1. Alma 43
2. Arapahoe National Forest 44
3. Avon 45
4. Boulder 45
5. Breckenridge 48
6. Central City 49
7. Como 50
8. Copper Mountain 52
9. Denver 53
10. Dillon 56
11. Erie 58
12. Estes Park 59
13. Evergreen 63
14. Fairplay 65
15. Fort Collins 68
16. Frisco 70
17. Golden 71
18. Granby/Grand Lake 74
19. Keystone 77
20. Leadville 79
21. Loveland 81
22. Minturn 83
23. Parshall 84
24. Pike National Forest 86
25. Rocky Mountain National Park 86
26. Roosevelt National Forest 87
27. Routt National Forest 88
28. Silverthorne 90
29. Twin Lakes 92
30. Vail 92
31. Wellington 96
32. Winter Park 97

AREA THREE

1. Cedaredge 99
2. Cortez 100
3. Creede 103
4. Crested Butte 107
5. Delta 108
6. Dolores 110
7. Dove Creek 112
8. Durango 113
9. Gunnison 120
10. Gunnison National Forest 123

11. Lake City 124
12. Mesa Verde National Park 127
13. Montrose 128
14. Ouray 130
15. Pagosa Springs 135
16. Rico 137
17. Ridgway 138
18. San Juan National Forest 140
19. Silverton 141
20. Spar City 144
21. Telluride 145
22. Uncompahgre National Forest 148

AREA FOUR

1. Alamosa 149
2. Antonito 151
3. Buena Vista 152
4. Canon City 154
5. Coaldale 157
6. Colorado Springs 157
7. Cripple Creek 160
8. Cuchara 161
9. Del Norte 162
10. Garfield 164
11. Green Mountain Falls 164
12. La Veta 166
13. Manassa 169
14. Manitou Springs 169
15. Monte Vista 170
16. Nathrop 172
17. Pitkin 174
18. Poncha Springs 175
19. Rio Grande National Forest 176
20. Salida 177
21. San Isabel National Forest 180
22. Silver Cliff 181
23. South Fork 183
24. Victor 184
25. Walsenburg 186
26. Westcliffe 187
27. Weston 189
28. Woodland Park 190

AREA FIVE

1. Akron 194
2. Arriba 194
3. Burlington 196
4. Cheyenne Wells 197
5. Deer Trail 198
6. Fort Morgan 200
7. Greeley 200
8. Julesburg 202
9. Kit Carson 205
10. La Junta 207
11. Pueblo 208
12. Rocky Ford 210
13. Trinidad 211
14. Wiley 213
15. Wray 214

GENERAL INFORMATION

This book is meant to help you in having more fun, and spend less having it, in Colorado. The state has so much to offer those who wish to save money and take part in activities that will be educational, interesting, and fun for the whole family. There are hundreds of bed and breakfast inns where you can be treated as family friends, thousands of places to explore the beauty and bounty of nature, and a million opportunities to learn something new and expand your horizons.

After personal experience, however, our family found that there was only one way to find out about these places. Ask! Everyone knows something about his or her home town that is not advertised in any way but would be fun for a tourist to do. We would gladly tell a vacationer about these things, but they never ask. We decided to do something about it. And, without further ado ladies and gentlemen, I give you the real Colorado.

P.S. Have Fun!

HOW TO USE THIS BOOK—It is very important that you take the time to familiarize yourself with the way this book is set up.

First, we have divided the state of Colorado into 5 sections, with number 5 being the whole eastern third of the state. This is done so that you will not have to search through the whole book to find the town you are interested in. If you are only traveling in one section of the state, you may want to read all about that one part. By putting all those towns together, you have much less flipping around to do and you save time also.

To find the town you want to read about, find out which section (one through five) it is in. Then look it up in that section alphabetically. The sections are indicated at the top of every page.

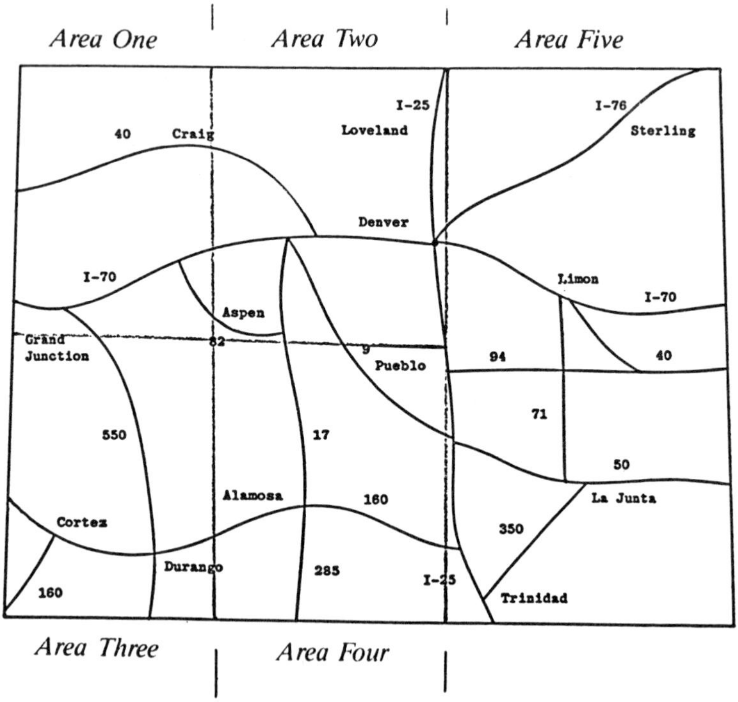

The information under each town contains a small introduction, things to see and do, and where to eat and sleep. Some towns may not have all of these, but by looking up nearby cities you can locate a restaurant or motel that is close by. National forests are listed like towns because they usually have their share of activities and attractions. Also, the forests do spread over more than one section, therefore each is given in the section where most of it lies.

Things to see and do. This part contains any local festivals and their approximate dates (the dates change year to year) and it is advised that you contact the Chamber of Commerce or pick up a local paper to find the exact dates. This segment also includes local activities that are enjoyed such as rafting or fishing. We have tried to give recommendations as to where these things may be done and who to contact if you need to rent equipment. Some scenic drives and places to explore (like forests or ghost towns) are also given in this part and a map will show you the route to take.

Where to eat and sleep. This section gives a short listing of restaurants which have unusual menus and low prices. Sometimes, a place is just too unique not to include, even if its prices are not budget. Motels, hotels, inns and campgrounds are included under where to sleep. We have tried to find the places that give the most service for the least money and believe we have been successful in this.

There are, of course, many more places to eat and sleep in most of these towns. What we have done here is given you a few alternatives to the expensive, chain establishments. Their prices are mostly budget, but do not rely on the rates quoted. Rates and prices do change and we have only given you the most recent we could find (as of December, 1986). If any of these have increased, it should not be dramatically.

Whatever you decide to do in each town, we know that you will save money and have more fun than you would have without this book. Remember, just have fun and enjoy the beauty of Colorado.

Bed and breakfast inns, campground and hostels are becoming more and more popular in America. There are many reasons for this but the main one has to be that they cost much less money than a big name or resort hotel. So much less in fact, that a family can afford to double their vacation with the money they save. The average bed and breakfast inn costs around $35.00 per room, and youth hostels cost about $10.00 per person and even less for members. Campgrounds are even less, averaging about $7.00 a night.

They also provide a family atmosphere that is becoming increasingly important to travelers who do not wish to be shut away from the community in which they are staying. They wish to learn about their chosen vacation spot and the best way to accomplish this is to associate with the local inhabitants. And what they find out is that there is a multitude of activities to be enjoyed. They also learn that these pastimes may be enjoyed for little or no money and are more rewarding and fun than going to a tourist trap which takes cash and returns very little in the way of entertainment.

By staying in a bed and breakfast inn, campground or hostel, the family has the opportunity to save money, learn about a region first hand and have more fun, all of which will lead to lasting memories. It is these fond thoughts of past experiences that truly show the worth of a vacation.

This book will provide you with a list of the bed and breakfast inns, campground, hostels and money saving motels around each town given. Keep in mind that some towns are small and may not have responded to our survey. Therefore, if there are no lodgings listed for a certain village you should look up other nearby towns to find accommodations. For a complete list of bed and breakfast inns and American Youth Hostels for the state of Colorado, please write to the following:

American Youth Hostels - Rocky Mountain Council
P.O. Box 2370
Boulder, CO 80306
(303) 442-1166

Bed and Breakfast Colorado
P.O. Box 20
Denver, CO 80220
(Enclose $2.00)
(303) 333-3340

An easy, free way to collect souvenirs is to find them, and what is a better souvenir of Colorado than a sample of one of the gems or metals which led to its development in the first place. It is called rockhounding and can provide hours of fun for the whole family. Both the plains and the mountains can yield a variety of gemstones, precious metals, petrified wood, antiques left by early settlers and more. Panning for gold is an interesting pastime which can be fun for everyone, even though you will probably not get rich from it. Most sporting goods stores and gift shops sell the pans complete with instructions and tools for around $6.00. There are also books on identifying the different specimens you find. A cheap investment for hours of fun, and we do mean hours because once the fever strikes, you won't want to quit. For additional information on the riches of Colorado, write the Colorado Division of Mines, 1313 Sherman St., Denver. CO 80203.

GOLD FEVER!

Ore Samples—an easy way to get some precious metal for free. Watch for mining roads where the ore trucks bounce a lot. *(see Silverton).* They are so full of ore that many of the rocks "jump" off. Walk along these roads (especially at corners) and look carefully for granite-like rocks which are usually white and gray. If the sun is shining, the metals in the rocks will sparkle. Important: Do not get so involved that you forget about the trucks which hurtle past at great speed. To test for deposits of pure gold, hold the sample next to some gold jewelry. If it is not the color of the jewelry, it is a combination of precious metals known as fool's gold. You can also find samples in ore bins next to abandoned mines. Another good place to look for these souvenirs is in the ravines below deserted mining operations; see the section on ghost towns for guidelines on how to do this.

Note: It is illegal to dig for and remove any native artifacts such as arrowheads from the state of Colorado on any lands other than private and then only with the owner's permission. Unauthorized persons who do so on public land are subject to fines and imprisonment.

Assay cups, core sample, narrow guage railroad spike and ore samples. All can be found near old mining operations.

Nothing is more eerie than trying to peer into the inside of an ancient, run-down building through an empty or broken window frame. And yet, almost nothing is more exciting. Ghost towns are as common as ants at a picnic in Colorado and offer more than just a shot of Adrenalin; they offer an education of our past.

An abandoned building shows much about the way we lived a hundred years ago. The architecture, furnishings (if any are left), tools, and more all tell us about the past as if we were actually there.

The gold rush brought settlers and dreamers from all over the world, hoping for a better life, and certainly a richer one, among the aspen and pine. They built many things which are no longer used but still remain to tell of their presence. Old towns where they lived, deserted mines where they worked, and unused and overgrown railways which they traveled are all still around for us to examine and explore. The old railroad beds often make a convenient road for hikers and backpackers. The old towns and mines are interesting places to search for souvenirs.

By souvenirs, we do not mean tear down or destroy the place in your search. Besides, it is often very dangerous to enter old mines because loose rocks, timbers, and toxic gases are often present. Many of the mines were little more than shafts several hundred feet deep. Many are covered with rotten timber, so never step on old planks unless you know exactly what is under them. What we suggest is to look around the grounds for discards from that past time. Old railroad spikes (sometimes selling for $5.00 in gift shops), miners tools like testing bowls or assay cups, ore samples rich in metals, old bottles, they all make interesting conversation pieces and are

"Keep Out" signs in Colorado are few and far between, but some territorial marmots go to extremes.

easily found.

One place miners were fond of discarding their useless items was in any nearby ravine. What was out of sight was out of mind and soon forgotten, but not by today's relic hunters. If you decide to try this mode of collecting souvenirs, be very careful on the way down because you could slip and injure yourself, wear long pants, sneakers or other tough shoes, bring water and a container for your finds, and go slowly. Watch out for animals, you are trespassing on their land. Remember how you descend so

Abandoned silver mines like this one are scattered throughout the state and are fun to explore.

that you can get back up to that spot. If you are careful, this should be a marvelous adventure. The best spot to choose for this is a small valley, gully or gulch below an old mine. Remember, the most important thing is to have fun; and who knows, you may find something valuable. In this book, we try to give a ghost town or abandoned mine for every town but you can ask any local residents or the Chamber of Commerce for others.

Your National Forests and Parks are a heritage for you, your children, and their children's children to enjoy. It is important to preserve these wild places because, as President Lyndon Johnson said, "If future generations are to remember us more with gratitude than with sorrow, we must achieve more than just the miracles of technology. We must also

The author takes a much needed break on the arduous Ice Lake Trail. Notice the Columbines, Colorado's state flower.

leave them a glimpse of the world as it was created, not just as it looked when we got through with it."

It is therefore important for you to experience what the world was like before man came along. *In Colorado there are over 14 million acres of National Forest,* making it an excellent place to enjoy the wilderness. Just a walk along one of the many trails will reveal a separate world of never before seen flowers, wild animals, and awesome vistas featuring mountains, streams and waterfalls.

The Forests are also full of campgrounds. Some of these are more modern than others, but they all afford an unforgettable experience. The best part about them is that they are very cheap as accommodations. In fact, if you set up camp in the Overflow Campgrounds, you can stay for *free.* You will have to take a walk to get to any facilities such as bathrooms and running water, but it is usually not more than a quarter mile and besides, walking is good for you. If you cannot find a space in either the regular or overflow grounds, you can always pack your tent into the woods for a night in the backcountry. If you don't have backpacks, you need only take the bare minimums or you could always go back for a second trip. Remember to follow all camping guidelines in regards to human waste and trash. Here is a list of all the Forest Service camgrounds in the state of Colorado, their Ranger District, name, number of units, and daily fee.

FOREST Ranger District Office Location	Campground Site Name	No. of Units	Daily Fee
ARAPAHO NATIONAL FOREST			
Clear Creek Idaho Springs	Cold Springs	47	$6.00
	Columbine	47	6.00
	Echo Lake	16	6.00
	Mizpah	10	6.00
	W. Chicago Creek	11	6.00
	Pickle Gulch	20	Group [1]
Sulphur Granby	Arapaho Bay	77	6.00
	Byers Creek	6	6.00
	Denver Creek	22	6.00
	Green Creek	83	Conc[2]
	Idlewild	24	6.00
	Sawmill Gulch	5	6.00
	St. Louis Creek	18	6.00
	Stillwater	148	Conc[2]
	Willow Creek	35	6.00
Middle Park Kremmling	Horseshoe	7	5.00
	South Fork	21	5.00
	Sugar Loaf	10	5.00
Dillon Silverthorne	Blue River	20	4.00
	Heaton Bay	83	6.00
	McDonald Flats	44	4.00
	Peak One	79	6.00
	Pine Cove	50	5.00
	Prarie Point	44	4.00
	Prospector	108	5.00
GRAND MESA NATIONAL FOREST			
Collbran Grand Junction	Jumbo	26	5.00
	Spruce Grove	16	5.00
	Carp Lake	20	5.00
	Crag Crest	11	5.00
	Eggleston Lake	6	5.00
	Island Lake	41	5.00
	Kiser Creek	12	5.00
	Little Bear	36	5.00
	Valley View	8	5.00
	Ward Lake	27	5.00
GUNNISON NATIONAL FOREST			
Taylor River Gunnison	Almont	10	5.00
	Cement Creek	13	5.00
	Dinner Station	22	5.00
	Dorchester	10	5.00
	Lakeview	40	5.00
	Lodgepole	16	5.00
	Lotis Creek	23	5.00
	Mosca	15	5.00
	North Bank	23	5.00
	One Mile	26	5.00
	Rivers End	15	5.00
	Rosey Lane	20	5.00
	Spring Creek	11	5.00
Cebolla Gunnison	Cebolla	5	4.00
	Deer Lakes	12	4.00
	Pitkin	22	5.00
	Quartz	10	5.00
	Slumgullion	18	5.00
	Spruce	9	4.00
	Williams Creek	29	5.00
PIKE NATIONAL FOREST			
Pikes Peak Colorado Springs	Colorado	63	5.00
	Meadow Ridge	19	5.00
	Painted Rocks	15	5.00
	South Meadows	57	5.00
	Thunder Ridge	21	5.00
	Pike Community		Group [1]
	Red Rocks		Group [1]
South Park Fairplay	Aspen	12	5.00
	Blue Mouintain	21	5.00
	Cove	5	5.00
	Fourmile	14	5.00
	Happy Meadows	6	5.00
	Horseshoe	19	5.00
	Jefferson Creek	17	5.00
	Lodgepole	35	5.00
	Michigan Creek	13	5.00
	Riverside	19	5.00
	Round Mountain	16	5.00
	Spillway	24	5.00
	Springer Gulch	15	5.00
	Spruce Grove	28	5.00
South Platte Lakewood	Baldy	8	5.00
	Buffalo	41	5.00
	Burning Bear	13	5.00
	Deer Crfeek	13	5.00
	Devils Head	22	5.00
	Flat Rocks	20	5.00
	Geneva Park	26	5.00
	Green Mountain	6	5.00
	Indian Creek	10	5.00
	Kelsey	17	5.00
	Kenosha Pass	25	5.00
	Lone Rock	19	5.00
	Meridian	18	5.00
	Tramway	6	5.00
	Bailey		Group [1]
	Redskin		Group [1]

San Isabel National Forest

Leadville	Baby Doe	50	7.00
	Baby Doe Annex	26	6.00
	Belle of Colorado	19	6.00
	Elbert Creek	17	5.00
	Halfmoon	24	5.00
	Lakeview	59	5.00
	May Queen	34	6.00
	Molly Brown	49	7.00
	Parry Peak	26	5.00
	Silver Dollar	45	6.00
	Twin Peaks	37	5.00
	White Star	64	5.00
	Printerboy		Group[1]
Salida	Angel of Shavano	17	5.00
	Cascade	23	5.00
	Chalk Lake	21	5.00
	Collegiate Peaks	45	5.00
	Cottonwood Lake	28	5.00
	Garfield	11	5.00
	Monarch Park	38	5.00
	Mt. Princeton	17	5.00
	Ohaver Lake	24	5.00
San Carlos Cannon City	Alvarado	47	5.00
	Bear Lake	15	5.00
	Blue Lake	15	5.00
	Cuchara	25	5.00
	Davenport	15	5.00
	Lake Creek	11	5.00
	Lake Isabel Cisneros	25	5.00
	Lake Isabel St. Charles	8	5.00
	Ophir	15	5.00
	Oak Creek	31	Group[1]

SAN JUAN NATIONAL FOREST

Animas Durango	Haviland Lake	45	5.00
	Junction Creek	34	4.00
	Purgatory	14	4.00
	S. Mineral	23	4.00
	Chris Park	50	Group[1]
Dolores	Burro Bridge	15	5.00
	Cayton	30	5.00
	Forks	6	5.00
	Manreeso	14	5.00
	Mesa	80	7.00
	Priest Gulch	18	5.00
	West Dolores	13	5.00
	Mesa Park		Group[1]
Mancos	Kroeger	13	4.00
	Thompson Park	51	4.00
Pagosa Pagosa Springs	Blanco River	18	4.00
	Bridge	19	4.00
	Cimarrona	21	4.00
	East Fork	26	4.00
	Teal	15	5.00
	West Fork	28	4.00
	Williams Creek	69	4.00
	Wolf Creek	26	4.00
Pine Bayfield	Florida	20	5.00
	Graham Creek	26	6.00
	Middle Mtn.	24	6.00
	Miller Creek	15	5.00
	North Canyon	22	5.00
	Old Timers	11	6.00
	Pine Point	30	6.00
	Transfer Park	25	5.00
	Vallecito	88	6.00

UNCOMPAHGRE NATIONAL FOREST

Norwood	Matterhorn	25	5.00
	Sunshine	15	5.00
Ouray Montrose	Beaver Lake	11	4.00
	Silver Jake	60	4.00
	Ampitheatre	3347	Conc[2]

WHITE RIVER NATIONAL FOREST

Aspen	Difficult	47	6.00
	Maroon Lake	44	8.00
	Silver Bar	4	6.00
	Silver Bell	4	6.00
	Silver Queen	6	6.00
Blanco Meeker	East Marvine	7	5.00
	Marvine	8	5.00
	North Fork	22	5.00
	South Fork	25	5.00
	Trappers Lake Bucks	10	5.00
	Trappers Lake Cutthroat	14	5.00
	Trappers Lake Shepperd Rim	20	5.00
	Trappers lake Trapline	13	5.00
	North Fork	47	Group[1]
Eagle	Fulford Cave	6	5.00
	Sweetwater Lake	9	Conc[2]
	Yeoman Park	24	5.00

Holy Cross Minturn	Blodgett	6	5.00
	Camp Hale	21	5.00
	Gold Park	14	5.00
	Gore Creek	17	6.00
	Hornsilver	12	5.00
	Tigiwon Community House		Group[1]
Rifle	Meadow Lake	10	5.00
Sports Carbondale	Avalanche	10	5.00
	Bogan Flats	37	6.00
	Chapman	42	5.00
	Dearhamer	13	5.00
	Janeway	9	5.00
	Little Mattie	20	5.00
	Little Maud	22	7.00
	McClure	19	5.00
	Mollie B	26	7.00
	Redstone	24	5.00
	Chapman		Group[1]
	Quarry		Group[1]

RIO GRANDE NATIONAL FOREST

Alamosa La Jara	Lake Fork	19	6.00
	Mix Lake	22	6.00
Conejos La Jara	Aspen Glade	34	6.00
	Conejos	16	6.00
	Elk Creek	45	6.00
	Mogote	20	6.00
	Spectacle Lake	24	6.00
	Trujillo Meadows	25	6.00
	Mogote Group		Group[1]
Creede	Marshall Park	15	6.00
	N. Clear Creek	23	6.00
	Palisade	13	6.00
	River Hill	20	6.00
	S. Clear Creek	6	6.00
	S. Clear Creek Falls	11	6.00
	Thirty Mile	35	6.00
Del Norte	Beaver Creek	20	6.00
	Big Meadows	50	6.00
	Cross Creek	12	6.00
	Park Creek	16	6.00
	Tucker Ponds	17	6.00
	Upper Beaver	15	6.00
Saguache	M. Crestone Creek	13	6.00

ROOSEVELT NATIONAL FOREST

Boulder	Camp Dick	34	6.00
	Kelly Dahl	48	6.00
	Olive Ridge	56	6.00
	Pawnee	55	6.00
	Peaceful Valley	15	6.00
Estes Poudre Ft. Collins	Ansel Watrous	19	6.00
	Big Bend	9	6.00
	Kelly Flats	23	Conc[2]
	Mountain Park	45	Conc[2]
	Sleeping Elephant	15	6.00
Pawnee Greeley	Crow Valley	5	6.00
Redfeather Ft. Collins	Aspen Glen	8	6.00
	Bellaire Lake	13	Conc[2]
	Chambers Lake	57	6.00
	Dowdly Lake So.	31	Conc[2]
	Dowdy Lake W.	24	Conc[2]
	Tunnel	49	6.00
	West Lake	29	Conc[2]

ROUTT NATIONAL FOREST

Bear Ears Craig	Freemen	17	4.00
Hahns Peak Steamboat Springs	Dumont Lake	12	6.00
	Hahns Peak Lake	26	6.00
	Hinman	13	5.00
	Meadows	33	6.00
	Seed House	25	5.00
	Summit Lake	17	4.00
	Walton Creek	14	6.00
North Park Walden	Aspen	7	4.00
	Big Creek lake	37	6.00
	Grizzly Creek	12	4.00
	Hidden Lakes	9	5.00
	Pines	10	5.00
Yampa	Blacktail Creek	8	5.00
	Cold Springs	5	6.00
	Gore Pass	12	5.00
	Horseshoe	7	6.00
	Lynx Pass	11	5.00
	Stillwater	29	6.00
	Toponas Creek	8	5.00

The great outdoors, our last bastion of freedom and wilderness. Picture yourself lying serenely beside a mountain stream as it burbles by quietly. You look up at the birds flitting back and forth among the evergreens, singing to their hearts content. You gaze into the water to admire the minnows swiftly darting between the reeds and what do you see? A beer can lying crushed on its side. Not a perfect picture, is it?

As you go into the natural world, a great responsibility falls upon your shoulders. It is to leave everything as true to nature as possible. Take all refuse back with you to civilization and dispose of it properly. Also, if you can, pick up after the ignorant, disrespecting slobs who went before you. You will be helping preserve something that your children will one day want to explore. Here are a few rules to follow if you venture into the wilderness, be it for a 20 minute hike or for a 3 day adventure.

1. Select a campsite away from lakes and streams. It should be away from any trail so that others may enjoy the solitude.

2. Use pack stoves when you can, especially in areas of heavy use. If you must build a fire, make it small and without rocks around it for they may be scarred. Remember to erase all signs of your fire when you leave.

3. Use biodegradable soap to wash yourself and your belongings. Make sure you wash at least 100 feet from any water source.

4. Bury human waste 6 inches below the surface at least 100 feet away from water so that it will not contaminate a water supply.

5. Pack out all trash you bring in and, if possible, any other trash you find along the way.

6. If you must take your pet with you, make sure it is on a leash. Domestic animals are not a part of the wilderness and they may disrupt the lives of forest animals. Better yet, leave your pet at home.

7. Always make sure someone knows of your plans, so they may watch for your safe return.

8. If you bring horses, stay on established trails, give hikers the right of way, and bring food for the horses as they should not be allowed to compete with the wild animals for food.

9. Remain quiet along the trail, especially if you are in a large group. This allows you and other hikers to enjoy the solitude and perhaps see a few of the inhabitants of the woods. Group size should be limited to less than 15.

There is also a code of responsibility for those who wish to take to the skis during their vacation. The Ski Safety Act of 1979 was approved and is enforced as Colorado state law.

1. Ski under control and in such a manner that you can stop or avoid other skiers or objects.

2. When skiing downhill or overtaking another skier, you must avoid the skier below you.

3. You must not stop where you obstruct a trail or are not visible from above.

4. When entering a trail or starting downhill, yield to other skiers.

5. All skiers will wear retention straps, ski brakes, or other devices to help prevent runaway skis.

6. All skiers shall keep off closed trails and posted areas, and observe all posted signs.

By following these guidelines, your vacation should be fun and safe, as well as memorable.

Hunting and fishing can be fun for the sportsman who follows state regulations, observes safety rules and has the proper licenses. Here are basic guidelines to big game hunting, small game hunting, and fishing in the state of Colorado. These are by no means complete and are only intended to give you an idea as to what will be required of you by the state. For a complete list of all requirements and the proper licenses, stop at any sporting goods store, hardware store, any authorized dealer or write the Division of Wildlife, 6060 Broadway, Denver, CO 80216.

Big Game Hunting—animals classified under big game are deer, elk, antelope, bears, mountain lions, bighorn sheep, and mountain goats. Licensing for some is limited to a certain number issued and must be applied for, while others are unlimited and may be obtained at any licensing agency.

Seasons vary on the different animals. Deer and elk seasons are held October to November. Bighorn sheep and mountain goat seasons open in August, antelope season in September. Black bear season is in the spring and during regular game season. Mountain lion seasons run concurrently with other big game seasons and in the winter months. There are special use seasons in which licenses are issued for hunting with archery equipment and muzzle-loading rifles. Hunters unfamiliar with Colorado's high mountains are advised to hire a guide or outfitter. Prices for licenses vary greatly between animal species and between resident and nonresident fees. For residents, they vary between $17.00 and $100.00. Nonresidents can expect to pay between $100.00 and $500.00.

Small Game Hunting—animals listed under this category include game birds like: turkeys, ring-necked pheasants, mourning doves, band-tailed pigeons, scaled quail, bobwhite quail, Gambel's quail, sage grouse, blue grouse, sharp-tailed grouse, and ptarmigan. Waterfowl are also listed under small game and include: ducks, geese, coots and a variety of shore birds. Small game animals include cotton-tail rabbits, snowshoe hares and squirrels. Animals classified as varmints are also under small game these include: coyotes, jack rabbits, prairie dogs and ground squirrels. Seasons are also held for trapping beavers, muskrats and weasels.

Pheasant and quail seasons are in November, waterfowl in October to mid-January, grouse in September, and small game seasons are usually held from September to February. Turkey seasons are in the spring and fall.

Again, prices vary for licenses to hunt small game. Resident $7.50 to $30.00. Nonresident $32.40 to $200.00.

Fishing—Colorado has over 2,000 lakes, natural and man-made, and more than 6,500 miles of stream and river. Almost any spot will get the angler some action and most old timers can give you a hint on local spots if they are so inclined. In these waters, it is possible to catch many kinds of trout, bass, walleye, fresh water salmon, bluegill, northern pike and numerous others. The state is best known for its trout, which naturally inhabit the streams and are also bred to stock the waterways and lakes. Special restrictions may apply to various waters, types of bait or lures permitted and breeds of fish. For a complete explanation of these restrictions, obtain a booklet on these matters from the Division of Wildlife or any sporting or hardware store. Anyone 15 years of age or older must have a valid Colorado fishing license. As with hunting, the price varies with resident, $2.00 to $15.00 and nonresident $3.00 to $35.00.

Resident status is determined by documents showing that a person has been living in the state for six months. These documents may be driver's licenses, vehicle registrations, rent or mortgage payments, voter's registration card, or paycheck vouchers. Three other groups of people are also considered to be residents of the state. They are members of the armed forces on permanent duty in the state, diplomatic personnel on permanent duty in the state, and students who are enrolled in or are attending any school within the state at least six months. Documentation is also required to prove these three categories.

Colorfest is the name of the celebration which marks the turning of the aspen leaves in the southwest section of Colorado. It is held from mid-September to mid-October and is marked by events such as jeep giveaways, tours, races, art shows, food festivals and Octoberfest activities. Of course, one can see the changing leaves wherever the aspens are found, but this extra effort to celebrate the harvest season and the coming of winter is certainly something that should not be missed if your trip coincides with this miracle of nature.

COURTESY OF COLORADO TOURISM BOARD

Sheep Mountain near Telluride during the Colorfest celebration.

COURTESY OF ASPEN RESORT ASSOCIATION

Fireworks rain over Aspen during Winterskol Festival.

AREA ONE

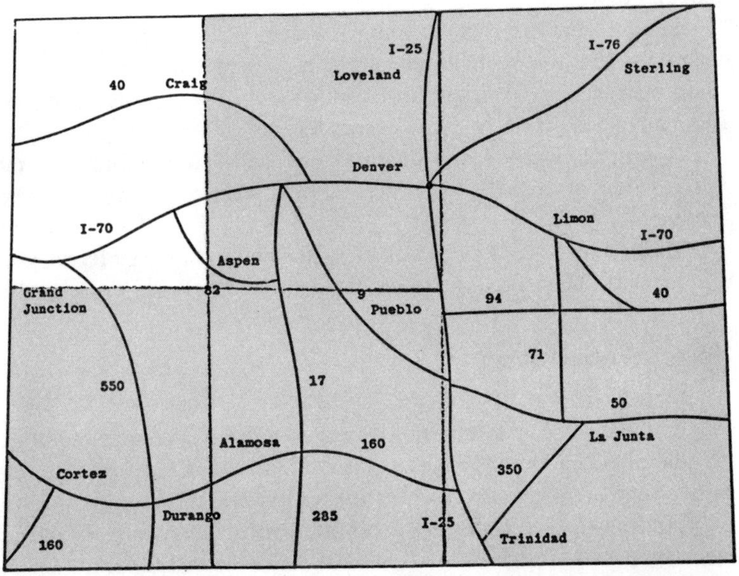

ASPEN—probably the ski capital of the Americas, this city is synonymous with snow. What many people do not know is that Aspen does not simply disappear when the snow melts. It is still there, and with a thousand things to do all through the warmer months.

Things to See and Do

Ski Season—the slopes have their opening day at the end of November. Aspen Mountain, Aspen Highlands, and Snowmass open with gala celebration while the Buttermilk area opens in the middle of December.

Winterskol—a five day festival in mid-January which features such events as a torchlight parade, fireworks, and other winter fun.

Aspen Music Festival—all summer long, it features various kinds of music like classical, opera, chamber, jazz, and contemporary. In all, the season presents 150 concerts and recitals which are performed under the music tent a short walk from the center of town and at the Wheeler Opera House. A visit at any time in the summer will be sure to coincide with a concert or two. For information, phone the Opera House at (303) 925-1940.

Hiking—the easy way to trek. Some ski lifts are open during the summer so that visitors may ride up the mountains (bring camera!) and hike down through the meadows of wildflowers or have a picnic. There are also many ghost towns to explore from the city's silver mining days.

Aspen/Snowmass International Wine Classis—in mid-June, over 60 vintners from around the world present their wares for tasting and give seminars.

Ghost Town—12 miles south of Aspen on Castle Creek Road, you will find this restored mining camp of the late 1800s. Price: *Free.*

Where to Eat and Sleep

There are, of course, many restaurants and lodges in Aspen. A full list may be obtained from the Resort Association and Chamber of Commerce. Here are a few whose prices are reasonable.

Andre's—312 S. Galena, in a historic Victorian building, it features the biggest breakfast menu in town and has a skiers special for $3.75. Weekend brunch includes free champagne with specials. Appetizers served in the piano bar in the evenings. Menu includes seafood, pasta and steaks. Hours: 7:30 a.m. to noon and 6 p.m. to 10:30 p.m. (303) 925-6200.

Asia—132 W. Main St., gourmet Chinese cuisine in a Victorian atmosphere. Specializing in Mandarin and Hunan. Price: entrees start at $6.95. Take out available. (303) 925-5433.

Eastern Winds—520 E. Cooper Ave., Mandarin and Szechuan cuisine, seafood, happy hour and daily lunch specials from $4.50. Lunch buffet during season. Take out available. (303) 5160. MC, V

Skier's Chalet Steak House—at the bottom of No. 1 Chairlift overlooking town at the top of South Aspen St. Known as having the best steak in town, it also features homemade bread, seafood, chicken, and salad prepared at your table. Open at 5:30 p.m. Price: $6.50 to $13.00. (303) 925-3381. MC, V

Alpina Haus—935 E. Durant St., friendly atmosphere, small rooms, bunk beds, 2 lounges with fireplace and cable TV, complimentary full hearty breakfast and more. Price: $44.00 to $59.00. (303) 925-7335.

Alpine Lodge—1240 E. Highway 82, Bavarian style lodge with rooms and cabins, optional full breakfast and dinner, lounge, family style main room to play cards, trivia or listen to your host, Hans Rieger, play the zither. Price: $30.00 to $50.00. (303) 925-7351.

Buckhorn Lodge—732 E. Cooper St., cozy rooms with private bath, cable TV, complimentaryu continental breakfast, one block from Aspen Mountain. Price: $38.00 to $68.00. (303) 925-7630. MC, V

Aspen Resort Association & Chamber of Commerce, 303 E. Main St., Aspen, CO 81611 (303) 925-1940

CARBONDALE—along with the nearby towns of Redstone and Marble, this area excels in beauty of many kinds. It is a young town and the average citizen is only in his or her mid-twenties.

Things to See and Do

Potato Day/Miners Day—founded in 1909 to honor the locals favorite crop, it has been held every fall since, except during World War I. Events include a parade, the crowning of a queen, a high school football game, dances a gigantic barbeque and the best baked spuds in the West!

Marble—30 miles south on 133, this high country town provided the marble used for the Tomb of the Unknown Soldier and the Lincoln Memorial. Although nearly a ghost town a few years ago, it is undergoing a revival and tourists can enjoy side trips into the mountains by jeep to visit the quarry and abandoned mines.

Hiking—there are many spots of interest near Carbondale and the Forest Supervisor or the Chamber of Commerce will be glad to give you information. Some special places to ask about are the Maroon Bells-Snowmass and the Hunter-Frying Pan Wildernesses, Thomas Lake, and Mt. Sopris.

Horseback Riding—the three following outfitters can provide your family with many enjoyable memories of the national forest and countryside in both summer and winter. Chair Moutain Stables, (303) 963-1232 in Redstone. Redstone Wagons and Sleigh, (303) 963-2526 in Redstone. Twin Pine Stables, (303) 963-1220 in Marble.

The Country Store—in Redstone, this remarkable curiosity shop can rent you anything to make your vacation better. From hiking and camping supplies to mountain bikes and cross-country skis, you name it, they got it! (303) 963-3409.

Where to Sleep

Crystal River Inn Bed & Breakfast—a Victorian farm house on 160 acres in the forest. There is great trout fishing in the river out back and, from the hen-house, farm fresh eggs on the table each morning. Four miles north of Redstone, (303) 963-3902.

Mountain View Inn—in Marble, 5590 County Road 3. Fish out back in the beautiful Crystal River and pick up a few of the marble souvenirs. (303) 963-1933.

Carbondale Chamber of Commerce, 590 Highway 133, P.O. Box 427, Carbondale, CO 81623 (303) 963-1890

CRAIG—the area abounds with wildlife like elk, deer, eagles, mountain lions and sandhill cranes. It is proud of its history in ranching and the cowboy way of life, and that of course includes the outlaws who roamed the area like Butch Cassidy, Tom Horn, and Anne Bassett who was called Queen of the outlaws.

Things to See and Do

Fall-Color Festival—mid-September brings a celebration of fall colors and it includes lots of fun things to do. These include a hospitality party, picking and fiddling contests, square dancing, games, a pancake breakfast, and more. Some proceeds go to the Interfaith Food Bank to bring others a happy fall. Call the Chamber of Commerce for information.

Craig City Park—at 6th and Rose, it is right behind the Marcia Railway Car and offers swimming, tennis, picnicking and the first home of Craig, the William Rose house.

Marcia Railway Car—Highway 40 and Rose, the personal car of the banker from Denver who was a driving force in the development of the railway system, David Moffat. It is lavish in its furnishing with mahogany from Africa and the Philippines, dining table for 12, brass, silk, and more. Tours are given, please call (303) 824-5689.

Moffat County Courthouse & Museum—221 W. Victory Way

(Highway 40), the second floor holds the history and lore of the area in four beautiful rooms full of antiques and artifacts. *Free admission daily.* (303)824-6360.

Trapper Mine— observe a real surface coal mine in action at this mine which produces 10,000 tons a day. It is 6½ miles southwest on Highway 13.

Wyman Elk Ranch & Pioneer Museum— take a guided tour through the beautiful Williams Fork Valley and its elk herds. Then stroll through the museum which shows life on the ranch as it used to be. To get there, take Colorado Road 13 south to Hamilton, then 317 east to just past Pagoda and then right to the ranch. Price: $1.00 per person. Picnic and overnight camping available, please call for information and reservations (303) 824-6431.

Lay Valley Bison Ranch— this family owned and operated ranch raises American Bison to sell as food and will gladly give tours. The bison was the original American cuisine and they have all nutritional information and recipes, too. Buy a couple of steaks and try it out. Take Highway 40 west of Craig for 18 miles to Lay, Colorado. (303) 824-9207.

COURTESY OF SOUTH PARK CHAMBER OF COMMERCE

Open range buffalo can be found throughout the state in small herds.

Sand Rocks Archaeological Site—between Pershing and Steele Streets and north of 10th Street, the morning is the best time to view these rock art styles of the Fremont, Ute, and Plains cultures.

Mount Harris Archaeological Site—7 miles east of Hayden off Highway 40, along the east side of the mountain there are painted figures and designs. Do not touch or deface these ancient drawings, please. Pictures only.

Fishing—try the Yampa River south of town and the Freeman Reservoir at Black Mountain or Elkhead Reservoir east of town. This area is famous for its gigantic Northern Pike, so be prepared for a fight.

Black Mountain—sightsee along this road as you head out to the mountain. Take Highway 13 north, from here you can go to a campground or a reservoir. Sawmill Creek Campground is 14 miles down Moffat County Road 27 which is 11 miles from town on the right. There are 6 sites with grills and toilets. The road to Freeman Reservoir is 2 miles past County Road 27. You will turn right on County Road 11 and then go 8 miles to the reservoir. There is a campground there which has 17 sites.

Elkhead Reservoir—this man-made lake offers boating, water skiing, picnicking, and fishing. Take Highway 40 east from town to County Road 29 and go north (left) to Road 28. Go right on 28 to the reservoir.

Where to Eat and Sleep

Banana Boat Deli—at 576 Yampa Ave., serves sandwiches, Mexican specialties, and pizza. Also homemade ice cream in 18 flavors. (303) 824-9380.

Desperado Restaurant—2045 W. Highway 40, serving steaks and seafood. (303) 824-6900.

Golden Cavvy Restaurant & Lounge—538 N. Yampa Ave., offering steak, seafood, soups and sandwiches. (303) 824-6038.

Annie Bassett's—in the Holiday Inn at 300 S. Colorado 13. Serves ribs, steaks, seafood, salad bar, and fresh baked goods. Price: breakfast and lunch $1.75 to $6.95, dinner $6.95 to $15.95. (303) 824-9455.

Adam's Fishing & Hunting Lodge—2400 Rio Blanco County Road 12 near Meeker, offers all kinds of wilderness adventures. A cabin with all the modern conveniences is only $30.00 to $55.00 a day. Or, you can take a pack trip to a nearby lake where everything is provided for you except sleeping bag and fishing tackle for $80.00 a day per person. There is a lodge which serves all three meals upon reservations (303) 878-4312,

878-4440 or 878-4338.

Best Western Inn—755 E. Victory Way, free cable TV, free continental breakfast, king/queen size beds, family rooms and more. (303) 824-8101.

Camping sites are available at Black Mountain, see above. For campgrounds, see Black Mountain above.

Greater Craig Area Chamber of Commerce, 616 East Victory Way, P.O. Box 1091, Craig, CO 81626 (303) 824-5689.

DINOSAUR—this town is named and known for its famous quarry where 2,300 fossil bones are on display. The dinosaur bones are over 140 million years old and the story they tell is amazing.

Things to See and Do

Dinosaur National Monument—the headquarters of the park are two miles east of the town of Dinosaur on Highway 40. From there the traveler may take a scenic drive north into the Monument on Harper's Corner Trail. To see the Visitor's Center where the bones are displayed,

COURTESY OF COLORADO TOURISM BOARD

The beautiful Green River flows through the Canyon of the Lodore.

one must go west on Highway 40 to the town of Jensen and then north on 149. Either way is a beautiful drive through scenery uncompared. The park offers many activities like boating, hiking, fishing, and sightseeing. For hikers there are four self-guided nature trails. After obtaining a permit, boaters can run the white water of the Green and Yampa rivers, and those with valid fishing licenses may try Jones Hole or the rivers for trout and catfish. Sightseers can observe the interesting and sometimes mystifying rock art of the Fremont people, an ancient Indian tribe of the region. There are various campgrounds and backcountry camping is allowed with a permit only. There are seven campgrounds, some of which are open all year. There are no hookups but RVs may be parked in some sites. Price: $5.00 a night per site. Backcountry permits are free. There are no gas, food or supply services in the park. Address: Dinosaur National Monument, Dinosaur, CO 81610. (801) 789-2115 or (303) 374-2216.

Where to Eat and Sleep

The town of Dinosaur has limited accommodations and unless one plans on camping at the monument with his own food, it is advised that one travel west to Vernal, Utah, or south to Rangely, Colorado.

EAGLE—the Eagle River Valley has a long and colorful history, being first settled by Ute Indians, then trappers and gold diggers. it has much to offer the traveler.

Things to See and Do

Scenic Drive—there are many. 1. *Brush Creek Road,* south of Eagle it offers several end points. 1A. *Hardscrabble Road*-turns off Brush Creek Road 5 miles out of town. 1B. *Sylvan Lake*-follow the signs on Brush Creek road to the perfect fishing spot. 1C. *Adam's Rib*-on the right side of the road heading toward Fulford, it is a proposed ski area where overnight camping is permitted. 1D. *Fulford*-historic mining town 17 miles from Eagle. 2. *Cottonwood Pass Road*-gravel road southwest of Eagle through Gypsum to Glenwood Springs, if offers wildlife and beautiful scenery. 3. *Deep Creek Road*-follow U.S. Highway 6 west of town past Dotsero and take the Sweetwater turnoff north to Coffee Pot/Deep Lake Road. It leads to some awesome wilderness hikes and fishing streams. 4. *Colorado River Road*-follow the river along the Dotsero turnoff 14 miles west of Eagle and get out the binoculars to spot golden eagles, ducks and other wildlife. Information on other scenic drives may be obtained from the Chamber of Commerce.

Jeeping—maps and advice can be gotten from the White River National Forest, Eagle Ranger District, Eagle, CO 81631. Ask for the Forest Service Map and the particulars on Red Table Road and Old Fulford Road. Or phone them at (303) 328-6388.

Fishing—angler's heaven! Try these streams and rivers: Eagle River, Colorado River, Brush Creek south out of Eagle, and Gypsum Creek south of Gypsum. Try these highcountry lakes: Lake Charles near Fulford Cave Road, Deep Lake west of Gypsum, Sylvan Lake south of Eagle, Sweetwater Lake on Sweetwater Creek Road, and Wilmore Lake 2½ miles west of Edwards off I-70.

Backpacking and Hiking—Eagle is a good base camp from which to explore the White River and Routt National Forests and their wilderness areas. See information under forest names.

Snow Skiing—Eagle is situated in an area well-known for its powdery slopes and bowls. Resorts abound all along I-70.

Horseback Riding—let outfitter Steve Jones take you through the wilderness the way it was done in the 1800s. Write to him at 5344 Brush Creek Road, Eagle, CO 81631 or phone (303) 328-6920.

Hunting—the Adam's Rib Recreation Area specializes in deer and elk hunting as well as pheasant hunting. Write Box 59, Eagle, CO 81631 or phone (303) 328-ADAM.

Annual Festivals and Events—*Snowmocarnival* in mid-December, *Tree Burning* the 12th night, *Cabin Fever Party* in February, *Saint Patrick's Day Parade and Social* on March 17th, *Ides of April* on the 15th of that month, and *Flight Days* in June which includes a rodeo, parade and live entertainment. Chamber of Commerce can be contacted for exact dates.

Where to Eat and Sleep

Winterhawk—at 700 Chambers Road, it specialized in Italian, German, Mexican, and American foods and has a bar

(303) 328-6950.

Dempsey's—at 201 Broadway, it h as a full menu of Mexican and American favorites. (303) 328-7381.

Valley Cafe—at 501 Highway 6 in Gypsum, it takes pride in its homestyle cooking. (303) 524-7350.

Reuben's—100 Chambers Place, it serves tasty lunch and dinner specials in a family dining atmosphere. (303) 328-7277.

Eagle Lodge Best Western—at the I-70 interchange. (303) 328-6316.

Yeoman Park Campground—take CR 307 south 12 miles, then FR 1546 south 1/10 mile. Run by the White River National Forest, it has toilets, tables, fire rings but no hookups. Price: $5.00

Eagle Valley Chamber of Commerce, P.O. Box 964, Eagle, CO 81631 (303) 328-5220.

FRUITA—the western portion of the state has much to offer the visitor and Fruita is a good place to make your base camp.

Things to See and Do

Colorado National Monument—explore the essence of Colorado, canyons, mesas, and the great outdoors. A good day trip, visitors can view the exhibits, take the scenic Rim Rock Drive, and hike on any of the numerous trails in one day. Remember to take water and your camera on the hikes. To get there, take 340 from Fruita to the Monument's scenic drive and Visitor Center. Address: Fruita, CO 81521.

Moon Farm—a great time for adults, but geared for the kids. Dozens of farm animals, pony rides, train rides and more. A day camp is available for children 12 and under which includes a lunch. For those who have frazzled nerves that come with traveling, especially with the kids, it is a great escape. Address: 1360 18½ Road, Fruita, CO. Take Highway 6 and 50 from Grand Junction, turn right on 19 Road, left on M Road, and right on 18½. Price: adults $2.00, children $1.00, day camp $8.00 a day. (303) 858-7176.

Where to Eat and Sleep

Fruita Junction RV Park—121 sites, some with full hookups. Price: $8.50 and up. Address: 607 Highway 340, Fruita, CO. 81521 (303) 858-3155.

Saddlehorn Campground—in the National Monument, 81 sites, no hookups, open all year, hiking trails. From town, take I-70 exit 4 and Highway 340 three miles south to the entrance of the Mounument.

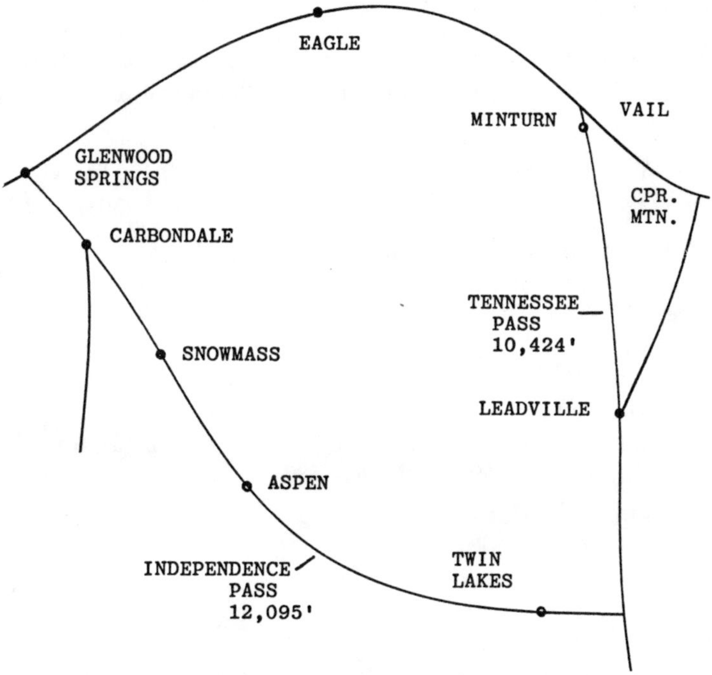

GLENWOOD SPRINGS—the springs here were used by Indians and cure-seekers from all over the world. Today the town is a resort at the edge of the White River National Forest where all the wonders of nature may be enjoyed.

Things to See and Do

Strawberry Days Festival & Roaring Fork Rodeo—the third weekend in June brings excitement to the town with dancing, a wild carnival and an even wilder rodeo. Enjoy the competition diving and swimming at the pools. Glenwood Hot Springs Pool—two gigantic pools fed by the hot springs below. There is a restaurant, bathhouse, and children's pool also. Rates vary. (303) 945-6571

White River National Forest—the largest in the state, with over 2 million acres for you to explore. Make Glenwood Springs your base and go forth each day to treasure hunt and explore the ghost towns and wilderness.

Where to Eat and Sleep

Village Smithy—26 S 3rd in nearby Carbondale, features excellent omelettes, soups and Sunday brunch. Eat on the patio if you like. Price: $2.00 to $8.00 (303) 963-9990.

Mr. Steak - 51701 US 6, the name says it all! Also has kids menu, seafood and salad bar. Price: $3.25 to $14.95 (303)945-6613.

Best Western Caravan Motel—1826 Grand Ave., close to the Sunlight ski area, hot tub, free coffee, cable TV, some oversize beds. Price: $37.00 to $59.00 (303) 945-7451 MC, V, AE.

Ami's Acres Campground—take I-70 exit 114. Go west 1 mile on Frontage Rd. Spacious, hookups, tent area, toilets, showers and tables. Price: $8.50 and up (303) 945-5340.

Glenwood Springs Chamber of Commerce, 1102 Grand Ave., Glenwood Springs, CO 81601 (303) 945-6589.

GRAND JUNCTION—at the joining of the Colorado and Gunnison rivers, this beautiful city is surrounded by mountains on all sides. There is an activity for everyone here.

Things to See and Do

Colorado National Monument—explore the essence of Colorado, canyons, mesas, and the great outdoors. A good day trip, visitors can view the exhibits, take the scenic Rim Rock Drive, and hike on any of the numerous trails in one day. Remember to take water and your camera on the hikes. To get there, take 340 from Grand

Junction to the Monument's scenic drive. Address: Fruita, CO 81521.

COURTESY OF COLORADO TOURISM BOARD

Independence Rock near Grand Junction is just one of the unusual rock formations found in the Colorado National Monument.

Grand Mesa National Forest—the world's largest flat top mountain awaits you at an altitude of over two miles. There are many lakes, 60 of which are stocked with trout. Drive to scenic 100 mile circle drive (from Grand Junction via Mesa over the Skyway Drive and back over Land's End to Grand Junction) which you will never forget for its wonderful views and grandeur. East of the city off of I-70.

Powderhorn Ski Area—lies on the north face of the Grand Mesa 40 miles from Grand Junction, take I-70 to exit 49, then Highway 65 to the resort area. As part of the National Forest, it offers some of the most scenic slopes around. Hours: 9:30 am to 4:00 pm (opens one hour earlier on weekends) from Thanksgiving to mid-April. Address: 744 Horizon Dr., Grand Junction, CO 81906. 1-800-233-9882 for reservations and information.

Dinosaur Triangle Trail Through Time—start in Grand Junction, Colorado with the Dinosaur Valley Museum open from 8 am to 4:30 pm, Memorial Day through September at the corner of 4th and Main. Price: adult $2.50, child $1.50. Next, the *Trail Through Time*—take the Rabbit Valley exit on I-70, 30 miles west of town. Now go to Price, Utah (I-70 to Utah Highway 6/191). In Price, take Highway 10 south for 30 miles and follow the signs to Cleveland-Lloyd Dinosaur Quarry. It has been excavated since 1928 and over 17,000 prehistoric bones have been discovered. It is open from Memorial to Labor Day, Thrusday through Monday, 9 am to 4 pm. Next travel back to Price and visit the College of Eastern Utah Prehistoric Museum. There you will see the bones from the quarry put together. Located at Main and 2nd East and open Monday to Saturday, 9 am to 5 pm. (801) 637-5060. Now travel northeast on 191 and 40 to Vernal, Utah and Dinosaur National Monument. In Vernal, take 40 to Jensen and 149 north to the Monument. It features a cliff wall where hundreds of bones are exposed. Open from 8 am to 5 pm daily. (801) 789-2115. To return to Grand Junction, take 40 east, 64 to Rangely and 139 south to Grand Junction. For brochure, call or write to the Chamber of Commerce.

Scenic Drives—the Chamber also provides a pamphlet of 8 drives around the city of Grand Junction. They vary from 39 to 280 miles long and take the visitor to valleys, canyons, mountains, rivers, and National Parks, Forests, and Monuments. Stop by and pick one up, call, or write the Chamber of Commerce.

Colorado Mountain Vineyards—10 miles east of town outside of Palisade. Take a tour, taste the wine, and take a little home for later. Address: 3553 E Road, open from Tuesday to Saturday, noon to 4 pm. Price: *Free.* (303) 464-7948.

Historical Residential Walking Tour—there are 35 homes from the turn of the century that are listed on the National Historic Registry. All are along North 7th St. Tour guide is available at the Chamber, Visitors Information Center, and other locations.

Moon Farm—a great time for adults, but geared for the kids. Dozens of farm animals, pony rides, train rides and more. A day camp is available for children 12 and under which includes a lunch. For those who have frazzled nerves that come with traveling, especially with the kids, it is a great escape. Address: 1360 18½ Road, Fruita, CO. Take Highway 6 and 50 from Grand Junction, turn right on

19 Road, left on M Road, and right on 18½. Price: adults $2.00, children $1.00, day camp $8.00 a day. (303) 858-7176.

Rafting—take a 2 to 5 day river trip through calm and white water. For reservations, brochure, and information, write: Adventure Bound, 649 25 Road, Grand Junction, CO 81505 (303) 241-5633.

Chili Cookoff and Pumpkin Harvest—this celebration takes place on Main St. at the end of October. (303) 245-2926.

Where to Eat and Sleep

G. B. Gladstone's—interesting decor and good food at reasonable prices. Address: 2531 N 12th St. (303) 243-3058.

Best Value Inn—133 units, restaurant, lounge, pool. Price: $15.95 to $21.95. Address: 718 Horizon Dr., Grand Junction, CO 81506. (303) 243-5080 MC, V, AE.

Big J Camper Court—160 sites with full hookups. Price: $9.50 and up. Address: 2819 Highway 50, Grand Junction, CO 81503 (303) 242-2527. MC, V.

Willow Cottages—bed and breakfast, 827 27 Road, (303) 242-6377.

Grand Junction Chamber of Commerce, 360 Grand Ave., P.O. Box 1330, Grand Junction, CO 81505 (303) 242-3214.

GRAND MESA NATIONAL FOREST—more than 340,000 acres in west-central Colorado, it is east of Grand Junction and north of Delta. There are picnic areas with grills, boat ramps, a visitor center, and many campgrounds all located on the largest flat top mountain. It is inhabited by elk, bear, marmot, squirrel, deer, and mountain lions. One attraction not to be missed is the Crag Crest National Recreation Trail which offers unique views of the area as well as an interesting display of our geologic history. It is 10 miles long, circular, and camping 300 feet from the trail is permitted. Those less used to exercise should take it slow and everyone using the trail should bring water. Campgrounds range in price from free to $7.00.

Grand Mesa Forest Supervisor, 2250 Highway 50, Delta, CO 81416.

MAYBELL—in northwest Colorado, this small town on the grassy plains is a perfect base from which to explore the wild canyons of the area.

Brown's Park—this National Wildlife Refuge lies on the Green River in the northwestern corner of Colorado between the Utah border and Dinosaur National Monument. There are 6,000 acres of wetlands for waterfowl like mallards, redheads, teal, canvasbacks, Canadian geese, wading birds, and others. There are also deer, antelope, partridge, grouse, elk, bighorn sheep, and hawks. There have been other visitors to this region also, and it is believed that Butch Cassidy and the Wild Bunch buried much of their loot in the area to escape the law. There is a tour road for your convenience and primitive camping facilities, remember to bring ample food, water and fuel. Take Colorado 318 northwest from Maybell to the refuge entrance on the left. It is approximately 50 miles from Maybell. (303) 365-3613.

Cross Mountain Archaeological Site—take Highway 318 northwest 10 miles, then Moffat County Road 10 about 6 miles then two tracks west to the base of the mountain. This requires a steep climb but you will see isolated panels of chipped and pecked human and animal figures. Please take only pictures and leave nothing.

Irish/Vermillion Canyon Archaeological Site—go northwest on 318 for 45 miles. At the south end of Irish Canyon is a BLM interpretive site with picnic sites and informational signs. There is pecked Fremont art on a boulder. Also in this canyon, 30,000 dollars in silver coins is believed to be buried so take your metal detector. Vermillion Canyon is 2 miles west and has some of the finest rock art around, you will have to hike into the canyon, please bring water, wear sunscreen or a hat and sturdy shoes.

Lay Valley Bison Ranch—this family owned and operated ranch raises American Bison to sell as food and will gladly give tours. The bison was the original American cuisine and they have all nutritional information and recipes too. Buy a couple steaks and try it out. On Highway 40 east of Maybell. (303) 824-9207.

Juniper—ghost town southwest of Maybell near Juniper Springs.

Maybell City Park Campground—in the town, you can stay at the park on US 40 from May to November. It has 30 sites, toilets, showers, tables and a playground.

Greater Craig Area Chamber of Commerce, 616 E Vistory Way, P.O. Box 1091, Craig, CO 81626 (303) 824-5689.

MEEKER—this town holds a lot of history within its limits. It was here that 1,500 troops were stationed to keep the peace with the Ute Indians. One can still see the Officer's quarters, just find the court-house at the old fairgrounds. There you will see the logs which mark the spot.

Things to See and Do

Range Call Celebration—on the Fourth of July the town explodes with exciting events. Enjoy them singly or obtain a low priced package ticket for all events including three rodeos, two parades, country music by well-known performers, barn dances, and fireworks.

White River Winter Rendezvous—this ten day festival starts in mid-January and hosts a multitude of events like cross country ski and snowmobile tours and races, dog sled races, hot air ballooning, ice and river fishing, black powder and archery contests, a lighted parade and crafts. There is something for everyone in the snow world of Meeker.

White River National Forest—make Meeker your base camp as you explore the beauty of the forest and the Flat Tops Wilderness Area. It is a flattened dome capped with lava, having wide canyons eroded by the elements over the centuries. One can backpack, horseback ride, fish, drive jeep trails, and sitesee throughout the wilderness. In the winter there is snowmobiling on over 200 miles of trail. The wilderness is accessible from US Highways 40, 6 and State Highways 131 and 132.

Spring Cave—30 miles east of town at the South Fork Campground in the National Forest (take Highway 13-789 2 miles east to County Road 8. Turn right for 20 miles to Buford and turn right on Buford-New Castle Road and take the first left beyond the Red Schoolhouse.) is the third largest cave in Colorado. Bring lanterns and flashlights to explore this barely developed cave which *has rope ladders* and *no paths, electricity or guides.* A spelunker's delight! Maps and history are available at the Chamber of Commerce.

The Devil's Causeway—a narrow basalt ridge which rises over 2000 feet above the valley in the Flat Tops Wilderness Area. It is accessible by foot and horseback.

Scenic Drives—through some of the richest cattle and sheep ranches in the state as well as some gorgeous forest. 1. *Drive to Rio Blanco* along Piceance Creek north to highway 64 and back to Meeker through Powell Park. 2. *Meeker Massacre Site*—take Highway 13-789 2 miles west to Highway 64 and go right 2 miles to the historical plaque on the left.

COURTESY OF SOUTH PARK CHAMBER OF COMMERCE

Ranching is an important business in Colorado and long horn cattle like these symbolize the West as it used to be.

Meeker City Park—in the middle of town one block south of Highway 13, it offers a stocked fishing pond for those 12 and under, horse shoe pits, barbeques, picnic shelters, and camping areas all within a short walking distance of downtown.

White River Museum—at 565 Park Street, it revisits the town's past with artifacts of local Indian tribes and early settlers including Nathan Meeker, the town's founder. Open 7 days a week from 9 am to 4 pm in summer and 10 am to 12 pm and 1 pm to 4 pm in winter.

Where to Eat and Sleep

Meeker Hotel—at 560 Main Street, it is on the National Register of Historic Places. Built in 1894, it has been lovingly restored into the truly elegant place it was in the past when it attracted famous guests like Teddy Roosevelt. Price: $18.00 to $40.00 for a two room suite. Write P.O. Box 1130, Meeker, CO 81641 or phone (303) 878-5061.

Meeker Chamber of Commerce, P.O. Box 869, Meeker, CO 81641. (303) 878-5510. Located at the corner of 7th and Market.

PALISADE—near beautiful forests and mountains, and yet close to plains and desert also. Palisade makes a good place to stay and explore the different types of terrain around.

Things to See and Do

Colorado Mountain Vineyards—10 miles east of town outside of Palisade. Take a tour, taste the wine, and take a little home for later. Address: 3553 E Road, open from Tuesday to Saturday, noon to 4 pm. Price: *Free.* (303) 464-7948.

Palisade Peach Festival—held the last Saturday in August, its events include a parade, river race, quilt show, square dancing, contests of all kinds, and the crowning of the peach king and queen, and the naming of the grouch of the year.

Old Wagon Trail—hike up this trail which was originally used to bring coal from the mountains by wagon.

Scenic Drive—over Orchard Mesa, especially in the spring, this drive starts over the Colorado River Bridge at 38 Road. Follow it through the blooming orchards of apple, pear, apricot, cherry and more.

Island Acres State Recreation Area—at the I-70 exit for Palisade (42), the recreation area is a favorite for all water sports like fishing, swimming and boating. There are also numerous hiking trails waiting to be explored. The campground has no hookups, but they do have toilets, tables and stores and cafes within a mile. Price: Free. (303) 464-7297.

Palisade Chamber of Commerce, P.O. Box 580, Palisade, CO 81526 or call the Town Hall (303) 464-5602.

RIFLE—this town offers a western atmosphere, as implied by its name, that is both friendly and casual. Although its altitude is over a mile high, it is unusual for there to be snow on the ground for more than a day. Even so, skiing, and ice skating are only minutes away. Perfect all the year round, the temperature averages between 40 degrees in February to 79 degrees in August.

Things to See and Do

Garfield County Fair & Rodeo Days—held on Labor Day weekend, this show is Colorado State Rodeo Association sanctioned and attracts professional riders from throughout the country.

Rifle Gap Falls State Recreation Area—with picnic and camping grounds north of town about 14 miles on County Road 325. Features trails, waterfalls, and even a few small caves to explore (remember the flashlight). Campsites here offer complete seclusion and some may only be reached by foot. Fees: entrance $3.00 and camping $6.00 in addition to entrance fee.

Rifle Gap State Recreation Area—offers activities in both summer and winter. A few are boating, water skiing, and ice fishing (regular fishing too, of course). A small herd of buffalo can even be observed at the northwest end of the park. Campsites are available. It is located 10 miles north of town on County Road 325. Fees: entrance $3.00

and camping $6.00 in addition to entrance fee.

Rifle Creek Trout Hatchery—16 miles north of town on County Road 325, this facility is one of the largest hatcheries in the world. Each year, it raises and releases over half a million trout, bringing joy to many an angler. Hours: 9:00 am to 5:00 pm daily.

Apple Pie Days—in July or August, contact Chamber of Commerce for dates. This celebration starts off with an apple pie baking contest, after which the pies are sold by the piece. Other events include a horse show, delicious Rotary barbeque and more.

Ghost Town—*Lacy* is on an old railroad track 3.5 miles west and *Una* is on a railroad near the south county line off Highway 6.

Where to Eat and Sleep

Fireside Inn—2 miles north of town on Highway 13, features lunch and dinner with cocktails, excellent food. (303) 625-2233.

The Mill Inn—1538 Railroad Ave., a fine family restaurant serving breakfast, lunch and dinner amid country decor. Good food at moderate prices. (303) 625-4331.

Martino's Pizzeria—851 Railroad Ave., serves more than just pizza, great spaghetti, sandwiches, salar bar and lasagne. Beer on tap. (303) 625-1666.

Lee Hayward's 96 Ranch—Horse rider's dream, pack trips and Champagne breakfast rides starting from $25.00. Weeklong trips for hunting or just riding start at $400.00 per person. Address: P.O. Box 248, Parachute, CO 81635, or phone: (303) 285-7439.

Coulter Lake Guest Ranch—located 21 miles northeast of Rifle, it offers weeklong packages (minimum stay is 3 days) that include 3 meals a day, lodging, maid service, riding, swimming, fishing, and hunting when in season (rates are higher for hunting). Price: per day: $78.00 to $97.00 for adults, $36.00 to $57.00 for children under 11, per week: $390.00 to $520.00 for adults, $180.00 to $305.00 for children under 11. Adress: P.O. Box 906, Rifle, CO 81650, or phone: (303) 625-1473.

La Donna Motel—½ mile west of Rifle on US Highway 6 at 520 Railroad Ave., cable TV, free coffee in room and free local calls. Price: $19.00 to $27.50. (303) 625-1741.

Shaler Motel—4 blocks north of Highway 6/I-70 on Highway 13 and 789, features cable TV, free coffee in room, free local calls, nearby restaurant. Price: $19.95 to $32.95. (303) 625-1777.

Red River Inn—in Rifle, room includes cable TV, continental breakfast, free local calls, hunting information, and horses for rent. Price: $22.50 to $30.50. (303) 3050.

For campgrounds, please see the Rifle Gap State Recreation Area and Rifle Gap Falls State Recreation Area above.

Rifle Chamber of Commerce, P.O. Box 809, 101 S Railroad Ave., Rifle, CO 81650 or phone (303) 625-2085.

STEAMBOAT SPRINGS—famous for its skiing; 9 national jumping records have been set here. It is also the location of the Routt National Forest's headquarters, making it the perfect place from which to explore the wilderness. There are also many ghost towns and old mines to investigate, as well as streams to try your luck at fishing or panning gold.

Things to See and Do

Skiing—famed for its white powder and cross-country, it has two ski areas. Howelson Hill is to the south off US 40 on River Road. It is used mostly for training and should be used by intermediate or advanced skiers. (303) 879-4300. Steamboat is to the east on US 40. Steamboat provides lifts, over 50 miles of trails, rentals, restaurants and lounges, a nursery and more. (303) 879-6111.

Steamboat State Park—north on County Road 129, it has facilities for boating, swimming, fishing, and waterskiing. Camping is permitted.

Scenic Drive—go east on US 40 over Rabbit Ears Pass (9,426 feet) and Muddy Pass (8,772 feet). Turn right on State Road 134 and go west over Gore Pass (9,524 feet) to Toponas. From here go north on 131, watch for Lone Spring Butte on your right. It is 10,228 feet high and is an impressive sight. When you meet up with US 40 again, go west back to Steamboat Springs.

Rabbit Ears Pass—(9,426 feet) many old mines are in the area of this pass over the Continental Divide. There are also rumors of lost and buried treasures. Take a pan or metal detector and try your luck.

Ghost Towns—*Butler* is believed to be 13 miles northeast of Steamboat Springs and *Trull* 5 miles to the northwest. The town of *Disney* is on an abandoned railroad track 9 miles to the south.

Fish Creek Falls—3 miles east on Fish Creek Falls Road, these magnificent falls drop more than 2000 feet. There is also a trail leading to the Continental Divide and picnic areas to enjoy. Price: *Free.*

Tread of Pioneers Museum—on 5th St., it houses many historical exhibits from the late 1800's. It is free, but donations are requested.

Where to Eat and Sleep

Cove—709 Lincoln, features Chinese cuisine at its best. Price: $4.75 to $9.25. (303)879-7720 MC, V, AE.

La Montana—2500 Village Dr., it serves Mexican specialties, and diners may choose to eat on the patio. Price: $4.50 to $18.95. (303) 879-5800 MC, V, AE

The Anch at Steamboat—at 1 Ranch Road, lots of extras at this year round resort, including cable, spa, fireplaces in some units and more. Price: $22.00 to $39.00 for 4. (303) 879-3000, 1-800-237-2624 in state, 1-800-525-2002 nationwide. MC, V, AE

Harbor—703 Lincoln Ave., it has 60 rooms with cable TV, pool, sauna, free continental style breakfast, oversize beds and library. Price: $52.00 to $58.00, higher during holidays, special ski rates. (303) 879-1522, in state 1-800-334-1012, nationwide 1-800-543-8888 MC, V, AE

Fish Creek Campground—1 mile east on US 40, has toilets, showers, store, ice, and tables. Fishing in the creek is a fun pastime. Price: $9.50 and up. (303) 879-5476.

WHITE RIVER NATIONAL FOREST—over two million acres in northwestern Colorado just waiting to be explored. The forest is actively used both summer and winter, in fact it surrounds some of the most famous ski areas in the world including Vail, Aspen, and Breckenridge. It has 17 wilderness areas for camping, backpacking, hiking, fishing, boating, kayaking, horseback riding, spelunking, and hunting. The wildlife abounds and one may see elk, bear, bobcat, mountain lion, bighorn sheep and mountain goat to name a few. The alpine vegitation and crystal clear mountain streams are sure to catch the eye and soul with their tranquility. Of course, the power of nature is also evident in this forest, along Highway 6 the roaring Colorado River carves its path through Glenwood Canyon. For campers there are 565 sites in the 36 designated campgrounds. Price: $5.00 to $8.00. The Forest is easily accessible by many main roads including I-70, Highway 24, Routes 131, 133 and 82.

Maps and brochures may be obtained at the ranger stations or by writing.

Forest Supervisor, Old Federal Building, Box 948. Glenwood Springs, CO 81602.

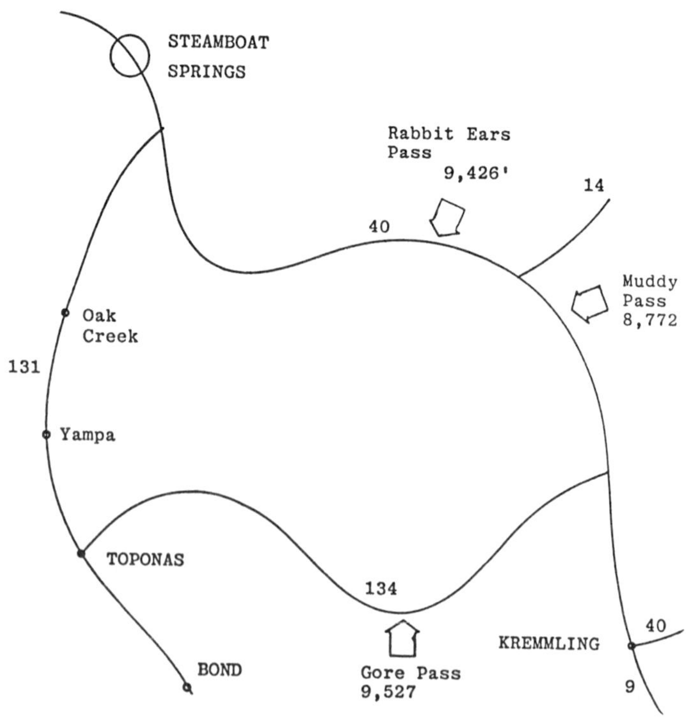

AREA TWO

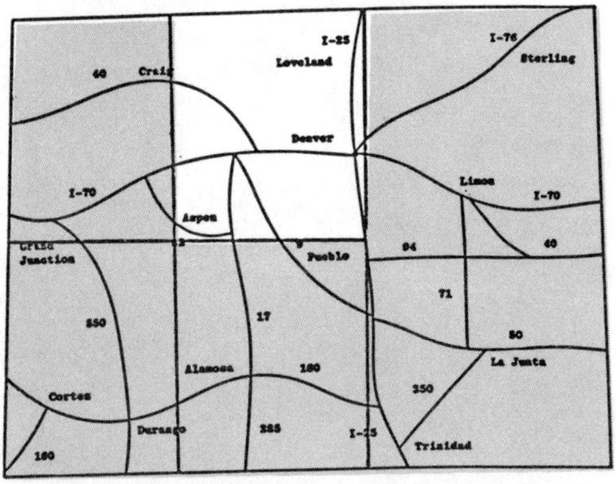

ALMA—this small village is actually a partial ghost town. It is also the highest incorporated town in the country at 10,400 feet. it is but 30 minutes away from some of the best known ski areas in the world.

Things to See and Do

South Park Valley— surrounded by mountains, this grassland spreads over 900 square miles at an elevation of 9,000 feet. It is home to many animals, including bighorn sheep, elk, deer, antelope, and buffalo as well as their predators, the bobcat, mountain lion, and bear.

Bristlecone Scenic Area—see the oldest living things on the Earth. These trees survive on the slopes of Mt. Bross, enduring winter cold, wind, rock, and altitude. North of Alma off of Highway 9.

National Forests—Alma has perfect access to three of Colorado's National Forests, the White River, the Arapahoe and the Pike.

Ghost Towns—the town itself is almost one and there are dozens more in the area to explore for souvenirs. Try the entrance of Buckskin Gulch 1 mile west of Alma for antique bottles. Some may be worth money, all are worth the memories.

South Park Chamber of Commerce, P.O. Box 312, Fairplay, Co. 80440 or contact the city clerk at (303)836-2622.

COURTESY OF SOUTH PARK CHAMBER OF COMMERCE

Bristlecone pine on the Limber Grove Hiking Trail near Horseshow Mountain.

ARAPAHOE NATIONAL FOREST—includes 1,009,000 acres of mountainous terrain. Within its boundaries are old ghost towns from the mining heyday and lively, elegant ski resorts. Activities available include hiking, backpacking, and pleasure driving. Local ranger stations can advise visitors of any regulations concerning these activities (camping permits are required for Indian Peak Wilderness).

Scenic Routes—modern route to the top of Mount Evans (14,260 feet above sea level).

Hiking—trails in the Forest are mostly high mountain routes on the Continental Divide. Hiking and backpacking may only be done by foot or horseback, no motorized vehicles are permitted (see ranger station for information on this as well as those rules governing fire, sanitation, and safety).

Camping—there are many campgrounds throughout the Forest which range from fully developed campgrounds with complete facilities to "walk in" tent camping with little or no facilities. Camping where there is no designated site is permitted in parts of the Forest, but rules and backcountry ethic must be observed. Fees: $5.00 to $7.00 a night. Permits are required for Indian Peak Wilderness.

Gold Panning—gold may be found in many of the streams within the Forest. It is recommended that prospectors contact the ranger station in the area they intend to search for information on land ownership, existing mining claims, and any restrictions.

Rafting—the Forest does not restrict rafting of any of the rivers, but a permit is required by the local county Sheriff's Office.

AVON—9 miles west of Vail, this town is also a skier's heaven.

Things to See and Do

Ice Skating—Nottingham lake, rentals are available.

Vintage Car Race/Concours d'Elegance—out of the past they race in all their glory. Vintage race cars zoom through the street and are shown for close-up inspection at Nottingham Park. Held in mid-July, phone (303) 949-5189.

Balloons, Bluegrass, & Barbeque—mid-August festival held in Nottingham Park features great music, food and sights in the sunny mountain air. (303) 476-1871.

Avon's Annual Fall Festival & Moretti Memorial—late August celebration which features a pancake breakfast, 5K and 10K races, bicycle parade, volleyball, horseshoes, concert in the park and more. (303) 949-4280.

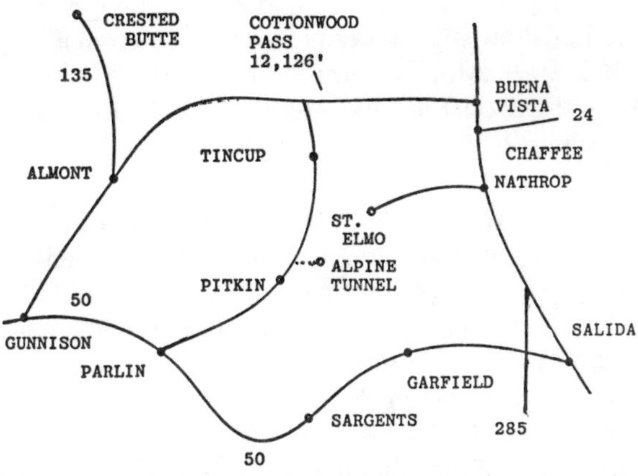

BOULDER—Boulder is a small but beautiful city situated at the foot of the Rocky Mountains just above Denver. There are innumerable things to see and do. The following are just a few of the more interesting and unusual.

Things to See and Do

Colorado Shakespeare Festival—Runs from early July until middle of August. Performances are given outdoors in the Mary Rippon Outdoor Theatre located on the University of Colorado campus. For information about next season's itinerary, write Colorado Shakespeare Festival Ticket Office, Campus Box 261, Boulder, Colorado 80309, or phone (303) 492-8181.

Colorado Gilbert and Sullivan Festival—Held during the early summer, performances are held in the Musical Theatre in the University of Colorado College of Music. For information on the coming season's itinerary, write Campus Box 301, Boulder, Colorado 80309, or phone (303) 492-7495.

National Center for Atmospheric Research—1850 Table Mesa Dr., has exhibits of research on weather, solar astronomy, weather balloons and a self-guided tour and slide show. Price: *Free.* (303) 497-8720.

Boulder Beer Tours—The brewery gives *free* tours of its facilities, as well as *free* samples of its product on Thursdays and Fridays from 11 a.m. to 1 p.m. The brewery is located at 2800 Wilderness Place, Boulder, Colorado 80301. You may write there for information or phone (303) 444-8448.

Leanin' Tree Museum of Western Art—Art depicting cowboys, Indians, the frontier, desert, and mountains of the West. To get there, follow Highway 19 north toward Longmont. Exit onto N. 63rd St. and go south to Longbow Dr. Take a right and the museum is on the right at 6055. It is open Monday thru Friday, 8:00-4:30, and Saturday, 10:00-4:30. Closed on Sundays, Holidays, and December 25 thru January 1. Admission is $2.00 for adults, $1.00 for seniors, and children under 16 are admitted *free.*

Snow Skiing—The closest slopes are the Eldora. About a half hour away from the city, they feature lots of easy skiing as well as new expert runs. For night skiing information, call (303) 447-8013 and for snow conditions and specific directions, (303) 447-8011. For more information on skiing, write the Chamber of Commerce.

Scenic Drives—*here are a few of the more interesting ones.*

Flagstaff Scenic Highway—west of town on US 26, take Flagstaff Highway to the top of the mountain and look down on the Continental Divide.

Peak to Peak Highway—Take Boulder Canyon Road (Hwy. 119) to Nederland, turn north on Highway 72, and follow it through Ward to Raymond. Then take Route 7 north through Allenspark to Estes Park.

Trail Ridge Road—From Estes Park, follow signs to Route 34. This road follows the north fork of the Colorado River and goes to the town of Granby. Take Highway 40 to I-70. From here you have two choices for the return trip to Boulder. The short route: take I-70 to Route 6. At Golden, go on Route 93 to Boulder. The long route: take Route 119 through Central City to Route 72 and back to Boulder.

Roosevelt National Forest Circuit—From Estes Park, take Route 34 to Loveland and Highway 287 north to Fort Collins. From here, follow Route 14 through Laporte, Rustic, Walden, and Coalmont. When it meets Highway 40, go south through Kremmling and Parshall to Granby. Follow 40 to I-70, go eat to 119 north. Then take Route 72 back to Boulder.

Nederland—deserted mining town, 16 miles west of Boulder on route 119.

Where to Eat and Sleep

Boulder Dinner Theatre—dinner and a great show from $18.95 to $22.95. Located at 55th and Arapahoe; phone: (303) 449-6000.

Burke's—at 1101 Walnut, one block off the Mall, affordable gourmet (veal, duck, fresh seafood, etc.) live jazz on the piano every night, happy hour. Price: $3.00 to $12.95. (303) 449-6661.

Fred's Restaurant—1308 Pearl St. on the Mall, oldest restaurant in the city. Lots of homemade goodies, including vegitarian specials. Price: $2.50 to $9.50. (303) 449-3183.

Kobe An—2010 14th St., just off the Mall, Japanese with Sushi, Mahi Mahi, and the more traditional. Price: lunch, $2.50 to $4.50; dinner, $7.00 to $14.00. (303) 449-4961.

The Red Robin—at 2580 Arapahoe, gourmet hamburgers, Sunday and Monday all-u-can-eat wings, happy hour with twofers all day long. Price: $3.35 to $7.00. (303) 442-0320.

Harvest Restaurant & Bakery—1738 Pearl St., a la carte, delicious breakfast, all natural dishes, and you can dine outdoors if you wish. Price: $2.00 to $8.50. (303) 449-6223.

American Youth Hostel—at 1107 12th St., two blocks from campus, bunks, communal kitchen, etc. (303) 449-6223.

Boulder Inn—at 770 28th St., restaurant and lounge, pool, hot tub/sauna, nearby university. Price: $40.00 to $75.00. (303) 449-3800.

Briar Rose Bed and Breakfast—at 2151 Arapahoe, 11 rooms, some with fireplaces, feather comforters, continental breakfast. Price: $49.00 to $95.00. (303) 442-3007

University Inn—1632 Broadway, bed & breakfast, continental style, TV, refrigerators, some oversize beds. Price: $39.00 to $44.00. (303) 442-3830.

NOTE: There are many more festivals, restaurants, hotels, and special events in this area, for a complete list write Chamber of Commerce, P.O. Box 73, 2440 Pearl St., Boulder, Colorado 80306, or phone (303) 442-1044. Request the booklet titled *Boulder, Colorado. Surprise!*

BRECKENRIDGE—This city is a 128 year old mining town. Its Victorian heritage lends to it a unique charm that attracts visitors to its famous ski slopes every year.

Things to See and Do

Snow Skiing—three interconnected mountains provide skiers with fine variety in slopes, bowls and cross country. Open from mid-November to mid-April. Price of full day lift ticket: $27.00. Contact the Breckenridge Ski Area, P.O. Box 1058, Breckenridge, Colorado 80424. (303) 453-2368.

Winter Sports—other than skiing, Breckenridge offers much more to do in the winter. For snowmobiling, sno-coach tours, and sleigh rides contact the following outfitter. Tiger Run Resort, 201 S. Main, (303) 453-2231. Breckenridge Nordic Ski Center, (303) 453-6855.

Helicopter Skiing—take scenic flights or ski down slopes from the tops of mountains. Scenic 30 minute flights are $85.00 per person. Single ski runs are $35.00 per person with full day runs between $175.00 and $295..00 which include a gourmet lunch, guide, safety equipment, and three to four runs. (303) 668-5600.

Winter Festivals—opening of ski area, mid-November.

Lighting of Breckenridge—mid-December when Santa arrives in a real horse-drawn sleigh, goes down Main Street where all the buildings are lit up in their Christmas finery.

Ullr Fest and World Cup Freestyle—late January, it honors the Norse god of winter, Ullr. Celebration includes parades, fireworks, and many other events. Entrants from eighteen countries compete for prizes in many Freestyle events.

Bicycle Touring—take a guided day tour of the town and surrounding National Forest. A day long adventure includes: mountain bike, water bottle, handlebar bag, rear seat pack, experienced guide, picnic lunch, and maps of the tour. Price: $25.00 per person for package or $9.00 per day without. (303) 453-2194.

Where to Eat and Sleep

Colts Sports Bar and Eatery—115 S. Main St. Breakfast to dinner, special kiddie corner, features food for all tastes. Price: $1.95 to $10.95. (303) 453-SHOE.

Whitney's Steak House—built in the 1860's, this place gained a reputation as Andrea's Pleasure Palace during the 1920's. Come and enjoy a little history. Prices for entrees are from $8.95 to $17.95, with a litre of Margaritas for $9.00. (303) 453-6921.

Gator's—upstairs in the Bell Tower Mall, it serves sandwiches, quiche, salads, burgers, Mexican specialties, and giant main courses. Price: $4.25 to $14.95. (303) 453-1760.

The Village Deli & Pizzeria—on the Pond Level at the Village, serving bagels and croissants for breakfast, big hot and cold sandwiches and pizza for lunch and dinner. Try the "Killer Pizza". (303) 453-0793.

Breckenridge Park Meadows—Traditional ski lodge, clean rooms, fireplace in main lobby. Prices: December and March $85.00 for four people. $75.00 at other times.

Fireside Inn—at 114 French St., a less expensive alternative to the big resorts, this cozy inn welcomes you. Price: winter $45.00 to $65.00, summer $24.00 to $29.00. (303) 453-6456. Write to them at P.O. Box 2252, Breckenridge, CO 80424.

Breckenridge Resort Chamber, Box 1909, Breckenridge, Colorado 80424, or phone (303) 453-6018 and ask for the booklet titled *Breckenridge, Genuine Colorado.*

CENTRAL CITY—an old mining town which was known for the unbelievable amounts of ore produced in the area. The area was also a favorite territory of outlaws like the infamous Reynold's gang who were believed to have hidden much of their loot in the area.

Things to See and Do

Central City Jazz Festival—the third weekend in August brings the hottest music from New Orleans to the mountains. (303) 573-0247.

Gold Mines—two local mines now give tours of their facilities and history. One is the *Bobtail Gold Mine* in Black Hawk, 1 mile east on Colorado 279 from Central City (303) 582-5866. The other is the *Central Gold Mine & Museum,* at 126 Spring St. (303) 582-5574.

Site of First Gold Load Discovery in Colorado—a stone monument marks the spot where gold was first found on May 6, 1859. At the boundary of Central City and Black Hawk.

Gilpin County Museum—228 E High St., in the school house you will find exhibits of early life in the county. The Historical Society maintains this museum. (303) 582-5283.

Old 71—on Spring St., see one of the engines which pulled its cars up the narrow gauge railroads.

Where to Eat and Sleep

Black Forest Inn—on Colorado 279 in Black Hawk, features lunch and dinner, German and American fare, wild game and entertainment. Price: $5.00 to $18.50. (303) 279-2333.

Golden Rose Hotel—at 102 Main St., Victorian style rooms, hot tub and cafe next door. Price: $48.00 to $77.00. (303) 825-1413, MC, V, AE

Columbine Campground—2 miles northwest on CR 279, has toilets, tables, no hookups. Maintained by Arapahoe National Forest. Price: $6.00

COMO—a partial ghost town that is a perfect place to search for pioneer artifacts.

Things to See and Do

South Park Valley—surrounded by mountains, this grassland spreads over 900 square miles at an elevation of 9,000 feet. It is home to many animals, including bighorn sheep, elk, deer, antelope, and buffalo as well as their predators, the bobcat, mountain lion, and bear.

Roundhouse—a real roundhouse, so important to the railroad industry because it saved time and money. This fine example has 6 stalls and is manufactured out of stone.

COURTESY OF SOUTH PARK CHAMBER OF COMMERCE

This roundhouse in Como is one of the few left in the United States.

Ghost Towns—many in the area as well as old mining sites. It is also rumored that the notorious Reynolds outlaw gang buried much loot in the area.

Where to Eat and Sleep

The Como Depot—restaurant and hotel in one. Restaurant has excellent food at reasonable prices. The building is set remotely in the South Park Valley and the rooms are clean and comfortable. The perfect base station for those who want to hike, explore and photograph the scenery, ghost towns, and wildlife. Price: $12.00 to $20.00.

South Park Chamber of Commerce, P.O. Box 312, Fairplay, CO 80440.

COPPER MOUNTAIN—the town is a resort in both summer and winter.

Things to See and Do

Snow Skiing—cross-country skiing is adjacent to the alpine ski area and lessons are available for those wishing to traverse the 74 trails. Downhill skiing from late October to early May on 1,470 acres with 19 lifts and dozens of slopes. The resort features "create your own vacation" packages custom designed to fit your needs from lodging to lessons. Price of full day lift ticket: $26.00. For parents, there are also day-care and baby-sitting services. Address: P.O. Box 3001, Copper Mountain, CO 80443. (303) 968-2882. In state 1-800-332-3828 and nationwide 1-800-525-3878.

Helicopter Skiing—take scenic flights or ski down slopes from the tops of mountains. Scenic 30 minute flights are $85.00 per person. Single ski runs are $35.00 per person with full day runs between $175.00 and $295.00 which includes a gourmet lunch, guide, safety equipment, and three to four runs. (303) 668-5600.

National Forests—Copper Mountain is surrounded by the White River National Forest, the Pike National Forest and the Arapahoe National Forest. This makes Copper Mountain the perfect base camp for you to explore the beauty of Colorado both in winter and in summer.

Fishing—try Ten Mile Creek for some of the finest fly fishing around.

Hiking—try the mountain without snow. Hiking the trails and slopes make for a day of exercise and fun.

Where to Eat and Sleep

There are many restaurants around the resort ranging from cafeteria style to gourmet dining. Here are a few.

Plaza Restaurant—serving gourmet cuisine with that Colorado touch in a quiet, intimate setting.

O'Shea's Copper Bar—barbeque deluxe and entertainment fantastic.

The Columbine Cafe—features gourmet burgers and dance music.

Rackets—located in the Athletic Club, it serves seafood and Oriental dishes.

Copper Mountain Resort—hotel rooms to 3 bedroom condos, children under 12 stay free, Athletic Club use included in price and optional meal packages in the American Plan style. Hotel room price: $65.00 to $140.00. 4 day, 4 night stay with lift tickets $145.00 per person. For package information write the resort at P.O. Box 3001, Copper Mountain, CO 80443, in state call 1-800-332-3828 and nationwide 1-800-525-3878.

Summit County Information Center, P.O. Box 214, Frisco, CO 80443. (303) 468-6205 or Copper Mountain Resort, address and phone numbers above.

DENVER—known as the mile high city, it is nestled in the most gorgeous of scenery. The plains stretch out to the east and the mountain rise in the west. As the capital of Colorado, Denver gives the tourist its hearty welcome and invites you to enjoy it and the state it represents.

Things to See and Do

NOTE: All suburbs and smaller cities in the immediate Denver area are designated by name.

Denver Information Center—225 Colfax, across from the U.S. Mint, it features over 400 pamphlets on attractions, accommodations, and restaurants, as well as other pertinent information on Denver and the state of Colorado. Hours: 8 am to 5 pm weekdays, 9 am to 4 pm in summer and 1 pm in winter, also open Sunday during the summer from 9 am to 1 pm. (303) 892-1505.

Colorado Renaissance Festival—during weekends in June and July, featuring outdoor fair with crafts, food and entertainment on the 14th, 15th and 16th centuries. In Larkspur at 2660 S. Monaco, 80222. (303) 756-1501.

Coors Brewery—at 13th and Ford St. in Golden, *free* 30 minute tours allow you to sample and learn about America's favorite beverage for football time. (303) 277-BEER.

Colorado State Capital—this building at Broadway and Colfax is a replica of the Capital Building in Washington DC and the 13th step is exactly 1 mile high. *Free tours* given weekdays 9 am to 3:30 pm.

Larimer Square—the 140 block of Denver's oldest street has been faithfully restored with courtyards, gas lamps, and Victorial architecture. *Free tour brochure* is available in many of the lovely shops and boutiques. There are also restaurants, arcades, and night clubs.

National Western Stock Show—at 1325 E. 46th Ave., the largest livestock show in the world is held here every January and has been for over 80 years. The rodeo is a classic example of this truly American sport. Price: Rodeo and grounds $6.00 to $8.50, grounds only $1.00 to $3.00.

Sakura Square—at 19th and Lawrence, this block is full of Oriental shops and restaurants, as well as a Buddhist temple and beautiful Japanese gardens.

United States Mint—at W. Colfax and Cherokee St., it contains the largest depository of gold outside of Fort Knox. *Free 20 minute tours* show how they produce 5 billion coins a year. Open 8 am to 3 pm weekdays, closed holidays.

Buffalo Bill's Grave & Museum—at the top of Lookout Mountain, take I-70 Exit 256. The museum honors the man who became a legend in his own time due to his skills as a scout and showman. Site gives magnificent view of Denver and surrounding area. Open 9 am to 4 pm daily, closed Mondays in winter. Admission charged for museum. (303) 526-0747.

Molly Brown House Museum—1340 Pennsylvania, the home of the woman who became known as the heroine of the Titanic, the "Unsinkable Molly Brown". Her unusual Victorian home is open daily 10 am to 4 pm, Sundays noon to 3 pm, closed Mondays. (303) 832-4092.

Colorado School of Mines Geology Museum—at 1500 Illinois Ave., it holds unusual fossils, rare rocks and gems, and historical information on the minerals and gems found in the state. Open Monday to Friday 10 am to 3 pm and Sunday 1 pm to 3 pm. Price: *Free.* (303) 279-0300.

Mount Falcon Park—trails for horse and hiker lead to historic sites and scenic vistas, plains and foothills. The abundant wildlife and flowers make this place a perfect one to relax. Off of State Highway 8 in Morrison.

Mount Evans Highway—the highest paved road for automobiles in the United States, it gives spectacular views along the way and at the mountain's summit (14,260 feet). Take I-70 west of Denver 60 miles, then Highway 103 south to the highway's beginning. Open June to September.

Where to Eat and Sleep

Please obtain a full list of restaurants and accommodations from the Visitor's Center.

Baby Doe's Matchless Mine—2520 W. 23rd Ave., serves lunch and dinner, dine and dance in an old silver mine and enjoy the view of downtown Denver. Price: $3.75 to $19.95. (303) 433-3386 MC, V

The Bay Wolf—231 Milwaukee, private, romantic setting, serving fresh fish and veal, light meals that are great tasting and low of calories for lunch and dinner. Jazz in the lounge. Price: $4.75 to $20.00. (303) 388-9221 MC, V, AE

Columbine Steakhouse & Lounge—300 Federal Blvd. is the home of great steaks for over 23 years. Salad, potato, and Texas toast with steak. Price: $4.35 and up. (303) 936-9110.

Duffy's Shamrock—1635 Court Pl., serving breakfast, lunch and dinner in a quaint tavern setting at yesterday's prices. (303) 534-4935.

94th Aero Squadron—10081 E. 25th in Aurora, overlooks Stapleton International with all its flight memoribilia and Sunday Champagne Brunch. (303) 344-4614.

19th Place Downtown—240 E. 19th Ave. at Grant, bed and continental breakfast, suites with kitchens, TV, parking, free local calls, etc. Price: $46.00 to $64.00. (303) 837-8694 MC, V, AE

Denver Inn—401 17th St., bed and breakfast continental style, one block from shopping mall. Weekly specials. Price: $49.00 to $67.00. (303) 296-0400 MC, V, AE

Hampton Inn—1500 S. Abilene Ave. in Aurora, room includes buffet breakfast daily, cable TV, and more. Price: $38.00 to $52.00. (303) 369-8400, nationwide 1-800-426-7866 MC, V, AE

Quality Inn North—110 W. 104th Ave. in Northglenn, bed and breakfast in the continental style, complimentary cocktails in the lounge or restaurant, sauna, whirlpool, lots more. Price: $47.00 to

$52.00. (303) 451-1234, nationwide 1-800-522-8111 MC, V, AE

Denver Metro Convention & Visitors Bureau, 225 W. Colfax Ave., Denver, CO 80202 (303) 892-1112. Ask about the ***Denver & Colorado Official Visitors Guide****, which is full of more restaurants, accommodations and activities, as well as money saving coupons.*

DILLON—on State Road 6 just off of I-70 (Interchanges 205 and 216) it is an area with an infamous past. There are old ghost towns (try the railroad south of town and you should find Dickey in about 3 miles) everywhere and mine on every hill. This was also a favorite area for outlaws like the Reynolds gang.

Things to See and Do

Snow Skiing—either cross-country out of town into the National Forests or visit one of the many nearby ski areas. Keystone Ski Area south on Highway 6 open from mid-October to early May, two day lift ticket $48.00, call 1-800-222-0188 or (303) 468-4242. Arapahoe Basin Ski Area south on Highway 6 open from late November to June, two day lift ticket $48.00, call 1-800-222-0188 or (303) 468-4242. Loveland Basin and Valley Ski Area east on I-70 to exit 216 open from mid-October to May, full day lift ticket $19.00, call (303) 569-2288.

Fishing—the Blue River from Hoosier Pass to the Colorado River has been proclaimed Gold Metal Water when it comes to angling. Try your luck anywhere along Highway 9 but make sure to obey signs indicating private property. There are various parking areas and river access points throughout town. Write the Town of Silverthorne for their fishing brochure.

National Forest—Dillon is situated between both the Arapahoe National Forest and the White River National Forest. Make the town your base camp and explore the beauty of either of these treasures, summer or winter.

Lake Dillon—huge lake created in 1965 to provide the area with water, it offers boating, sailing, fishing, and other water sports.

Yacht Charters—take your honey on a beautiful sailboat for island punch and hors d'oeuvres from only $15.00. Also offered are dinner cruises and private charters. (303) 468-3077 or 468-5665 ext. 077.

Balloon Rides—imagine floating over the Aspen forests, sipping champagne, and admiring the view. It can all be yours from Balloon Colorado. Price: adult $150.00, child $100.00. Address: Box 1364, Dillon, CO 80435. (303) HOT-AIRE.

COURTESY OF BALLOON COLORADO

A different way to take a scenic trip.

Burros Over the Summit, A Cracker Jack Event—held in June, the race features jockeys and their nimble, if sometimes uncooperative, mounts going for the gold with gusto. Laughs galore and fun too.

Mid-Summer's Eve—mid-June celebration of epic proportions, with a street dance and home style barbeque.

Ghost Towns—*Dickey,* on railroad 3 miles south and *Braddocks* 2 miles further. *Keystone* on a railroad spur 2 miles east. *Breckenridge,* on Highway 9 on the Blue River south of Dillon.

Where to Eat and Sleep

Pug Ryan's Steak House—at 101 Dillon Mall, with all the goodies traditionally at any steak house, including lobster, trout, prime rib, filet mignon, and gigantic T-bones. Happy hour Monday to Friday from 4 to 5:30 pm. Dinner served from 5:30 to 10 pm. (303) 468-2145.

Ptarmigan Mountain Bed & Breakfast—reservations are a must for a stay in this 7 bedroom, 4 story home nestled in the trees. They serve skiers in the winter and sailors in the summer and are only 5 minutes from town and Lake Dillon. Price: $25.00 to $70.00. Call for reservations: (303) 468-5289.

ERIE—is a small town that is directly north of Denver and east of Boulder. It is an old coal mining town and there are many old mines in the area.

Things to Do and See

October—Eerie Erie, 5k and 10k races on the closest Saturday to Halloween.

September—Erie County Fair, parade, contests, games, etc.

First Rural School of Colorado—plaque near Highway 52 on County Line Road marks its site where it was organized in 1861.

Erie Town Hall—the old building is on the National Register of Historic Places and was once a school for the area's children.

Scenic Drive—take Road 8 west to Highway 287 and go north to Longmont. Past there, take US 36 west. When you get to Estes Park, take US 34 west (portions are closed in winter so check weather conditions) into the Roosevelt National Forest and the Rocky Mountain National Park. The scenery is uncompared, watch for ghost towns and mines. Then head south on 34 to Granby. Here take US 40 southeast to I-70 and go east. Take State Road 119 north from Idaho Springs through Boulder to State Road 52 and go east to 287. Take US 287 south to Road 8 and go east to Erie.

Where to Eat

The Convair Restaurant—*the restaurant itself is an airplane* that was used as a passenger plane. Come and enjoy the excellent fare, there are parking facilities for both cars and planes. There is entertainment on the weekends, located at the public airport in the residential airpark, 3000 Airport Drive.

Greater Erie Chamber of Commerce, P.O. Box 625, Erie, CO 80516.

ESTES PARK—a place to spend a few days and remember a lifetime. In fact, archeologists find that Indians have spent their summer vacations here for as long as 20 thousand years! Estes Park was homesteaded in 1869 by scout and fur trapper, Joel Estes. Only 71 miles from Denver, it is the gateway to Rocky Mountain National Park, white water rafting, dude ranches, and snow skiing just to name a few.

Things to See and Do

Rocky Mountain National Park—located on the Front Range of the beautiful Rocky Mountains, it contains 107 named peaks over 11,000 feet. Its diversified wilderness offers so many unique sights that the park offers a guide for photographic drives. The self-guided tours range from 49 miles to 18 miles in length. For *"Picture-taking in the Rockies"* brochures, write the Estes Park Chamber of Commerce.

Cowpoke Corral—2 locations in the National Park offer horseback riding. The National Park Village Stables, near the north entrance on Highway 34 (303) 586-5890 and Cowpoke Corner Corral near the south entrance, take Highway 36 to 66 (YMCA Rd.) at Glacier Lodge, (303) 586-5890. Both offer half-day, full-day, breakfast and supper rides, and overnight trips. Ponies are available for children.

COURTESY OF COLORADO TOURISM BOARD

Longs Peak and Nymph Lake, one of the many spectacular views in Rocky Mountain National Park.

Aerial Tramway—visit the top of Prospect Mountain via the tree tops. Upon reaching the peak, visitors can picnic in the pines, feed chipmunks, and hike the many trails. Located 1 block south of the Estes Park post office at 420 E. Riverside Dr. (303) 586-3675.

Lazy "B" Ranch—have dinner and a show, Western style! Family entertainment featuring Tom Justin and the Lazy "B" Wranglers, a true western singing group who have performed at the White House and the Grand Ole Opry. Menu includes barbequed beef simmered in the Lazy B's own special sauce, baked potatoe, beans, biscuits, cake and lemonade or coffee. Price: adults $9.00, kids under 10, $5.00. Hours: From early June to Labor Day, gates open at 5:30 pm with dinner at 7:00 pm. Located 1½ miles from Sombrero Stables off Highway 34. Phone: (303) 586-5371, in Colorado 1-800-228-2116.

Ski Estes Park at Hidden Valley—10 miles from town in the National Park, a family place with European alpine slopes from beginning to expert. Rentals, snack shop and cafeteria, ski school, and a nursery for the little tots. For information write: Estes Park Recreation & Park District, Box 1379AC, Estes Park, Colorado. (303) 586-8191, winter (303) 586-4887.

Trout Haven Ponds—guaranteed to catch fish or you pay nothing! *Free* use of tackle, *free* storage and freezing, *free* packing. Fees are charged by the inch and there is a pondside cafe to prepare your catch. Located on Highway 36 W. and open from 8:00 am to sunset, call (303) 586-2944 for information.

Estes Park Area Historical Museum—at 200 4th St. and US 36, learn more about this fascinating area and its past. Hours: daily 10 am to 5 pm, Sunday 1 to 5 pm. (303) 586-6256.

Peak to Peak Highway—scenic vistas are yours for the taking, with a camera that is. Drive south along Highway 7 down to Central City, a historic mining town. Take Highway 7 to Highway 72 and then to Highway 119. Go east on 119 and you are on the peak to peak highway.

Horse Shows—Estes Park has a multitude of equestrian events throughout the year. June brings these shows: Westernaires, Arabian, Miniature. July: Morgan Horse, Rooftop Rodeo, Silver Dollar Hunter competition, and Estes Park Classic Hunter Jumper show. August: Paint horse, Trail Ridge Riders, Appaloosa shows.

Where to Eat and Sleep

Lazy B Ranch—see above.

The Big Cheese/Deli—the slogan of this shop is, "We don't make sandwiches — we build them!" and, boy, do they! Have your favorite custom-built from 8 choices of meat and cheese and go on a mountain picnic. For more elegant fare the gourmet section will tempt any palate. Located at 213 W. Elkhorn Ave. (303) 586-4016.

The Black Canyon Inn & Restaurant—a romantic, Victorian place to stay and eat. *The restaurant:* pink linen, fine art, stone fireplace, elegant. Lunch is in the best of English pub tradition while dinner is set in the romantic main dining room. There is also brunch on Sunday. Dinners: $9.50 to $25.00. *The Inn:* ½ mile north of town, it overlooks the Black Canyon and historic MacGregor Ranch, it covers 14 acres of vacation paradise. Bed and breakfast to condos with kitchens. Prices are $20.00 to $75.00 a night. Address: Box 4654AC, Estes Park, CO. (303) 586-8113, in Colorado, 1-800-423-7444, ext. 8113, and nationwide, 1-800-762-5698, ext. 8113.

Heidi's Family Restaurant—a family of 4 can eat for under $20.00 and choose from pancakes to pizza so even those picky eaters will be satisfied. Located across from the big slide under the Aerial Tramway in Piccadilly Square. Hours: 7:00 am to 10:00 pm daily. (303) 586-6318.

The Inn at Glen Haven—restaurant and accommodations. *The restaurant:* gourmet, featuring Steak Escoffier, Smoked Pheasant in Morel Mushroom Sauce, Bouillabaise, and many more too delectable to print on anything but a menu. Hours: lunch, Wednesday to Sunday 11:00 am to 4:00 pm., dinner daily from 4:00 pm to 10:00 pm. Reservations: (303) 586-3897. *The Inn:* famous in the 1920's as a speakeasy and bordello, it has an elegant atmosphere, a wine tasting room, antiques, and guests are welcome to fish, hunt, hike, and ride horses nearby. Bed and breakfast packages and its open all year. Price: $40.00 to $70.00 a night. Located 7½ miles north of Estes Park, their address is:

Box 19AC, Glen Haven, CO 80532. (303) 586-3897.

The Mountain Man Family Restaurant—all three meals served in family style at family prices. Wednesday is Mexican Day, sports lounge features large screen TV and Old Style Beer is $.75 during Cubs games. Live entertainment from June to September 1. Hours: 6:00 am to midnight. Located at the intersection of Highways 34 and 36. (303) 586-8646.

The Aspen Lodge—full American Plan accommodations, features sauna, jacuzzi, horseback riding, cross-country skiing, snowmobiling, sleigh rides, barbeques, and much more. Price: weekly, $500.00 to $650.00 and daily, $70.00 to $100.00. Address: Highway 7, Longs Peak Route, Estes Park, CO 80517. (303) 856-8133.

The Ptarmigan Room—features steak and lobster, trout Almondine, and wild game dishes. Lounge features live entertainment Friday and Saturday nights and there are buffet specials and Sunday brunch. Price: $10.00 to $30.00 in the Aspen Lodge. (303) 586-8133.

Brookside Resort—offers clean cabins with and without kitchens, and a private pier on the Big Thompson River. Price: $28.00 to $55.00. Located 1 mile west of Estes Park (toward the Rocky Mountain National Park) at 725 Riverside Dr. Address: Box 1982AC, Estes Park, CO. (303) 586-4669.

Estes Park Campground—open June 1 to September 1, tent campers have access to hot showers, modern toilets, and picnic grounds. Price: $9.00 a night. Located 1 mile past YMCA at the west end of Highway 66. Address: Box 3517AC, Estes Park, CO. (303) 586-4188.

National Park Resort—on a mountainside among the pines and next to the Rocky Mountain National Park, it offers cottages, motel rooms, and campground spots. Price: cottages $44.00 and up, motel $30.00 and up, campground $10.00 and $11.00. Located on Fall River Road. — Moraine Route. AC. (303) 586-4563.

Estes Park Chamber of Commerce and Visitor Information Center, P.O. Box 3050-B, Estes Park, Colorado 80517. In Colorado 1-800-654-0949, and nationwide 1-800-621-5888.

EVERGREEN—has access to the big city life of Denver as well as the beauty, mystery and isolation of the high country. There are many legends of lost mines, buried treasure and ghost towns filled with riches.

Things to See and Do

Colorado Philharmonic Orchestra—June thru August, concerts are given at the Evergreen High School and other locations. Call for schedule: (303) 674-5161.

Summerfest Evergreen—music and arts, food and displays around the 4th of July are celebrated in Heritage Grove, Meadow Drive.

Mountain Rendezvous & Evergreen Rodeo—early August gives way to many festivities. In honor of the gathering of mountain men in the early 1800's, there is singing, dancing, trading, and tale telling (the taller the better)! There are demonstrations of pioneer and mountain skills, lots of food and continuous entertainment. The rodeo and its downtown parade are the highlight of the weekend held at the El Pinal Arena. (303) 674-5238 for information.

Winterfest Faire—the beginning of December brings 50 local artisans out to display their wares to prospective Santas. Unique gifts for everyone. Held at the Jefferson County Open Living High School, Highway 73 and Buffalo Park Rd. (303)674-4625.

Means Meadow Park—there are trails, wild flowers, wildlife, and horseback riding. Hiking brings one to elevations where terrain changes and cool mountain breezes blow. Take Highway 74 north from Evergreen 2 miles.

Arapahoe National Forest—any road west to Evergreen will bring the vacationer to mountains over 14,000 feet, hiking, cross-country skiing, horseback riding, camping, scenic views and much more.

Hiwan Homestead Museum—at 4208 S. Timberline off of Meadow Drive, the visitor will find a 17 room log mansion built in the 1880's. It is the perfect place to dream and get architectural designs of your own, not to mention to admire the precious antiques within. A true masterpiece on the National Register of Historic Places. Hours: Tuesday to Sunday, noon to 4 pm. Price: *Free.* (303) 674-6262.

Scenic Drive—take Highway 74 north to Highway 103 which winds through the mountains and back to I-70. Take I-70 west to Highway 9 (exits 203 and 201) and go south through Alma. Just past Fairplay take US 285 northeast across the valley and watch for the herd of elk which grazes here. Keep on 285 as it heads into the mountains. Go north on 74 at Conifer and back to Evergreen.

Where to Eat and Sleep

The Davidson Lodge—3/4 mile east of Evergreen on Highway 74 at 27400 Lower Bear Creek. Cabins are of logs with fireplace, cable TV, kitchenette and all modern conveniences on beautiful Bear Creek. Perfect for a family vacation or a memorable honeymoon. Price: $42.00 to $52.00 per night. Reservations and information (303) 674-3442.

Highland Haven Resort Motel—4395 Independence Trail, turn on the road across from the Phillips 66 station. Cottages, rooms and suites are available, some with kitchens and fireplaces. Weekly rates available. Price: for 2 people, daily $34.00 to $60.00, weekly $288.00 to $360.00. (303) 674-3577.

COURTESY OF DAVIDSON LODGE

Lower Bear Creek is at your back door when you stay at Davidson Lodge.

Mount Evans Campground—10 miles west on Highway 74 to Upper Bear Creek Rd., this primitive camping area is high in the mountains, has 15 tent sites only. Fishing and hiking nearby is a good pastime. Price: *Free.*

Evergreen Chamber of Commerce, P.O. Box 97, 3951 Colorado Highway 74, Evergreen, CO 80439. (303) 674-3412.

FAIRPLAY—the area around this town is full of riches. Almost any stream will give the prospector some gold and the ridges in the high country or any rock slide is likely to yield a few precious gems like amethyst, topaz or turquoise. There are also many ghost towns in the vicinity to explore.

Things to See and Do

Burro Pack Races—during the last full weekend of July, the first race takes participants through 28 miles of rough riding. From downtown to the summit of Mosquito Pass (10,000 feet) and back. In existence for more than 30 years, it brings the spirit of the West to Fairplay every year. The second race is during the last week of September featuring both men's and women's events and is for the championship. Its starting point alternates each year between Fairplay and Leadville but follows the same 23 mile route over Mosquito Pass.

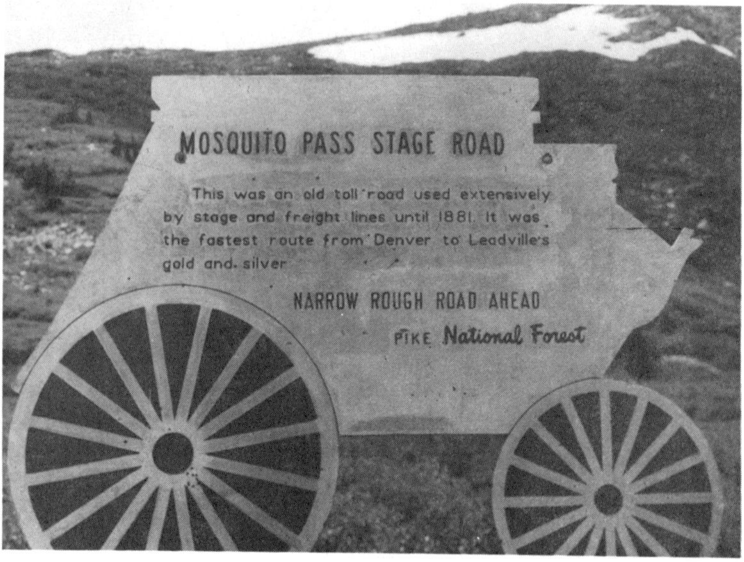

COURTESY OF SOUTH PARK CHAMBER OF COMMERCE

Mosquito Pass Stage Road is the highest pass with a road in Colorado. Travel by foot or 4 wheel drive in the summer.

Dog Pull—this nationally recognized event takes place the first weekend in April. It tests the strength and endurance of both man and beast.

Sheldon Jackson Memorial Church—this church was dedicated in 1874 and its architecture is a beautiful example of those times. Its bell tower and fine detail make it a most handsome religious monument. Regular services are held each Sunday.

Gold Panning—free to anyone with the *"fever",* try the Platte River just south of town or Beaver Creek to the north on Highway 285.

Ghost Towns—the Chamber of Commerce has maps and directions to most of the abandoned towns and most roads are accessible during the summer. The Chamber can also give information on hiking and backpacking along the old mining roads and abandoned railroad tracks where the foot traveler can see one or more of the towns.

Handmade Pottery & Fur Company—buy that perfect gift for him or her from a full selection of earthernware of beautiful fur products.

Fairplay Courthouse & Schoolhouse—the oldest in Colorado in continuous use. Built in 1874.

Fairplay Flume—the weekly newspaper for this town has been published continuously since 1879. Pick up a copy.

South Park City Museum—is an outdoor museum showing 19th century life in a Colorado mining town. It features a trapper's cabin, pioneer homes (some on their original sites), a drugstore, bank, railroad, brewery, and much more. Hours: May 15 to October 15, 9 am to 5 pm. Price: adults $2.50, children 5-12 and seniors $1.25, under 5 *free*. (303) 836-2387.

South Park Valley—surrounded by mountains, this grassland spreads over 900 square miles at an elevation of 9,000 feet. It is home to many animals, including bighorn sheep, elk, deer, antelope, and buffalo as well as their predators, the bobcat, mountain lion, and bear.

Bristlecone Pine Trees—these trees are the oldest living things on the Earth and can be seen throughout the South Park area along both major and minor roadways. They are known for their extraordinary ability to withstand the most adverse of weather conditions.

Old Ute Indian Natural Fort—taking Highway 9 south to Hartsel gives the visitor a view of fort-like rock formations used by the Ute Indians to battle invading Indians who tried to take over the land.

Prunes Monument—this monument erected at Front St. next to the Hands Hotel honors the life of Prunes, a burro which packed supplies to the mines in the area.

Where to Eat and Sleep

J Bar J—this restaurant features excellent homemade food. Price: average meal — $5.00 to $8.00. (303) 836-9971.

Aspen Leaf—home cooked meals. Price: for two people — $13.00 to $15.00. (303) 836-2673.

Boardwalk Cafe—excellent food cooked the old fashioned way, *GREAT!* Price: average meal — $6.00. (303) 836-2882.

COURTESY OF SOUTH PARK CHAMBER OF COMMERCE

South Park Valley is the burro capital of the world.

Fairplay Hotel and Restaurant—excellent food at about $14.00 for two people to eat, located in downtown Fairplay, it is a clean and historic restored hotel. Price: $15.00 to $40.00. (303) 836-2565.

Brown Burro—modern conveniences with a rustic western atmosphere. Prices: $25.00 and up. (303) 836-2291.

Western Inn—modern motel units with phones, very new and very clean. Price: $35.00 and up. (303) 836-2026.

South Park Chamber of Commerce, P.O. Box 312, Fairplay, CO 80440 or contact the city clerk at (303) 836-2622.

FORT COLLINS—established in the winter of 1836 by a party of French trappers who buried supplies there to lighten their loads.

The area attracted settlers and became the base for an army camp in 1864. Unlike many Colorado towns, its early trade was not precious metals but granite, sandstone, marble, and agriculture. It is 65 miles north of Denver on Highway 287.

Things to See and Do

Power Plant Visual Arts Center—in the old power plant on north Highway 287, it houses 5 galleries, a children's museum, an art library, and learning facilities. There is a sculpture garden being planned for the grounds.

Fort Collins Museum—at 200 Matthews St., Indian artifacts, antique farming and military equipment all in the fort that gave the town its name. Price: *Free.* (303) 221-6738.

Pioneer Museum—219 Peterson St., it presents the first cabin ever used in the town and other historical exhibits including a gun collection. Open Monday to Saturday 1 to 5 pm. Price: *Free.*

Horsetooth Reservoir—at the western edge of town, it provides excellent fishing, water skiing, boating, hiking, rock climbing, and more.

Colorado Trout Route—nine miles northwest of Fort Collins along the beautiful Poudre River and Canyon. it offers prime fishing and outdoor fun for all. Bring the camera!

Lory State Park—22 miles west of town, it offers hiking, horseback riding with cross country trails and jumping courses, mountain bike trails, and the opportunity to view the wilderness, its inhabitants and vegitation. For guided tours, call (303) 493-1623.

National Forests—within a short drive from Fort Collins are Rocky Mountain National Park, the Rawah Wilderness Area and Roosevelt National Forest.

Where to Eat and Sleep

A full list of all the area restaurants may be obtained at the Chamber of Commerce.

Elizabeth St. Guest House—at 202 E. Elizabeth, it specializes in bed and breakfast with no costly frills. Weekly rates available. Price: $28.00 to $38.00, reservations recommended, call (303) 493-2337.

Town and Country Motel—at 1513 N. College, has kitchen facilities, weekly rates in winter and a restaurant across the street.

Price: $24.00 to $28.00. (303) 484-0870.

Winchester Inn—at 409 Centro Way, it has weekly rates, water beds in some rooms, group rates, and a restaurant nearby. Price: $20.00 to $26.00. (303) 493-7701.

El Palomino Motel—at 1220 N. College, it has group rates, kitchen facilities, pool, weekly rates, and a restaurant. Price: $20.00 to $26.00. (303) 482-4555.

Fort Collins Chamber of Commerce, 225 South Meldrum, Drawer D, Fort Collins, CO 80522. (303) 482-3746.

FRISCO—the area is full of tales about outlaws, buried treasure and lost mines. There should be some gold in just about any stream and some souvenirs in the many ghost towns which dot the area.

Things to See and Do

Show Skiing—cross-country skiing is unbelievably popular in Frisco, in fact they have set aside the Frisco Cross Country Recreational Area for that very purpose. It offers daily groomed, scenic trails for beginning through advanced skiers. Lessons and beginner's packages are available at the Main Center. To find the park take Highway 9 south from Frisco. Price: daily pass for adults $4.00, children $2.00. (303) 668-5276.

Frisco Gold Rush—the last Sunday in February brings the oldest and biggest cross-country race for citizens in the Rocky Mountains! A 10 kilometer course through the awesome Arapahoe National Forest and over Lake Dillon. Proceeds help high school racers in the Junior Olympics Championships and assist the US Ski Team.

Arapahoe National Forest—Frisco is situated in the middle of this spectacular wild area, making it the perfect base camp from which to explore its beauty in both winter and summer.

Where to Eat and Sleep

Charity's Saloon—on Old Main St., serving favorite finger foods like nachos, hearty Mexican specialties, and burgers galore (try the blue cheese bacon burger) as well as American favorites like steak. Price: $4.00 to $12.95. (303) 668-3644.

Golden Annie's—at the east end of Old Main St., it offers lots of munchies like fried clams, chicken stix and tater skins, Mesquite grilled seafood and steaks, and barbequed goodies also. Price: $3.95 to $13.95. (303) 668-0345 MC, V, AE

Whiskey Creek—in Antler's Trading Post on Summit Blvd. Specialties include Mexican combos, salads, house favorites at excellent prices. Price: $3.75 to $7.25. (303) 668-5595.

Frisco Lodge—at 321 Main St., it is centrally located and loding includes a continental breakfast, cable TV and free movies. Price: $18.00 and up. (303) 668-9815.

MarDei's Mountain Retreat—221 S. 4th Ave., bed and breakfast at its best, choice of private or shared baths, continental morning meal, and winter ski packages available. Two day minimum stay during Christmas holidays and February 15 to April 15. Price: $10.00 per person to luxurious rooms for two at $70.00. (303) 668-5337.

Snowshoe Motel—521 Main St., cable TV, some rooms with kitchenettes, waterbeds, or jacuzzi. Price: $22.00 to $49.00. (303) 668-3444.

Camping facilities may be found in the White River National Forest campground 2-1/4 miles southeast on Highway 9.

Town of Frisco, P.O. Box 370, Frisco, CO 80443. (303) 668-5276.

GOLDEN—historic city with many sights and activities. Also, home of the world famous Coors Brewery.

Things to See and Do

Buffalo Bill Days—festival in mid-July includes pancake

breakfast, arts and crafts, carnival, parade, and more. For information: (303) 279-3113.

Rocky Mountain Scottish Highland Games—beginning of August brings out the bagpipes and traditional Scottish and American games and events held at Brooks Field.

Octoberfest—one of the best in the country held in mid-September. Traditional German everything right down to keg-tapping, music, food, and fun.

Colorado Railroad Museum—1 mile east of the city on 44th Ave. It is a replica 1880 depot housing rare papers, photos, artifacts and books. Hours: 9 am to 5 pm daily. (303) 279-4591.

Adolph Coors Company—on 12th and Ford St. Tour the factory and see how Rocky Mountain spring water is turned into this universally known beer. Children must be accompanied by an adult and any adult may sample complimentary glasses of Coors' many products. Tours are *FREE* and can be arranged for hearing or motor impaired persons as well as foreign visitors. Hours: open daily except Sundays and holidays. For information: (303) 277-BEER.

Foothills Art Center—at 15th and Washington. Housed in historic church and a beautiful Victorian house, it displays many nationally known exhibits. *FREE* to the public. (303) 279-3922.

Pioneer Museum—at 911 10th St. The early days of Golden are kept safe for us to see in this unique museum. Hours: Monday to Friday, 10 am to 5 pm in summer and 1 pm to 5 pm in winter. *FREE* to the public. (303) 279-3331.

Buffalo Bill Museum—at the top of Lookout Mountain off of I-70. The museum holds many artifacts of the famous frontiersman as well as his grave. Hours: daily from 9 am to 5 pm in summer and 9 am to 4 pm in winter. Price: adults $1.00, children 6-15 $.25, under 6 *free*. (303) 526-0747.

Lariat Trail—an alternative route to the Buffalo Bill Museum. Start at 19th St. west of Golden. Drive carefully because it rises 2,000 feet in 5 miles!

Rock Flour Mill Warehouse—at 8th and Cheyenne, it is the oldest industrial building in the city, built in 1863 on red granite rock. Today it houses many offices and antique shops worth investigating.

Heritage Square—1 mile west of Highways 6 and 40 Interchange, it is a turn of the century shopping and entertainment village. Many fine shops and excellent restaurants, and an opera house which specializes in Victorian scripts and humor along with dinner. For reservations (303) 279-7881.

Golden Gate Canyon State Park—15 miles northwest of Golden, take Highway 93 north of the city and turn left on Golden Gate Canyon Road, it offers the beauty of the Rockies year round. Also visit White Ranch Park off of the Golden Gate Canyon Rd. It offers horseback riding, trails, camping, and all with no road traffic through the area.

Colorado School of Mines—at 15th St. and Illinois, this educational facility is dedicated to training mineral and energy engineers. Tours of the campus are available, and be sure to see the Geologic Museum to learn more about mining, paleontology and minerals. Also see the USGS National Earthquake Information Center. *Both the museum and the center are free to visit.* This makes a great stopping point for those who wish to find some of the gems or metals of Colorado as they will learn how to do so and see samples of them. (303) 273-3000, 1-800-446-9488.

Where to Eat and Sleep

Golden Natural Foods—1205 Cheyenne, offers health foods, vitamins, trail mixes, delicious sandwiches, and fruit shakes. Carry out. Hours: Monday to Friday 10 am to 7 pm, Saturday, 9:30 am to 5 pm. (303) 279-3420, MC, V

Hilltop House—Golden Tea Room — 1518 Washington in a three story mansion. Also art gallery. Hours: Continental breakfast 9 to 11 am, lunch from 11 am to 4 pm. (303) 279-8151. MC, V

Kenrow's Restaurant—718 12th St. The menu is a food festival all day, every day. Features a grand salad bar, complete regular bar and Mexican, American, and Italian specialties. Hours: 6 am to 11 pm daily. (303) 279-5164.

Old West Pizza Company—714 14th St. in a historic home. Serves gourmet pizza, calzones, pasta, salads, soups, sandwiches and desserts inside or on the patio. Complete bar. Hours: Monday to Wednesday 11 am to 8 pm, Thursday to Saturday 11 am to 10 pm, closed Sundays. (303) 278-1581. MC, V, AE

The Dove Inn—711 14th St. Bed and breakfast in a Victorian Inn. Centrally located in downtown Golden. Price: $29.00 including breakfast. (303) 278-2209. MC, V, AE

Iron Horse Motel—17115 W. 44th Ave. 13 rooms available during summer, singles, doubles, kitchenettes, free coffee. Price: $24.00 to $30.00. (303) 279-1071. MC, V

Foothills Ramada Inn—11595 W. 6th Ave. Luxury to the Maximum with fireplaces, waterbeds, pool, health club, restaurant, lounge with live band. (303) 238-7751. All credit cards.

La Quinta Motor Inn—at Exit 264 and I-70. Cable TV, nonsmoker and handicapped rooms, pool, restaurant and free morning coffee in lobby. Price: $41.00 and up, kids under 18 free with parent. (303) 279-5565 or 1-800-531-5900. All credit cards.

Golden Chamber of Commerce, 1204½ Washington Ave., P.O. Box 1035, Golden, CO 80402. (303) 279-3113.

GRANBY/GRAND LAKE—This area is a recreational dream, both in winter and in summer. There are many miles of cross-country ski trails in the three major touring centers as well as in the Rocky Mountain National Park and Arapahoe National Forest. Grand Lake is considered the snowmobile capital of Colorado and has more than 100 miles of maintained trails for their use. It even hosts the annual March of Dimes Snowmobile Marathon.

In the spring and summer, there are also numerous activities available. There are miles of trails for hiking, horseback riding, and backpacking in the nearby forests and parks. There are several lakes and reservoirs available for water sports and fishing, as well as rivers for white-water rafting.

All of this is located in the heart of the Rockies, 8300 feet above sea level. It is accessible via I-70 (Exit 232) and U.S. Highway 40, west over Berthoud Pass.

Things to See and Do

Trail Ridge Road—opens officially on Memorial Day, climbs to 12,183 feet. To go over this scenic ridge, take Highway 34 north from Granby or Grand Lake and through Rocky Mountain National Park.

Winterfest—held during the second week of February, this celebration includes every conceivable winter sport or event possible from sled dog races to sleigh rides to snow sculpturing.

Fourth of July—features parade, Bar-B-Que, rodeos, live music, and fireworks.

Ghost Towns—*Gaskill,* north of Grand Lake. *Lulu City,* 20 miles north of Grand Lake. *Willows,* on railroad 4 miles west of Granby *Dexter,* 7 miles north of Granby. *Spitzer,* on railroad 3 miles northeast of Granby. *Elk,* on railroad 3.5 miles southeast of Granby.

Where to Eat and Sleep

Soda Springs Ranch—9921 US Highway 34 in Grand Lake, Sunday Brunch and nightly specials from $7.95. (303) 627-3486.

El Monte Ranch Kitchen—in the Best Western, hearty food in the old world style, Sunday Champagne Brunch from $7.95. (303) 887-3486.

The Country Boy Cafe—in the Granby mini mall, serving Belgian waffles all day, homemade ice cream, Hunter's Breakfast special $3.65, and more. (303) 887-2429.

Windy Gap Inn—on Agate Ave. in Granby, the town's favorite night spot for food, entertainment and music. Family style meals a standard all day long, live music on weekends. Price: $2.00 to $5.95 and up for dinner. (303) 887-3693.

Shue's Motel—in nearby Parshall just west on US 40, no phone, no TV, lots of relaxation! The Colorado River, picnic tables, and Bar-B-Que's are in the back yard, as well as the deer that visit the property for treats. Restaurant two blocks away serves burgers and Mexican favorites for $3.00 to $5.00. Williams Fort Reservoir is 3 miles away, downhill skiing is 19 miles away and Hot Sulphur Springs is only 5 miles from the motel. Rooms have refrigerators and coffee pots, a few have single space kitchenettes and there is one small two bedroom house perfect for a family of 6. Located on U.S. Highway 40, 16 miles west of Granby. Prices: daily — $18.00 for two, $30.00 for four; weekly — $100.00 for two, $175.00 for four, house is $60.00 a night and $300.00 a week. 25% deposit required. Rates are subject to change, so write, Shue's Motel, Parshall, CO 80468, or phone (303) 725-3481 for information and to make reservations.

Shadow Mountain Ranch—bed and breakfast, log cabins built in the 1930's, fireplace in the main lodge. The ranch specializes in fishing and maintains stocked ponds, as well as having streams that

COURTESY OF SHUE'S MOTEL

Early morning visitor to Shue's Motel attracts the attention of one of its year-round residents.

cross its borders. Location: 5 miles north of Granby on Highway 125 in the scenic Willow Creek Valley. Prices: $25.00 per person/double occupancy includes bed and breakfast with lunch and dinner at additional charge. Write: Shadow Mountain Ranch, P.O. Box 4022, Silvercreek, CO 80446, or phone: (303) 887-3411.

Granby Chamber of Commerce, P.O. Box 35, Granby, CO 80446. (303) 887-2311, in state 1-800-325-1661.

KEYSTONE—a ski resort with that special style that makes you want to return again and again. Skiing takes place in a variety of settings which guarantee to be perfect for each member of the family.

Things to See and Do

Snow Skiing—the Keystone Mountain, North Peak, Arapahoe Basin ski area offers three sets of slopes and cross-country by sun or moonlight in the beautiful Arapahoe National Forest. Open from early November to early May. Price of a two day lift ticket good at all three slopes: $48.00. Write or call for information on package rates. Address: Box 38, Keystone, CO 80435. (303) 468-2316 and nationwide: 1-800-222-0188.

Helicopter Skiing—take scenic flights or ski down slopes from the tops of mountains. Scenic 30 minute flights are $85.00 per peson. Single ski runs are $35.00 per person with rull day runs between $175.00 and $295.00 which includes a gourmet lunch, guide, safety equipment, and three to four runs. (303) 668-5600.

Rollerblade—rent roller or iceskates by the hour, day or week. Price: $3.00 to $21.00. Located 1 mile east of Keystone stoplight on Highway 6 at Mountain View Plaza. (303) 468-0396.

Mine Sightseeing Tour—tour old mines, railheads, ghost towns, and more. Starts every summer Tuesday at 10 am at the Keystone Resort Activities Center. Price: $10.00 per person. (303) 468-4130.

Where to Eat and Sleep

The Navigator—at the center of Keystone Village, elegant dining and fine seafood, a legendary salad bar and New England Clam Chowder. Live entertainment at the piano bar Tuesday to Saturday from 7:30 pm to Midnight. Price: $12.95 to $26.75. (303) 468-5600.

Keystone Lodge—a full service hotel with spectacular mountain

COURTESY OF KEYSTONE RESORT

North Peak at Keystone Resort is a hot skier's playground with steep moguled terrain to challenge the most advanced skier.

view. Some rooms have sitting room, loft bedrooms, and the lodge has a heated indoor/outdoor pool, sauna, hot tub, three restaurants, two lounges. Price: $125.00 nightly, $494.00 weekly. There are also condominiums for rent. (303) 468-4242, 1-800-222-0188.

Summit County Information Center, P.O. Box 214, Frisco, CO 80443. (303) 468-6205.

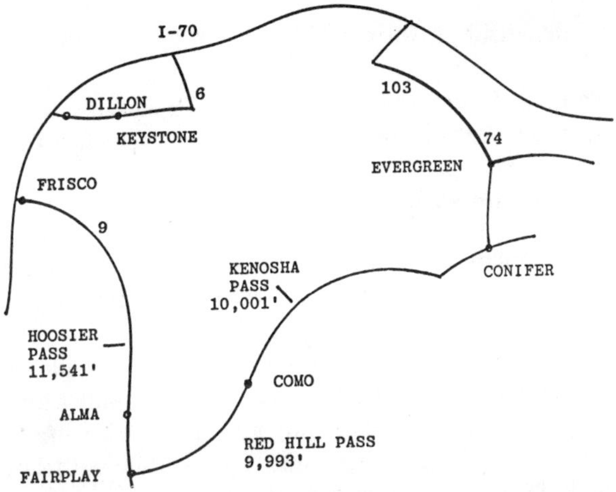

LEADVILLE—One of the most famous and infamous mining camps in our nation's history, Leadville was the richest silver camp in the country. Nearly a billion dollars in minerals was taken from the mountains around the town.

Things to See and Do

Sled Dog Races—in February at the Mt. Massive Golf Course, 3½ miles west on County Road 4, phone (303) 486-2998 for information.

Oro City—in June and July, the rebirth of a Miner's Camp, story telling, arts and crafts, mining, music, sporting events, and more. For exact information on dates, phone (303) 486-2015.

Boom Days Celebration—first weekend in August, has a street fair and entertainment, mine drilling contests.

International Pack Burro Race—22 mile race to over 13,000 feet, starts at 10 am at 6th and Harrison, approximately the 9th of August, contact Chamber of Commerce for exact dates.

Annual Victorian Homes Tour—early December. Christmas Arts and Crafts Fair, and Rekekah Bazaar.

U.S. Fish Hatchery—tours of the hatchery are *free* during the hours of 7:30 to 4:00, Monday thru Friday during May to October. Located 4 miles south of Leadville on U.S. 24.

H.A.W. Tabor House—at 116 E 5th, this historic Victorian home built in 1877 belonged to Horace and Augusta Tabor. Hours: daily 9 am to 5 pm. (303) 486-0551.

Healy House-Dexter Cabin—912 Harrison, a real 2 room miner's home on the outside, luxurious Victorian antiques on the inside. (303) 486-0487.

Turquoise Lake—four miles west of Leadville on Sixth St. Boating, water skiing, fishing, camping and picnicing are allowed.

Where to Eat and Sleep

Golden Burro Cafe and Lounge—710 Harrison, specializes in family atmosphere and dining with homemade pies and cinnamon rolls. (303) 486-1239.

Delaware Hotel—at 700 Harrison Ave., Leadville, Colorado 80461, phone (303) 486-1418. Has its own mini-mall with adorable gift shops and restaurants including an ice cream parlor and a Victorian restaurant with daily specials. Rooms filled with antique furniture include continental breakfast. Price: $35.00 to $45.00 for individual room to $65.00 to $75.00 for a two-room suite.

Mountain Mansion Bed & Breakfast—129 W 8th St., romantic little inn. Some suites and rooms with fireplaces, antiques, Argentine style breakfast or coupon to eat at a nearby American restaurant included with lodging. Special packages available at times throughout the year. Prices: The whole 8 bedroom, four fireplace, 2 kitchen home for $200.00 a night (rates get better the longer your stay). A small room for 2 with fireplace is $35.00 a night. Room or suite for 4 with fireplace and private bath is $48.00 and up. For information, write them at: 129 W 8th St., Leadville, CO 80461 (303) 486-0655.

Inn of the Black Wolf—in nearby Twin Lakes. Feather beds and breakfast, this hotel is a 100 year old stage coach stop and brothel. It holds its own special events throughout the year. Prices include a two day special, $44.95 per person which covers two night's lodging, one dinner, and one breakfast. Write the inn at Highway 82, Twin Lakes, Colorado 81251, or phone (303) 486-0440.

Sugar Loafin' Campground—go south on US 24 to 6th Ave. and go west to County Road 4. Go northwest on 4 to the campground. No hookups, separate tent area, store, grills, wood, showers. Price: $11.00 and up. (303) 486-1031.

Leadville Chamber of Commerce, P.O. Box 861, Leadville, Colorado 80461, or phone (303) 486-3900 or stop by their offices at 809 Harrison Avenue.

LOVELAND—is a rapidly expanding city 50 miles north of Denver, it is in the foothills of the Rocky Mountains. This group of people is a most serious bunch, especially when it comes to the name of its town. Yes, this is the place where you send Valentine cards to be remailed with a handstamped romantic postmark (address and stamp your cards, place them in an envelope and send it to Postmaster, Attn. Valentines, Loveland, CO 80537 by February 7. They also re-send wedding invitations and any other mail.)

Things to See and Do

Sweetheart Balloon Rally—weekend closet to St. Valentine's Day, color fills the sky over Loveland. Local businesses sponsor each aircraft and often raffle off a ride.

Sculpture in the Park & Arts and Crafts Show—mid-August showing of the work of local artists, demonstrations, and tours of a local Art Castings Foundry. Held at Benson Park and North Lake Park (both at 29th and Taft). For information call (303) 667-6311 or (303) 667-9211.

Corn Roast Festival—lots of fun for everyone at this late August party. Starting early, attend the bed race and parade, then watch or participate in the contests. Contests: lip-sync, horseshoes, mud wrestling, fiddling, *sexy legs* (for men only), and corn eating (most ears, most creative style of eating, cleanest ear).

Stone Age Fair—late September, it includes displays of Indian artifacts and demonstrations. It is sponsored by the Loveland Archaeological Society. (303) 669-7149.

12 Scenic Mountain Circle Trips—the Chamber of Commerce has provided a pamphlet listing 12 drives which give the visitor an excellent opportunity to explore the area's beauty. One of the drives is this. Take US 34 south 2 miles and turn left on County Road 19-E. Continue to a T intersection and turn right on County Road 20. Turn left on County Road 29 and then right on County Road 18-E until the intersection with County Road 31 and go right to Lake Carter. Take County Road 8-E and Colorado Road 56 east into Berthoud then north on US 287 to Loveland. This drive is great for later afternoon. Stop by the Chamber of Commerce for more information on scenic drives.

Loveland Museum—503 Lincoln Ave., it contains an art gallery, a gigantic map of the Thompson Water Reclamation Project and many antiques from the late 1800's. Price: *Free.*

Ghost Towns—there are quite a few of these as well as abandoned mines in the area. The towns of *Birds, Gove* and *Office* are located a few miles east of Loveland. Ask a few local residents or the Chamber of Commerce for exact directions to these and others in the area.

Where to Eat and Sleep

Heartland Cafe—301 E 4th St., serves family style meals with homemade flair. (303) 669-1400.

Josie Dillon's—530 N Cleveland Ave., the best in homemade food. (303) 669-6787.

Village Inn Pancake House—1225 W Eisenhower Blvd., any kind of pancake you want and more. (303) 667-8555.

Fireside Motel—6850 Highway 34 W, 8 rooms with fireplaces, some kitchenettes, AC, color TV, no pets. Price: $25.00 and up. (303) 667-2903. MC, V, AE

Lakeview Motel—768 W Eisenhower Blvd., newly remodeled

with some suites, cable TV, Free breakfast for 2 with coupon from motel manager and receipt. Price: $20.00 and up. (303)663-2600 MC, V.

Loveland Super 8 Motel—1655 E. Eisenhower Blvd., brand new motel with queen size beds, some king size, non-smoking rooms, free coffee and local calls. Price: $21.88 to $30.88. (303) 663-7000. Major credit cards.

Riverview Campground—7806 W. Highway 34, 6 miles west of town, open year round, BIG trees, full hookups, hot showers, camping and RV supplies, grills, game room, weekly and monthly rates available. Price: $7.75 to $10.75 for 2 people. (303) 667-9910.

Loveland Chamber of Commerce, 114 East 5th St., P.O. Box 7058, Loveland, CO 80537. (303) 667-6311.

MINTURN—Located just five miles west of Vail, this town plays host to a variety of activities.

Things to See and Do

Fourth of July—Minturn Volunteer Fire Department puts on a Bar-B-Que and fireworks display.

Minturn Crafts Fair—early September, features homemade Mexican food, live entertainment, a pancake breakfast, and a parade in addition to the many arts and crafts displays.

Senior Citizens Luncheon—every Tuesday and Thursday at the Minturn Town Hall.

Lost Crazy Woman Mine—it is rumored that this mine was in the Minturn area and had extremely rich ore. Who knows what those hikes in the woods might bring you. Take the pan and try your luck in a stream.

National Forests—Minturn sits right between the White River and Arapahoe National Forests and makes the perfect base camp from which to explore them both. NOTE: The regional office of the Forest Service is located in Minturn and offers great advice on hiking, trails, campgrounds, and woodcutting and Christmas tree permits, etc.

Where to Eat and Sleep

Minturn Country Club—choose and cook your own steaks, fish, Shish K-Bob, or chicken over the charcoal grill yourself. Steaks from rib eye by the ounce to the 16 ounce Porterhouse . . . Prices: $3.25 to $11.95. Located in downtown Minturn on Main St. (303) 827-4114.

Turntable Cafe—one of the last "great American diners" this place serves excellent breakfasts, sandwiches, burgers, and entrees that are served with soup or salad, potatoe, vegetable, and rolls. The menu is also full of trivia and tips from local old timers. Prices: $3.05 to $10.95, children's menu under $3.00. Located at Exit 171 in Minturn. (303) 827-4164.

The Saloon—Mexican food from tacos and burritos to local favorites like steak and quail and all possible combinations of the above. Price: $7.95 to $17.95. Located at 146 S Main. (303) 827-5954.

Eagle River Inn—newly remodeled hotel only 10 minutes from Vail and Beaver Creek ski resorts with 4 nearby restaurants. Two surrounding national forests make this the perfect place to use as a base camp from which to explore the wilderness. Price: seasonal from $75.00 to $100.00. (303) 827-5761.

Town of Minturn Chamber of Commerce, Minturn, CO 81645. (303) 476-1000.

PARSHALL—close to all major attractions of the state, snow skiing, forests, fishing and prospecting. It is small enough to be a quite place to stay but without being totally isolated.

Ghost Towns—*Pearmont* is 10 miles to the northwest. *Troublesome* is on an old railroad track just a 5 mile hike west. Ask the residents for their directions, as well as about other ghost towns in the area.

Williams Fork Reservoir—south of Parshall, a great place to fish, hike or relax in the beautiful Arapahoe National Forest.

Shue's Motel—in Parshall on US 40, no phone, no TV, lots of relaxation! The Colorado River, picnic tables, and Bar-B-Q's are in the back yard, as well as the deer that visit the property for treats. Restaurant two blocks away serves burgers and Mexican favorites for \$3.00 to \$5.00. Williams Fork Reservoir is 3 miles away, downhill skiing is 19 miles away and Hot Sulphur Springs is only 5 miles from the motel. Rooms have refrigerators and coffee pots, a few have kitchenettes and there is one small two bedroom house perfect for a family of 6. Located on US Highway 40, 16 miles west of Grandby Prices: daily — \$18.00 for two, \$30.00 for four; weekly — \$100.00 for two, \$175.00 for four, house is \$60.00 a night and \$300.00 a week. 25% deposit required. Rates are subject to change, so write Shue's Motel, Parshall, CO 80468, or phone (303) 725-3481 for information and to make reservations.

COURTESY OF COLORADO TOURISM BOARD

Magnificent view of the Pike National Forest and its famous mountain, Pikes Peak.

PIKE NATIONAL FOREST—this forest consists of over a million acres west of Colorado Springs. As is indicated by its name, it was christened after Zebulon Pike who tried to climb the mountain which is now named after him. Pike's Peak is not the tallest mountain in the United States, but it is impressive because it rises from the plains so majestically. The top of it can be reached by car, railroad or foot.

The region is also famous for its gold and silver production, which led to its development in the late 1800's. The road to Cripple Creek and Victor will give to visitors some appreciation of the hardships indured by the miners who lived here. Along the way, watch for ghost towns and likely streams to pan.

The forest is also home to the oldest living things on Earth, the Bristlecone Pines. You can find them along the Windy Ridge Bristlecone Pine Scenic Area. It is in the western most portion of the forest and can be reached from Fairplay.

Camping is permitted in the forest and there are 37 designated campgrounds. Most are very primitive with only camper disposal facilities, but they are an excellent bargain at $5.00 a night.

Forest Supervisor, 1920 Valley Dr., Pueblo, CO 81008

ROCKY MOUNTAIN NATIONAL PARK—a true treasure, it preserves the alpine wilderness of the mountains it is named after. One third of its total area is above the tree line and snow capped peaks are everywhere. The park also holds one of the most famous scenic drives in the world, the Trail Ridge Road. Take US 34 between Estes Park and Granby to enjoy this picturesque highway, but remember that it is open from June to September only because of its high altitude.

The wildlife also abounds here and birdwatching, hiking, and fishing often are rewarding pastimes that bring nature to you. Remember to be quiet in the woods and the animals will be less likely to run away. There are numberous hiking trails throughout the park which connect mountain lakes and lead to glens and valleys full of lost mines and gold.

The winter also brings activity to the park. Local skiers have long known it as a perfect place for cross-country skiing and ice skating.

A pass is required to enter the park. It is $2.00 and certainly worth the price.

COURTESY OF COLORADO TOURISM BOARD

Horseshoe Park is one of the many beautiful vistas seen within the Rocky Mountain National Park.

ROOSEVELT NATIONAL FOREST—this forest was originally part of the Medicine Bow Forest Reserve, in 1910 it became the Colorado National Forest. In 1932, President Herbert Hoover renamed it in honor of President Theodore Roosevelt who was most responsible for the creation of the National Forest system. The region is dotted with alpine lakes, high mountains and deep canyons. There are even a few small glaciers and the remnants of ancient icefields to see. Activities available include hiking, backpacking, mountain climbing, camping, fishing, hunting, photography, and pleasure driving. Local ranger stations can advise visitors of any regulations concerning these activities.

Things to See and Do

Scenic Routes—take State Road 14 over Cameron Pass to adjoining Routt National Forest. Or take State Road 7 to SR 72 to SR 119 to see the famous mining town of Central City.

Hiking—trails in the Forest range in type from grasslands to high mountain routes on the Continental Divide. Hiking and backpacking may only be done by foot or horseback, no motorized vehicles are permitted (see ranger station for information on this as well as those rules governing fire, sanitation, and safety).

Camping—there are many campgrounds throughout the Forest which range from fully developed with complete facilities to "walk in" tent camping with little or no facilities. Camping where there is no designated site is permitted in parts of the Forest, but rules and backcountry ethic must be observed. Fees: $5.00 to $7.00 a night.

Gold Panning—gold may be found in many of the streams within the Forest. It is recommended that prospectors contact the ranger station in the area they intend to search for information on land ownership, existing mining claims, and any restrictions.

Rafting—the Forest does not restrict rafting on any of the rivers, but a permit is required by the local county Sheriff's Office. White water rafting can be done on the Poudre River.

Supervisor's Office, Roosevelt National Forest, 240 W. Prospect, Ft. Collins, CO 80526. (303) 224-1277.

ROUTT NATIONAL FOREST—this forest has one of the longest lists of things to do; it can become a whole vacation in itself.

Anyone who is a fishing addict could easily spend a lifetime in this area, and for campers, hikers and backpackers its a dream come true! Of course, for the person who prefers to spend his vacation in a hammock, it also has its appeal.

Fishing—after the spring run-off and after the water has slowed down is the best time to dig out the tackle box. In the Routt National Forest and the surrounding area, there are many breeds of fish to catch such as cuttroat, rainbow, brook, lake, and brown trout, Kokanee Salmon, Grayling, Pike, and a host of others. Lakes and streams may be used for bait fishing, but in some areas only artificial flies and lures are allowed. Every person over 15 years old must have a valid Colorado fishing license, whether they are a resident of the state or not. Specific information and licenses may be obtained at any sporting goods store in the state or by writing the Division of Wildlife, 606 Broadway, Denver, CO 80216. Visitors to the forest may also obtain information from the ranger stations, or by writing (be sure to ask for Carl Creel's pamphlet of favorite fishin' holes and tips).

Hunting—Write the Division of Wildlife in Denver for the Colorado Hunting Information Guide. It gives all information needed to hunt in the state's big game seasons, including rules on antler restrictions, combined seasons, different weapons, and applications for each season.

Mt. Zirkel Wilderness—this part of Routt National Forest straddles the Park Range of the Continental Divide and ranges from spruce/fir forests to alpine meadows. There are 14 mountain peaks near or over 12,000 feet, more than 65 lakes, herds of elk and mule deer, ptarmigan and pika just to name a few. Points of interest include Slavonia Mine (8 miles up Gold Creek) and Ute Pass which was used by Indians. Three of the access points afford easier travel for automobiles. For a pamphlet, write the forest. This is just one fine example of the many wilderness areas here.

Hiking—Routt National Forest contains 130.6 miles of trails which are mapped out and described in detail. The shortest of these is 2.8 miles and is rated moderate for difficulty. Longest is the Wyoming Trail, which at 47.3 miles is rated more difficult. The trails also are rated of use which is from light to very heavy. For a list of trails, write the forest.

Winter Activities—cross-country skiing can be done throughout the forest in designated areas and equipment may be rented for around $10.00 per day. Snowmobiling is also available, but visitors may only go on guided tours and cannot rent equipment alone. Sleigh rides can be taken and are offered with or without dinner. In the Routt National Forest, there are 286 campsites in 26 different campgrounds. Facilities differ from one to the other and there are no showers, flush toilets, or hookups. The campgrounds collect fees from July 1 through October and many of the no-fee grounds are self-service or no-service, so be ready to carry out all refuse. Fees range from $4.00 to $6.00. For a complete list of campgrounds and their various attractions, visit the ranger stations or write: Supervisors Office, 29587 W. US 40, Steamboat Springs, CO 80487, or phone (303) 879-1722.

SILVERTHORNE—originally a mining town, like many others it has become a resort community with many activities available for the tourists.

Things to See and Do

Snow Skiing—either cross-country out of town into the National Forests or visit one of the many nearby ski areas. Keystone Ski Area south on Highway 6 open from mid-October to early May, two day lift ticket $48.00, call 1-800-222-0188 or (303) 468-4242. Loveland Basin and Valley Ski Area east on I-70 and exit 216 open from mid-October to May, full day lift ticket $19.00, call (303) 569-2288.

Fishing—the Blue River from Hoosier Pass to the Colorado River has been proclaimed Gold Metal Water when it comes to angling. Try your luck anywhere along Highway 9 but make sure to obey signs indicating private property. There are various parking areas and river access points throughout town. Write the Town of Silverthorne for their fishing brochure.

National Forests—Silverthorne is situated between both the Arapahoe National Forest and the White River National Forest. Make the town your base camp and explore the beauty of either of these treasures, summer or winter.

Scenic Drive—go north on State Road 9 to US 40. Along 9 you should be able to see many mines and ghost towns. The streams were said to blind people with their riches, so stop and give panning a

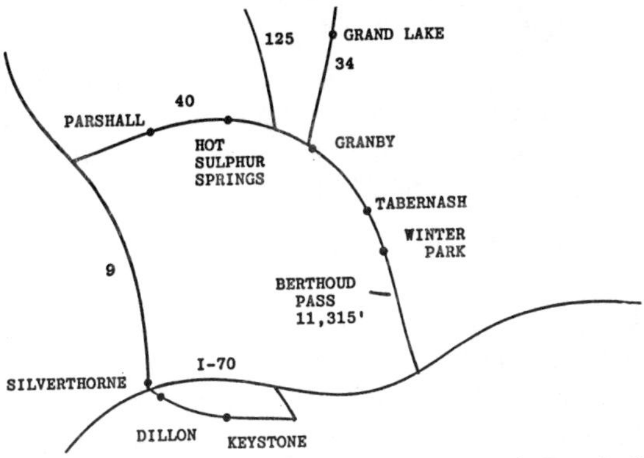

try in any of the streams you pass. Go east through Parshall to Hot Sulphur Springs. From here you can continue on 40, or, if your car is in shape, try the road over Cottonwood Pass to the right as you get to town. You will meet up with US 40 again, head southeast through Tabernash and Fraser. You will then go over the famous Berthoud Pass (11,314 feet). When you reach I-70, go west back to Silverthorne.

Where to Eat and Sleep

Fun Hog Ranch Bar & Grill—3/4 mile north of I-70 on the Blue River Parkway, hearty meals for the skier, happy hours, 4 TV's, pool tables, darts, and more. Food features burgers, munchies, omelettes and pancakes. Hours: 6:45 am to whenever at night. Price: average meal $4.75. (303) 468-2457.

The Mint Country Club—at 341 Blue River Parkway. The only thing missing is the golf course, but it does feature a 20 item salad bar, big steaks, and lots of homemade soups and desserts. Hours: daily for lunch and dinner. Price: average meal $8.95. (303) 468-5247.

Willow Creek Cookery—1½ miles north of I-70 on Highway 9, it has elegant dining with vegetarian specials and country cookin'. Hours: daily for breakfast, lunch and dinner. Price: $4.00 to $16.50. (303) 468-8432.

Sunshine Cafe—in the Summit Place Shopping Center, serving gourmet burgers, omelettes, and other goodies. Hours: daily 7 am to 8 pm. Price: $2.50 to $6.50. (303) 468-6663.

Eagle's Nest Resort or
Silverthorne Lodge or
Wildernest. Call for reservations: (303) 468-5289.

Ptarmigan Mountain Bed & Breakfast—reservations are a must for a stay in this 7 bedroom, 4 story home nestled in the trees. They serve skiers in the winter and sailors in the summer and are only 5 minutes from town and Lake Dillon. Price: $25.00 to $70.00. Call for reservations. (303) 468-5289.

TWIN LAKES—a famed gold and silver camp, it boasted many a boisterous crowd in its heyday. Today, the town has calmed down only a little and anyone looking for fun time should check it out.

Twin Lakes Reservoir—two lakes merged into one provide enjoyment for the angler and boater. They are stocked with mackinaw trout but fishermen are limited to one apiece 20 inches or more. The north shore of the lakes is available for picnicing and has grills. Campsites are available.

Tomatoe War—mid-September, the Inn of the Black Wolf annually sponsors this war between Colorado and Texas, who practice *"tomatoe ballistics"* with lethal results. After the last tomatoe has exploded the first day, the truce is called and one and all join for a rock and roll party. The dawn, however, does not bring peace and the battle begins anew. To join the army, a soldier must pay the $39.00 entry fee which buys him a T-shirt, entrance in the three day battle, and an *unlimited supply* of ammo.

Inn of the Black Wolf—Feather beds and breakfast, this hotel is a 100 year old stage coach stop and brothel. It holds its own special event throughout the year. Prices include a two day special, $44.95 per person which covers two night's lodging, one dinner, and one breakfast. Write the Inn at Highway 82, Twin Lakes, Colorado 81251, or phone (303) 486-0440. Remember to inquire about the special events which are all just as fun and exciting as the tomato war listed above.

VAIL—100 miles west of Denver on I-70, this well-known resort town is easy to get to and fun to visit year round. Probably best known for its world class skiing, this town has still more to offer during the spring, summer and fall. Located in the center of the White River National Forest, Vail provides a convenient base from which to explore the wilderness around it. Luxury is the key word here. The town has 72 world class famous restaurants, cozy resort lodges, and perfect weather for that intimate walk for two in the woods.

COURTESY DAVIS LOKEY

Bright winter day downtown in the village of Vail.

Things to See and Do

Snow Skiing—season is from late November to mid-April and 8:30 am to 3:30 pm each day. A multitude of possibilities await the skier on more than 10 square miles of ski terrain from beginner's courses to expert runs. There are more than 60 miles of trails and two vast powder bowls. Ten miles west is Beaver Creek with its 750 acres of skiing. For full brochure, write: Vail Resort Association, 241 E. Meadow Dr., Vail, CO (303) 476-5677, nationwide 1-800-525-3875; Beaver Creek Central Reservations, P.O. Box 915, Avon, CO 81620, (303) 949-5750, nationwide 1-800-525-2257.

Ski Tours—take a cross-country ski trip from 4 to 6 days or more. Stay in beautiful lodges each night and cross silent, awesome landscapes each day. Price: $350.00 a day for 1 to 4 skiers, each additional person $95.00 a day. Write: Paragon Guides, P.O. Box 130, Vail, CO 81658.

Gondola Rides—enjoy a ride to the top of Vail Mountain all year round. Ride back down or hike it in summer. Winter perhaps provides the fastest way down the mountain, bring your skiis. There are two restaurants at the top to eat at and enjoy the view. Hours: summer 10:00 am to 4:30 pm, and winter 8:30 am to 3:30 pm. (303) 949-5750, ext. 4580.

Colorado Mountain College—in west Vail in the Cascade Village Complex, it offers courses, workshops, and seminars all year round. Subjects are fly fishing, wine tasting, photography, area history, ethnic cooking, and kayaking to name a few. (303) 476-4040.

Balloon Colorado—the highest balloon port in the world offers everything including Champagne flights both winter and summer. Address: Box 1364, Dillon, CO 80435. (303) 476-0808. MC, V, AE

Winterfair—mid-January festival which is highlighted by International Ski Races and ice and snow sculpturing contests.

Hiking—Vail Mountain offers marked trails ranging in length from .4 miles to 4.6 miles. If you hike up the mountain, the gondola ride down is *free.*

Vailfest—3-day, mid-September celebration which gives emphasis to the beauty of the changing Aspen leaves. Events include a walkfest, 5K and 10K runs, lawn party, music, barbeque, and a mountaintop dinner at Eagle's Nest. Special event: Annual Vail High School Marching Band and Jazz Competition. (303) 476-1000.

Ski Hall of Fame—just east of Vail, it gives historical exhibits about skiing and its past as well as films on the sport. Price: *Free.* (303) 476-1876.

Where to Eat and Sleep

Alfie Packer's—sit on the deck and sun yourself or watch the widescreen TV. Serves seafood, prime rib, steak, and salad bar. Next to the gondola in Lionshead, open for lunch and dinner. (303) 476-2121. MC, V, AE

Bart and Yeti's—inside and outside, sit and eat the fine sandwiches and barbeque ribs in log cabin atmosphere. Open for lunch and dinner. Address: 553 E. Lionshead Circle. (303) 476-2754. MC, V, AE

D. J. McCadams—breakfast anytime with delicious omelette specialties, and great lunches and dinners too! Located in the Concert Hall Plaza at the west end of Lionshead, 616 Lionshead Circle (303) 476-2336.

Marriott's Mark Resort—the restaurant, actually there are 5. *Shadows*-nightspot, dancing. *Windows*-roof-top dining, steak by the ounce. *Center Court*-country, fire-side setting breakfast to late night snacks. *The Oasis*-exotic drinks and sandwiches poolside. *Luigi's* ***PIZZA!*** ('til 3:00 am yet!)

The Resort prices:

Winter	Hotel	1 Bedroom	2 Bedroom	3 Bedroom
Nightly	115-175	150-290	220-425	300-600
Weekly	528-738	650-1140	510-869	475-825
Summer				
Nightly	95	145	220	300

Package specials available during summer vary, contact Resort at (303)476-4444.

Sitzmark Lodge—183 Gore Creek Dr., ski packages, cable TV, pool, whirlpool, sauna, free continental breakfast, some oversize beds, refrigerators. Price: nightly $41.00 to $107.00. (303) 476-5001.

Gore Creek Campground—take Highway 67 northeast 3 miles, then FR 370 east 8 miles. Run by the national forest, it has toilets, pull-thru's, tables and fishing but no hookups. Price: $6.00. Open June to September.

For complete listings of rates, both winter and summer, for all hotels in the Vail area, please write to the Chamber of Commerce. The rates above do show the feasibility of a summer stay in Vail.

Vail Chamber of Commerce and Resort Association, 241 E. Meadow Dr., Vail, CO 81657. (303) 476-5677, nationwide 1-800-525-3875.

WELLINGTON—is a small village in the north central part of the state. It is the home of Chief Justice Byron "Whizzer" White and there is a park dedicated in his honor in the town.

Things to See and Do

Pawnee National Grasslands—take Interstate 25 south to Highway 14 and go east. Watch the plains for wildlife such as buffalo.

Roosevelt National Forest—take I-25 south and Highway 14 west. This will take you to some beautiful forest and a well-known scenic route.

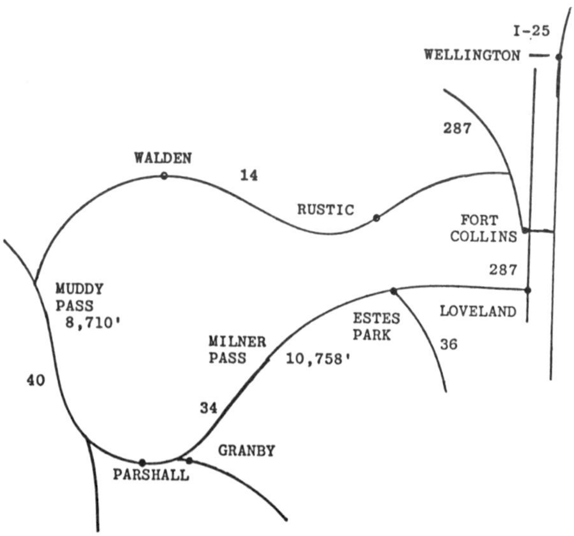

Scenic Drive—follow Highway 14 west to Highway 40. Go southeast on 40 to 34. Highway 34 goes northeast through Roosevelt National Forest and Rocky Mountain National Park. This is closed in winter as Trail Ridge Road is snowed in over the Continental Divide. In summer it gives the driver a spectacular view so remember the camera and for the safety of everyone, only stop your car at designated overlooks. Stay on 34 until you reach I-25 and go north back to Wellington.

Well-O-Rama—the third weekend in June bursts forth in Wellington with a demolition derby, tractor pulls, dances, arts and crafts, and a variety of other games and activities.

Anheuser-Busch Brewery—6 miles away on I-25, this is the newest and most modern of all the company's facilities. Tours are *Free.*

Where to Sleep

Kamper Kountry—take I-25 to exit 278 then take CRF 5 east 14 mile. Has full hookups, store, tables, showers, toilets and pool. Price: $9.00 and up. (303) 568-7486.

WINTER PARK—the town is a ski resort with all things revolving around the slopes.

Things to See and Do

Snow Skiing—for cross-country at its best, contact Snow Mountain Ranch/YMCA of the Rockies, P.O. Box 169, Winter Park, CO 80482 (303) 887-2152 for information on lodging, groomed trails, and rentals. Or just take off in either of the adjacent National Forests. For down hill skiing, there are some beautiful slopes on the combination of Winter Park Mountain and Mary Jane Mountain containing 1028 acres, 18 lifts, and programs for beginning and advanced skiers. Open from Mid-November to mid-April. Price of a full day lift ticket: $24.00. 1-800-453-2525 or (303) 726-5587.

Winter Festivals—Christmas Eve Torchlight Ski Down, December 24. Winter Wild West Week, last week in January. Colorado Ski Week, beginning of April.

Professional Snow Skiing Races—First Interstate Bank Cup, beginning of February. Mascot Race, beginning of April. Golden Bunny Race, Easter Sunday. Many more.

Where to Eat and Sleep

Beaver Village—½ mile south on US 40. Has rooms, condos with kitchens up to 4 bedrooms, pool, sauna, cafe. Prices: Lodge $25.00 to $48.00, condos $42.00 to $122.00. (303) 726-5741, 1-800-525-3561. MC, V, AE

Idlewild National Forest Campground—1 mile south on US 40, tents and RV's welcome, tables, wood. Primitive but gorgeous. Price: $6.00 (303) 725-3301.

Robber's Roost National Forest Campground—5 miles south on US 40, tents and RV's welcome, tables, wood. Price: $6.00. (303) 725-3301.

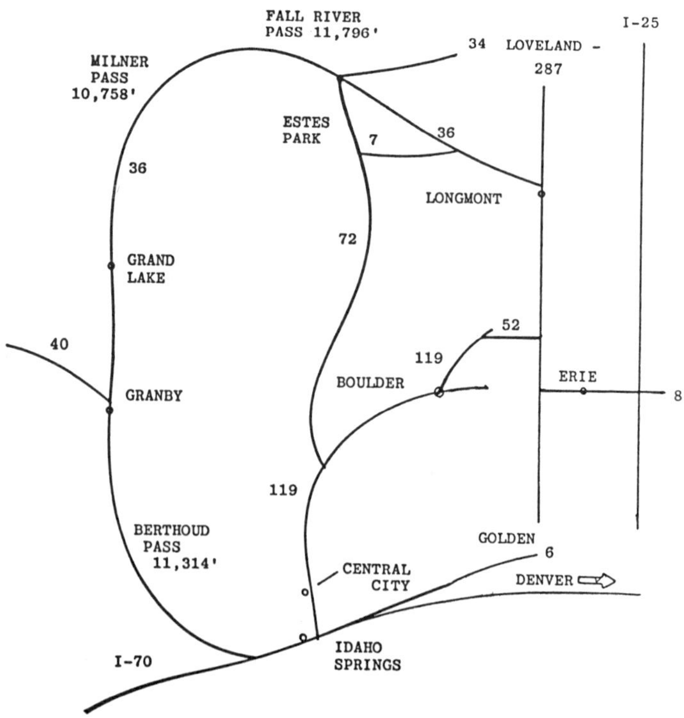

AREA THREE

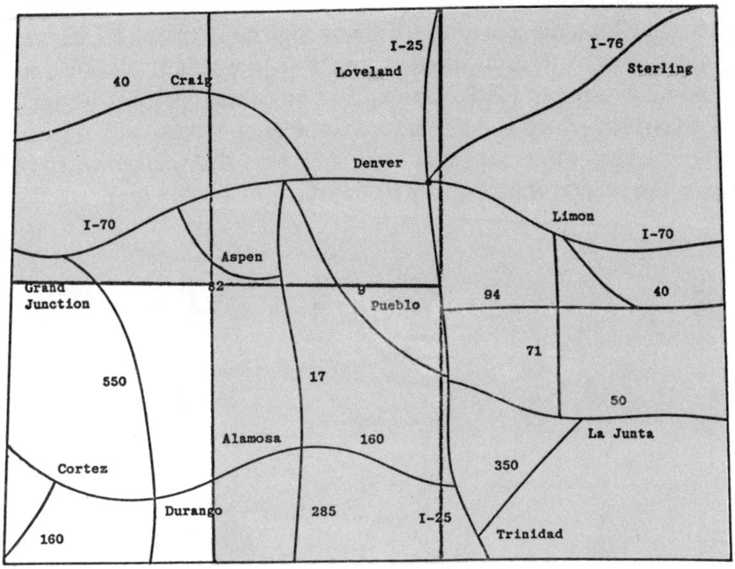

CEDAREDGE—known as the southern gateway to Grand Mesa, the 10,000 foot high flat-topped mountain, it is much more than only the entrance to a natural wonder. It and its surrounding small towns of Austin, Cory, Eckert and Orchard City fill the Surface Creek Valley with good people and lots to do.

Things to See and Do

Hart's Basin Reservoir—one mile southeast of Eckert provides boating and water skiing and other water oriented sports.

Surface Creek Festival—the second week in July, it brings dancing, a barbeque, a parade, a pancake breakfast, and a fantastic art show to the valley. This is all capped off by the Little Britches Rodeo.

Apple Festival—in October, Cedaredge comes alive again with apples. There are apple judging and pie eating contests, square dancing, and apple dunking. The streets are also lined with arts and crafts booths.

Grand Mesa National Forest—more than 340,000 acres in west-central Colorado, it is north of Cedaredge on Highway 65. There are picnic areas with grills, boat ramps, a visitor center, wildlife galore, and many campgrounds. Don't miss Crag Crest National Recreation Trail which offers unique views of the area.

Fishing—the many lakes atop the mesa and the nearby streams give the angler choice spots from which to try his luck.

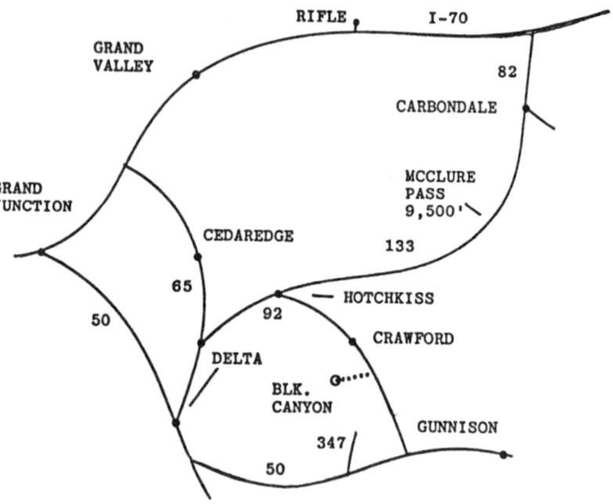

Scenic Drive—take Highway 65 south to Highway 92 and go east to Hotchkiss. At Hotchkiss, take Highway 133 northeast through the awesome Gunnison, White River and Grand Mesa National Forests. They all border the highway along this route which travels over high mountain passes. In Carbondale, take Highway 82 north to I-70 and head west. At Interchange 49, take Highway 65 back to Cedaredge.

Cedaredge Chamber of Commerce, Box 278, Cedaredge, CO 81413.

CORTEZ—this town grew because of its trade in sheep and cattle, but now is more noted for playing host to people visiting Mesa Verde National Park.

Things to See and Do

Mesa Verde National Park—located in the high plateau country of southwestern Colorado, between the cities of Cortez and Mancos off of US 160. Park headquarters are located 21 miles from the entrance. Hiking and camping are permitted in designated areas only. Some Recreational Vehicles and trailors may be restricted because of road conditions, parking is available. Cliff dwellings may only be entered when accompanied by a ranger. The entrance station can provide the visitor with information, maps, and schedules for tours and lectures. Price: $2.00 per vehicle, .50¢ for bus passengers.

COURTESY OF COLORADO TOURISM BOARD

Looking down at Cliff Palace in the beautiful and mysterious Mesa Verde National Park.

Ute Mountain Tribal Park—south of Cortez on US 666 at Towaoc, reservations are required because a tribal guide must accompany each group of visitors. The park has been set aside by the tribe to preserve prehistoric Indian dwellings. Camping, hiking tours, and backpacking are permitted. For more information, write: Ute Mountain Tribal Park, Towaoc, CO 81334, or phone (303) 565-3751, Ext. 282.

Four Corners—take US 160 southwest and follow the signs to the only spot in America where four state corners meet. Have your picture taken of you in four states at one time.

Four in one, strike an interesting pose at Four Corners.

Lowry Pueblo Ruins—take US 666 northwest to Pleasant View then go 9 miles west on the county road. See the sacred kivas of the Anasazi Indians. Bring water, lunch and a camera. Price: *Free.*

Hovenweep National Monument—take 666 northwest to Pleasant View, then 5 miles west on County BB, then County 10 south for 20 miles. The ruins include cliff dwellings, pueblos, a self-guided trail and camping facilities all year round. (303) 529-4461.

Where to Eat and Sleep

McDonald's—the Golden Arches on the main street going through town have one thing going for them that most fast food places don't, live entertainment. That's right, because the vacant lot next door is home to hundreds of prarie dogs which put on quite a show. The food is standard fast food, but the window seats make it worthwhile.

Homesteaders—45 E. Main, serves American favorites and Mexican goodies also, and summer brings melodrama to the restaurant. Live entertainment, fresh baked breads and buffets make it good dining all around. Price: $2.15 to $5.95 for breakfast and lunch, $3.95 to $9.50 for dinner. (303) 565-6253. MC, V

Sands of Cortez—1000 E. Main St., this Best Western has indoor pool, oversize beds, satellite and cafe. Price: $46.00 to $55.00. (303) 565-3761. MC, V, AE

El Capri—2110 S. Broadway, has free coffee in rooms, pool, playground, cable TV and picnic grills. Price: $30.00 to $36.00. (303) 565-3764. MC, V, AE

Lazy G Motel & Campground—at the intersection of Highway 145 and US 160, east of Cortez. has sauna, jacuzzi, pool, full hookups, showers, tables, ice. Price: $9.00 and up. (303) 565-8577.

CREEDE—this town is nestled in the bosom of the historic, boom-town area. It was started as a silver mining camp around 1889 and was visited by many of the famous and infamous characters of the old west such as Bob Ford, the killer of Jesse James (Ford himself was killed in Creede and a marker in the cemetery shows where he was buried before his remains were taken to Missouri), Bat Masterson, Calamity Jane, and Alferd Packer (who was tried in Creede and sentenced to hang for cannibalism) just to name a few. This town also boasts of a few visitors who don't happen to be among the living and guests in some of the older hotels may meet up with a ghost if they're lucky, or unlucky as the case may be. These spirits are reputed to be those of Bob Ford and various miners.

Things to See and Do

Rio Grande River Raft Races—early June, on the river between Creede and South Fork. Both amateur and pro races and a first place prize purse of $1000.00!

Raft Race Dance—first night of the races at the Elk's Hall in Creede.

Creede Repertory Theatre—giving excellent performances of five different plays throughout the summer, it was noted in an article of New York City's Backstage magazine (March 22, 1985 issue) because of its ongoing commitment to present new plays. Opens in early June and closes on Labor Day, tickets are priced at around $8.00. Phone: (303) 658-2540.

COURTESY OF JOHN GARY BROWN AND CREEDE CHAMBER OF COMMERCE.

Creede Opera House, home of the Creede Repertory Theatre.

Fourth of July/Days of '92—after the traditional parade, the real celebration starts in Creede. Mining contests such as machine, single and double jack drilling, machine and hand mucking (shoveling ore), and the Miner of the Year Award are presented. Fireworks, dances, and parties go far into the night.

COURTESY OF MINERAL COUNTY MINER

Days of '92 mining contest.

Wolf Creek Ski Area—east on 149, then south on 160 (40 miles altogether) takes the skier to challenging, but little known slopes which are big on excitement and small on lines.

Bachelor Loop—scenic drive past mines, ghost towns, wildlife, and breathtaking mountain landscapes. The complete circle takes 1 to 2 hours and is 11.2 miles long. Remember to check your vehicle's brakes beforehand as much of the trip is up and down steep inclines. Take the road past the courthouse at the north end of town, when it forks take the left branch. You then take West Willow Road up the steep incline of the mountain. Follow the road as it leaves Willow Creek and bear left at the switchback and as you cross West Willow Creek. The Bachelor Townsite is in a large clearing, a magnificent place to picnic and take in the view of the Rio Grande Valley far below. Return to town the way you got there. The Chamber of Commerce can provide a detailed description of all the sights on this drive and many others in the area.

Inspiration Point Trail—take the trail up the hill behind the school. It has a magnificent view of the countryside, and the balance of the day should be given to this venture. Bring your camera and pack a snack to enjoy at the Point, but remember to take all garbage back with you. A complete guide to this and other hiking trails can be found in the Mineral County Miner paper or through the Chamber of Commerce.

Where to Eat and Sleep

The Bristol Inn—located 18 miles southwest of Creede on 149, this restaurant offers casual elegance and meals that include a salad, entree, vegetable, rice or potatoe, homemade bread, and tea or coffee. Open Wednesday to Saturday from 5:30 to 9:30 pm, and on Sunday from 11:00 am to 6:00 pm for a buffet.

The Lighter Side—part of the Bristol Inn, this part of the restaurant offers a sunroom and a lighter (of course) menu including soups, sandwiches, salads, and light entrees, as well as appetizers and desserts. Open Wednesday to Saturday from 5:30 to 9:30 pm. Reservations suggested, *no tips please.* Prices: $3.00 to $10.00. Phone: (303) 658-2455.

The Golden Nugget—located in downtown Creede, this establishment serves breakfast and lunch from 7:00 am to 2:00 pm and from 5:00 to 9:00 pm for dinner and after the theatre. Family-style fare that can't be beat. Phone: (303) 658-2385.

Antler's Ranch—5 miles south of Creede on Highway 149. Cabins and efficiency units on the Rio Grande provide backdoor fishing at its best. Reservations required. Rates: $40.00 to $54.00 a night with weekly rates available. Address: Box 310, Creede, CO 81130, or phone (303) 658-2423.

Continental Ranch—30 miles north of Creede on 149, 11 primitive cabins with lakes and streams nearby for fishing. Rates: $12.00 for singles, $15.00 for doubles. Reservations required, address: Continental Ranch, Creede, CO 81130, or phone (303) 658-2257.

Wason Ranch—2 miles southeast of Creede on the Rio Grande River, many of the 22 cabins have fireplaces and guided fishing is available. Rates: riverside cabins $85.00 a day (minimum of 5 days), smaller cabins: weekly rate of $34.00 a day. Address: Box 220, Creede, CO 81130, or phone: (303) 658-2413.

Snowshoe Motel—at the southeastern edge of town, this motel offers cable TV, a gift shop, and all-electric heat. Rates: $19.50 to $28.00 a night. Address: Box 305, Creede, CO 81130, or phone: (303) 658-2315.

Creede Chamber of Commerce, Box 580, Creede, CO 81130. (303) 658-2343.

CRESTED BUTTE—surrounded by National Forest, this old mining town with Victorian atmosphere is perfect as a base for exploring nature both summer and winter.

Things to See and Do

Crested Butte Ski Area—being far away from other, more famous ski resorts is an advantage here because there are virtually no lift lines or any lines at all for that matter. Trails specially designated for beginner and intermediate skiers are available as well as steep, challenging terrain for those who are advanced. Open from late November to mid-April. Price of a full day lift ticket: $25.00. Contact the resort by P.O. Box A, Mt. Crested Butte, CO 81225. 1-800-525-4220 or (303) 349-2222.

Winter Festivals—College Ski Week, January. Flatlanders Ski Association, January. Flauschink, its out with winter and in with spring at this early April celebration.

National Forests—Crested Butte happens to be close to the Gunnison National Forest, the White River National Forest, and the San Isabel National Forest, which makes it the perfect base from which to explore the trails, streams, and beauty of Colorado both in winter and summer.

Where to Eat and Sleep

Penelope's—at 120 Elk Ave., serving continental style fare for breakfast and dinner and specializing in steaks, seafood, and fresh baked goods. Price: breakfast $2.00 to $5.50, dinner $7.95 to $16.00. (303) 349-5178. MC, V, AE

Rozman's Crested Butte Motor Inn—on Highway 135, weekly rates, ski packages, cable TV, refrigerators, cafe and bar. Price: $38.00 to $50.00, kitchen units more. (303) 349-6669.

Cement Creek Campground—take Highway 135 southeast 7.5 miles, then Forest Road 740 northeast 4 miles. Has no hookups but has toilets, pull-thrus, tables, fire rings. Price: $5.00.

Crested Butte, P.O. Box A, Mt. Crested Butte, CO 81225. (303) 349-2222 or nationwide for reservations: 1-800-525-4220.

DELTA—some things you will not find in Delta and its area are congested highways, dirty air, unchecked crime, and urban sprawl. What you will discover is a friendly little town with big ideas for having fun all year round! With an average of 205 sunny days a year and an altitude of 4,980, Delta has found its place in the sky.

Things to See and Do

Deltarado Days—celebration during the last week of July which includes PRCA Rodeo (with the 2nd largest purse in the state), arts and crafts, and the renowned mud volleyball tournament.

Ute Council Tree—located just off US 50 in north Delta, it is the sight where the ute Indians held their meetings, including those of war and peace. The famous chief Ouray and his wife, Chipeta (the only woman ever allowed to attend) were among the people who visited the meetings.

Crag Crest Trail—a National Trail atop Grand Mesa, it is a 10 mile loop. Starting at 9500 feet and climbing to over 11,000 feet, only persons in reasonably good shape should attempt it. Parking lots and bathrooms are at each end and are just off of Highway 65 across from Island Lake (watch for turnoff signs).

Black Canyon of the Gunnison—one of the deepest, steepest, wildest, scenic canyons in the world. It became a National Monument in 1933. Go south from Delta on Highway 50 to Montrose. Its visitor center is east 15.2 miles from Montrose on Colorado Road 347. There are scenic drives, hiking, climbing (for professionals only), picnicing, and camping.

Scenic Drives

Escarpment Circle Drive—from the Delta KOA, drive west on Highway 92. Turn north on Highway 50 (watch for Ute Council Tree signs) to LN G92 Lane. Follow the Lane to Road 1550 which meets at Highway 50. Go north approximately 25 miles to Lands End Road and drive the 22 miles up to the top of Grand Mesa. Along the way are many hiking trails and picnic areas. Follow the signs to the Visitor Center which is open from 8:00 am to 8:00 pm, snow-end to snowfall. Follow the road on to Highway 65 and go south to return to Delta.

Black Canyon's North Rim—this is a combination driving/hiking tour. First, take Highway 92 west through Hotchkiss and Crawford. When you pass Crawford Reservoir, watch for the Black Canyon entrance sign on the right side. Turn right onto the gravel road and after passing the entrance take the right fork which goes to a campground. Keep to the road to the Chasm View Trail sign where there is a 4-page introduction to the sights along the trail. Unpack the camera, lock the car, and begin your hike. This trail is not as strenuous as most and almost anyone can handle it, but parents should keep children close because of the dropoffs.

Delta Dobie Darter—a rare species of owl (possibly related to the Southern Snipe) which has become the mascot of the county, it may be seen swiftly bouncing along the forest rails or roadsides. Although not known to be a flyer, Air Force pilots have made unconfirmed reports of their presence at high elevations during subsonic flight. Known primarily for its fondness for apples, this furry rascal has been blamed for many a picnic basket theft. Many are concerned about their community and are registering to vote, one is even considering public office. *Sightings* occur mainly at night south of town in or near Sweitzer Lake State Park.

Thunder Mountain Lives Tonight—the county's historical drama, it includes 60 residents who perform the saga of the old west in all its glory, humor, and beauty. Through the summer, performances are given Tuesday through Saturday in the Delta Roundup Club Arena at 8:00 pm. Price: adults $9.00, children $4.50. Write the Delta Chamber of Commerce for information.

Gunnison River—catch "Gold Medal Trout" in a picturesque setting. From Delta, go east on Highway 92. Drive 14 miles to the sign for "Gunnison Forks Wildlife Area River Access" and turn onto the gravel road, go 1 mile and you are at fishermen's paradise.

Where to Eat and Sleep

Cher's Restaurant & Lounge—located at 220 Main St., it specializes in Mexican food as well as seafood, steaks and sandwiches. Live entertainment on Friday and Saturday nights, the lounge is open from 5:00 pm to 2:00 am. Restaurant hours: 6:00 am to 9:00 pm daily. Price: $1.25 to $12.95. (303) 874-9001.

Mary's Cafe—located at 155 Highway 92, has a complete menu, family atmosphere, home-style cooking and low prices! Price: $.60 to $7.95. (303) 874-7237.

Riverwood Inn & Restaurant & RV Park—all located at 677 1575 Road. The restaurant: steaks, seafood, crepes, Omelettes, soup and sandwiches all to be eaten out on the deck by the river. Dinner music is provided on the weekends, open from 7:00 am to 9:00 pm Monday through Saturday and 7:00 am to 5:00 pm on Sunday. Price: $2.00 to $11.95. The Inn: all the luxuries and more, bed and breakfast, cable TV, even waterbeds available. Price: $28.00 to $39.00, extra person $5.00 (price includes breakfast). The RV Park: launder, showers, tent spaces, and more. Price: $10.00 full hookup, $7.00 tents. (303) 874-3854. Mc, V

Westways Court—1030 Main St., it has modest facilities and excellent family packages. Price: $20.00 to $26.00, $34.00 for the family. (303) 874-4415. MC, V

Delta/Grande Mesa KOA Kampground—at 1675 Highway 92, it has cabins, jacuzzi, pool, showers, tents, teepees, and more. Price: $9.25 for 2 adults, $2.00 each extra person and each additional hookup. (303) 874-3918. MC, V

Delta Chamber of Commerce, 224 Main St., Delta, CO 81416. (303) 874-8616.

DOLORES—near many Indian ruins, including Mesa Verde National Park 20 miles south.

Things to See and Do

Mesa Verde National Park—take 145 south, then 160 east. Follow signs to entrance. The park is a true treasure of history, the ruins tell of the earliest Americans and their way of life. Hours: All year 8:00 am to 5:00 pm. Price: $2.00 per car.

San Juan National Forest—make Dolores your base camp and go out northward on 145 each day to the trails (there are hundreds to choose from) for a hike or to the streams to fish or pan for a little gold. Try the Dolores River.

Monument Valley Scenic Tour—take visitors to the beautiful harsh deserts of the U.S. Watch the deserts along the way for their unique wildlife including Prairie Dogs, Prong-horned Antelope, and Roadrunners. 285 miles round trip, there is gas along the way and make sure your car is able to make the trip. Take 184 west from Dolores to Highway 666 and travel northwest into Utah to Monticello. Go south on Highway 163. You might want to tour some of the attractions on the way like Manti-la Sal National Forest, Edge of the Cedars National Monument, and the Navajo Indian Reservation. Going south on 163 to Kayenta, Arizona. Now take Highway 160 back northeast. Take time to stop and take your pictures at Four Corners, the only point in the U.S. where four state corners meet. After that, keep heading northeast on 160 to Cortez. Just past Cortez, take 145 north to Dolores.

Scenic Circle Drive—see the essence of the mining town on this trip. Go north on 145 to Placerville, east on 62 to Ridgway, south on 550 through Ouray and Silverton to Durango. Next, travel west on 160 toward Cortez. Before Cortez, turn North on 145 and head back to Dolores. On the way, think about the fact that this area was frequented by outlaws like Butch Cassidy, miners in search of treasure, and good people seeking the promised land. Watch for ghost towns and abandoned mines, stop and explore the trails around the various campgrounds you pass, or just stop at the designated pull-offs to admire the view.

Escalante Ruins—were discovered by Father Silvester De Escalante in 1776. The Heritage Center there now displays artifacts found at the site and should be open in the spring of 1987. The ancient structures, built and abandoned for unknown reasons around 900 AD by the Anasazi Indians, can be seen by taking Highway 184 west 3 miles from Dolores.

Fishing—along any nearby stream or try these local favorites. Groundhog Reservoir 31 miles north of Dolores, Miramonte State Recreation Area 46 miles north, the Dolores River east and west forks, and Summit Lake 9 miles southeast of town.

Escalante Days—during the second weekend of August, it commemorates the arrival of the good Father in 1776. Events include games, a parade, a dance, and arts and crafts booths.

Where to Eat and Sleep

Sandwich Works—at 310 Railroad, deli style food. (303) 882-7674.

Rio Grande Southern Hotel & Restaurant—101 S. 5th, good boarding house and motel in a historic building in downtown Dolores. Price: $20.00 and up. Restaurant serves excellent home cooked meals. Price: $3.00 to $7.00. (303) 882-7527.

Outpost Motel—1800 Central, excellent accommodations along the Dolores River and RV spaces. Price: $20.00 and up.

Priest Gulch Ranchcamp—15 miles north on 145, has full hookups, tables, toilets, showers and a store. Price: $7.00 and up.

Delores Chamber of Commerce, Dolores, CO 81323, or phone the Dolores Star at (303) 882-4486.

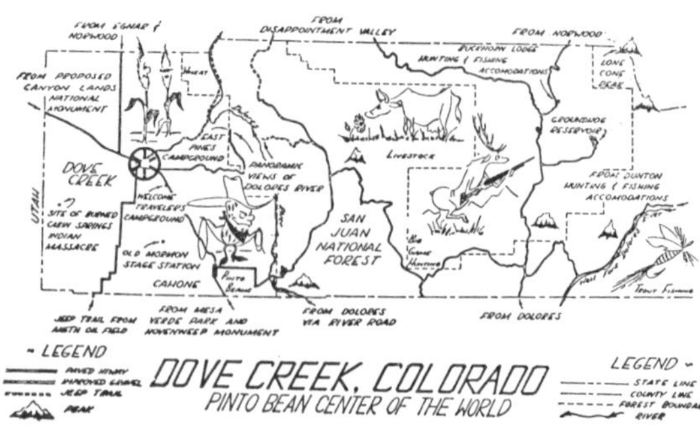

COURTESY OF DOVE CREEK CHAMBER OF COMMERCE

DOVE CREEK—the pinto bean capital of the world is located in the southwest part of the state, in fact the town saying is "Happiness is a crock of beans". It is the sight where Zane Grey wrote, *Riders of the Purple Sage.*

Things to Do and See

Pick' N' Hoe Celebration—held on July 4th, there is a free Bar-B-Q at noon, a parade, games and fireworks. Sometimes, the party gets out of hand and lasts for three days!

Dolores Canyon Overlook—two miles east on Highway 666, take the canyon entrance on the left. The overlook is quite spectacular and gives proof that this is the "Grand Canyon" of the Dolores. There is camping available in this recreation area.

San Juan National Forest—just to the northeast lies this beautiful forest with all its animals, trails both for hiking and jeeping, mountains and semi-desert terrain. Take Highway 666 east and then any road north to get to the forest.

Scenic Drive—go west on 666 to State Road 141 and go north. When you reach US 50 in Whitewater go southeast through Delta to Montrose. Here, take State Road 90 southwest through the Uncompahgre National Forest and over the Plateau of the same name. When you reach 145 you can take 141 back to Dove Creek or follow 145 east and then south through Ophir, Rico and Dolores. Just after Dolores, take 184 west to 666 and back to Dove Creek. Taking the long way will show you through the San Juan National Forest and all its inherent beauty.

Western Cafe—open all day.

Blue Mountain Cafe—famous for their Navajo Taco.

Country Campground & Store—at the west city limit on 666, overnight camping facilities and grocery. (303)677-2850.

Dove Creek Chamber of Commerce, P.O. Box 613, Dove Creek, CO 81324.

DURANGO—one of the most interesting places in the state, it is full of fun things to do, a multitude of places to eat, and hotels everywhere. The following are just a few things to do in this historic town.

Things to See and Do

Durango—Silverton Narrow Gauge Railroad—this famous railroad connects the two towns in its name by 45 miles of track weaving through the awe inspring San Juan mountains to a height of

9,318 feet. The views along the way are spectacular, of white water rapids and water falls, high mountain chalets and ghost towns, snow capped peaks in July, and Quaking Aspens everywhere. The only round trips can be taken from Durango, but a visitor may stay overnight in Silverton for as much as 30 days by arranging with the depot there the date of return to Durango. Backpackers can purchase tickets to Elk Park and Needleton from Silverton. Allow the whole day for a round trip. Hours: May to October. Times of departure vary with season, but averate 7, 8, 9, and 10 am from Durango. Tickets must be purchased in advance, the farther the better, because seating and choice of seat are limited. Price: adult $28.10 ($48.30 in parlor car where only adults over 21 are allowed), children $14.10. Address: 479 Main Ave., Durango, CO 81301. (303) 247-273

Silverton—the town itself is something to do, in fact, the whole place is a Registered National Historic Landmark. There are countless gift shops and curios but if you don't want to spend money, the town offers Victorian age buildings to admire like the old jailhouse, the courthouse, and most of the hotels and houses. The hotels are often famous for having been bordellos and saloons, especially along Blair St. A walking tour pamphlet is available from the Chamber of Commerce, the courthouse, the depot, or various stores. Silverton was named the county seat in 1876 after an all-night blow-out in Howardsville (then the county seat) caused the disappearance of county records. They turned up in Silverton and have been there ever since. Take the time to explore thoroughly part of your American heritage.

Mesa Verde National Park—take 160 west to the park, the entrance of which is just after Mancos. See the cliff dwellings of the ancient who abandoned it centuries ago. Or take a helicopter tour of the area. The price varies between$25.00 and $125.00. Contact Four Corners Helicopters, 7553 CR 25, Cortez, CO 81321. (303) 565-8994.

Rafting—from white water kayaking to canoeing, Durango has it all. The Animas River shows evidence of this sport's popularity as it flows through town, bringing crafts and people with it by the dozen. Here are a few of the outfitters who specialize in supplying rafters and their average prices. Easy trips — Mountain Waters Rafting, 108 W. 6th St., P.O. Box 2681, Durango, CO 81302. (303) 259-4191, 1983. Price: full day, adults $40.00, children $35.00. Colorado River Tours, P.O. Box 1386, Durango, CO 81301 (make reservations at 15th and Main) (303) 259-0708, 1-800-451-0708. Price: full day, adults $45.00, children $40.00. Rapids - Flexible Flyers, 2344 County Road 225, Durango, CO. 81301 (303) 247-4628, 8131. Price: 2 hours, adults and children $15.00. Four Corners Kayak School, P.O. Box 379, Durango, CO. 81302 (303) 259-3893, in state 1-800-492-8080, nationwide 1-800-4CORNER. Price: for three day novice clinic $225.00.

COURTESY OF MINERAL COUNTY MINER

Enjoy the sport of river rafting throughout the state.

Skiing—just north of Durango is the famous Purgatory ski area with its slopes and cross-country trails ranging from beginner to expert. The lift lines are shorter here because the mountain is uncrowded. Reservations are a must. The Purgatory/Durango Central Reservations booking agents will arrange everything including lift tickets, ski school, ski rental, and lodging at discount prices. Call them at (303) 247-8900, in state 1-800-358-3400, nationwide 1-800-525-0892. Purgatory's reservation and information number is 1-800-247-9000. Prices and packages vary greatly, so call for information.

Aztec Ruins—see the Great Kiva and Indian ruins of a lost tribe. Take Highway 550 south 35 miles. Hours: daily 8am to 5pm. Price: $.50 per person or $1.00 per car load. (303) 334-6174.

Fishing—try these local favorites. Pastorius Lake south of town off Highway 550, Vallecito Lake 18 miles northeast on County Road 240 then 5 miles north on County Road 501, Lemon Lake 12 miles northeast on 240 and 3 miles north on 243, and Haviland Lake 20 miles north on 550.

Chuckwagon Dinner—just what you need to make that trip to the west complete. Enjoy an old fashioned cowboy feast and show. Contact *Bar D Chuckwagon Suppers,* 8080 County Road 250, Durango, CO. 81301 (303) 247-5753. Price: adults $9.00 , children under 8 $5.00. Bar D's menu includes sliced beef in barbeque sauce, baked potatoe, baked beans, homemade biscuits, applesauce, old fashioned cake, coffee or lemonade. *The Cowboy,* 11920 County Road 240, Durango, CO. 81301 (303) 247-4948. Price: adults $10.00, children 10 and under $6.00. The Cowboy's menu includes cowboy steak cooked over oak fire, Mama's chili beans, tossed green salad, French bread, blueberry donuts, coffee or punch.

Shopping—there is a street in Durango that is full of unique shops and excellent restaurants. It is Main Avenue and is a lot of fun even if one just looks. There are leather shops, antique shops, art galleries, an awesome chocolate shop, deli style cafes, and unbelievably good Mexican restaurants.

La Plata Canyon—drive through scenic beauty where many old mines and streams just right for panning gold are everywhere. Start 11 miles west of Durango on US 160.

San Juan National Forest—make Durango your base camp and go out each day to the trails for a hike or to the streams to fish

Unused church on La Platta Canyon Road west of Durango.

or pan for a little gold.

Million Dollar Highway—this circle drive takes you through some of the beautiful San Juan National Forest, on the gold and silver ore that is the highway. Take 550 north through Silverton and Ouray to Ridgway, then 62 west to Placerville, 145 south through Rico and past Dolores. Upon reaching 160 go east and back to Durango. On the way, think about the fact that this area was frequented by outlaws like Butch Cassidy, miners in search of treasure, and good people seeking the promised land. Watch for ghost towns and abandoned mines, stop and explore the trails around the various campgrounds you pass, or just stop at the designated pull offs to admire the view.

From the Million Dollar Highway, one can see the city of Silverton nestled in its valley.

Colorfest—mid-September brings the change in the Aspen leaves. This beautiful sight brings celebration to Durango with tours, marathons, triathlons, the Mayor's Ball, hot air balloon rally, kite festival, and more for a whole month.

Hiking, Jeeping—many trails for walkers and riders can be found near Durango in the San Juan National Forest. A map which identifies trails, campgrounds, and roads is available from each ranger district for $1.00. Or write, call, or stop by for general directions from the Durango Chamber of Commerce. Ask for the pamphlets called *"San Juan National Forest Hiking Trails (Durango Area)"* and *"San Juan National Forest Off Highway Vehicle Opportunities (Durango Area)".*

Ghost Towns—these small abandoned towns are rather common to the area because after the booms for precious metals died, so did they. When an area was emptied of its metal, the people moved on to found yet another future ghost town. In fact, there are 97 ghost towns or mining camps in the Durango area alone. For detailed directions to these legacies of the past write, call or stop by the Durango Chamber of Commerce. Ask for the Dave Curtin article titled *"The Lure and Lore of Ghost Towns"* which was published in The Durango Herald on Sunday, April 20, 1986 or *"Jeep Roads & Ghost Towns of the San Juans"*.

Where to Eat and Sleep

There are many restaurants in Durango, for a full listing contact the Chamber of Commerce. Here are two the author tried.

Francisco's Restaurante Y Cantina—619 Main Ave. If you like Mexican food, mild to hot and spicy, this is **THE place!** Also a kids menu, steaks, seafood and delicious appetizers and margaritas. Price: average meal $6.00 to $11.00. (303)247-4098.

Rosewater's Deli—across from train station, serving breakfast and lunch to go (for the train) BIG sandwiches, vegetarian dishes, imported beers, fresh fruit and juice. Deli atmosphere. Price: average meal $2.00 to $6.00 (303)247-8788.

Camping—camping is permitted in the park on 501 in north Durango.

Victorian Inn—bed and breakfast $45.00 to $55.00 (303) 247-2223.

Scrubby Oaks—bed and breakfast $25.00 to $40.00 (303) 247-2176.

The Strater Hotel—near the station, a traveler's paradise since 1887, it retains its Victorian charm. Rooms are furnished with antiques and there is an old west saloon for guests to enjoy. Price: $49.00 to $85.00 (303)247-4431.

Five Branches Camper Park—4677 County Road 501-A in Bayfield, take 501-A north of Durango, on Vallecito Lake and Pine River, boating, fishing, horseback riding, cabins and full hookups. Price: camping $6.00 to $15.00, cabin $45.00 and up. (303)884-9631, 884-2582. Again, a full listing of lodgings and their costs may be obtained at the Chamber of Commerce.

Durango Chamber of Commerce, 111 S. Camino del Rio, P.O. Box 2587, Durango, CO. 81302 (303)247-0312.

GUNNISON—there is always something to do in Gunnison country. The summer is filled with rodeos, barbeques, dances, and festivals. Winter gives no respite to the busy schedule of summer because it features many social meetings, tournaments, theatre, and snow skiing (when you have the time).

Things to See and Do

Cattlemen's Days—5 day festival in mid-July is good old country fun. Activities include horse shows, hog, sheep, and steer marketing, rodeo events all week both amateur and professional, branding contests, dances, parade, chariot racing and (believe it or not) much, much more.

Hunter Hospitality Days—in October the weekend before season opens, local merchants and the Chamber of Commerce provide snacks, coffee and ice, informational brochures, *freebies* (pens, key chains, etc.), grab bags, safety films by the Division of Wildlife on field dressing and hunter safety.

Winter Wonderful Week—first week in February, this celebration starts with a stuff yourself pancake breakfast (with sausage, coffee, orange juice, tea, and milk) for about $3.00. Also featured are dog sled races, sleigh rides, barbeques, snowshoe races, snow sculpturing, and the Grand Finale, the Annual Gunnison Snowmobile Gran Prix Classic! For information and to register for events, contact the Chamber of Commerce (303)641-1501.

Curecanti National Recreation Area—offers sightseeing, boating, hiking, camping, swimming, and hunting to name a few. It was formed when 3 dams were built to provide water and power. Trout of 4 species and Hokanee Salmon are waiting for anglers. Winter brings in big game, cross-country skiing, and snowmobiling. Take Highway 50 west of Gunnison. Campgrounds are abundant, for information (and reservations at the East Elk Creek Campgrounds) call (303)641-2337.

Black Canyon of the Gunnison—formed by erosion over the millennia, this scenic wonder is a National Monument. Its Rim Drive

COURTESY OF GUNNISON CHAMBER OF COMMERCE.

Bar-B-Q in progress during Winter Wonderful Week.

gives the vacationer a view never to be forgotten. The visitor center provides information on the drive and park activities. Hiking trails are all along the rim, none longer than 1.4 miles but remember to inform the ranger station of your position if you plan to hike into the canyon or back country. Camping is available on a first-come first-serve basis, so reserve a spot early if you plan to stay overnight in the Monument. To get to the Monument, take Highway 50 west from Gunnison to 347 and go north 3 miles. Information: P.O. Box 1648, Montrose, CO. 81401.

Pioneer Museum—includes many rare and unique items, including Cinder Ella, the last train to go through the Alpine Tunnel. There is memoribilia from mining operations, the town's citizens, and from around the county.

Ghost Towns—there are literally dozens of these little deserted villages, sometimes having no more than one or two buildings. They were usually hastily built to shelter miners during the long winters. Most were constructed between 1880 and 1890. A few of the easier to find are: *Sargents*—30 miles east of Gunnison on Highway 50 at the foot of Monarch Pass. *White Pine*—just east of Sargents, take the side road to the left, when it forks take the right fork. *Gothic*—from Gunnison, go north to Crested Butte on 135. Go past the cemetery and ski area and follow the road to the ghost town. *Castleton* and *Baldwin*—take 135 north from Gunnison and turn off on Ohio Creek Road. Follow it to the towns. Many others are along the way, ask an old timer where he or she would go and discover your own ghost town.

Scenic Drives—the Chamber of Commerce has put out a brochure of 20 circle trips around the county. Many go by ghost towns, mines, National Forests, Monuments, lakes, high country passes, the Alpine Tunnel, just to name a few. Drop by the Chamber, call or write for the pamphlet on "20 Circle Tour Trips".

Alpine Tunnel—said to be *haunted* by the ghosts of workers who perished there, this was the world's highest tunnel. It was bored through 1800 feet of solid rock. Abandoned in 1910, so many had died there or in the vicinity it was said to have a curse upon it. Take 50 east to Parlin and turn north toward Pitkin. The entrance road to the tunnel is 2.4 miles north of Pitkin on the right.

Boating & Fishing—the river flowing through the Black Canyon is available for your sightseeing and angling pleasure, as are Morrow Point Lake and Blue Mesa Lake. Contact Elk Creek & Lake Fork Marina, 46 Apache Road, Gunnison, CO. 81230. The rates are reasonable, a 1½ hour tour is $6.50 for adults, $3.75 for children and $5.85 for seniors. Reservations required. For reservations, call after May 1st: (303)641-0707.

Jeeping, Rafting, & Fishing—exploring the back country can be fun and exciting, however the average family car won't get very far. Three Rivers Resort can outfit you and guide you to that special fishing spot, float you to that perfect picture, or just let you roam the back country 4 wheel drive style. Price: jeeps: 3 hours between $15.00 and $30.00 per person, rafting: $8.00 to $12.00 for kids, $12.00 to $18.00 for adults, fishing: floating—$50.00 to $135.00 a day, group rates lower, walking—$125.00 for one, $190.00 for three. Address: PO Box 336, Almont, CO. 81210, 10 miles north of Gunnison on Highway 135. (303)641-1303.

Where to Eat and Sleep

Last Chance—at 9th and Rio Grande, it specializes in Mexican food at reasonable prices. Its lounge is open from 3pm to 2am. It serves dinner from 5 to 9pm. Price: $1.85 to $8.85. (303)641-9834.

Sidewalk Cafe—at 113 W. Tomichi, breakfast and lunch served on the patio. Open daily at 6am. Price: $1.75 and up. (303)641-4130.

Tomichi Village Restaurant—on E. Highway 50, its casual setting is relaxing.. It serves breakfast and lunch from 6:30am to 2pm and dinner from 5 to 9pm. Price: $5.95 and up, dinner. (303)641-4130.

The Trough—1 mile West on Highway 50, it is fine dining at its best and entertainment too on Wednesday through Saturday. Prime rib, steak, seafood, chicken, reservations suggested. Price: $7.75 and up. (303)641-3724.

Cattlemen Inn—at 301 W. Tomichi, the *restaurants*—they serve three meals a day with fast and friendly service. A lounge and salad bar, seafood and steak are featured. Price: $3.00 and up. *The Inn*—conveniently located in Gunnison with great rates. Price: $18.00 to $36.00. (303)641-1061.

Waunita Hot Springs Ranch—8 miles north of Highway 50 between Gunnison and Monarch Pass, the turnoff is marked ½ mile west of Doyleville at mile marker 176. Winter rates for rooms and meals only are $45.00 a day per person. The summer changes to the American Plan, which includes all activities like horseback riding, float trips, cookouts, hayrides, etc. Price: $495.00 a week per person. For reservations, write: 8007 County Road 887, Gunnison, CO. 81230. (303)641-1266.

Three Rivers Resort—10 miles north of Gunnison on Hwy. 135, modern cabins to tent sites, lots of National Forest, activities, and fun. Price: $7.00 to $65.00. (303)641-1303.

Gunnison Chamber of Commerce, P.O. Box 36, Gunnison, CO. 81230 (303)641-1501.

GUNNISON NATIONAL FOREST—over one and a half million acres await the traveler with easy access via Highway 50, and State Routes 114, 133, and 149. It contains many wilderness areas with high mountain meadows, deep canyons, and dense forest. The forest also is one access point to the famous Alpine Tunnel, said to be haunted by the ghosts of men who died during its construction (at the town of Pitkin, go north 2.4 miles and the turn-off is on the right. Follow the signs). There are many ghost towns in this area and gold panning is a popular activity among the forest's visitors. Anglers will find their dream fish in the many pristine, alpine lakes and hunters can get the big ones in any of a number of animals and fowl. Camping fees range from free to $7.00.

Gunnison Forest Supervisor, 2250 Highway 50, Delta, CO. 81416.

LAKE CITY—a boom town during the late 1800's, this small mountain-surrounded village is today Colorado's largest National Historic District. As freelance writer, Barbara Fretwell, puts it, "This small enclave in the Colorado mountains has that magic power to banish tension, to recharge the mind, and to remind the visitor just what it is about life that is truly wonderful." What more need we say?

COURTESY OF SILVER WORLD PUBLISHING CO.

The Lake City business district had a booming appearance when this photo was taken in 1877. One and two story false front frame buildings were hurriedly built to cater to the influx of miners and prospectors. By 1878 the town, which started with a population of fewer than 100 in 1875, had grown to 5,000.

Things to See and Do

Colorado State Snowmobile Convention—mid-February brings special tours of more than eighty miles of trails along the Continental Divide. Come and enjoy the winter beauty of the mountains while you explore the wilderness on these neat machines. (303)944-2369.

Historical Society's Victorian Banquet—mid-July, the town of Lake City is the perfect place to hold this dinner because many of its buildings were built during the 1800's. In this authentic setting, you will enjoy an old-fashioned feast which the English Queen Victoria would have envied. (303)944-2514.

Alferd Packer Jeep Tour & Barbecue—mid-September, tour the site just south of town where Hinsdale County lost 5 of its Democrats to the infamous cannibal, Al Packer. The barbeque promises to be in a lot better taste, as it were. (303)944-2679.

Arts and Crafts—the Lake City area has more than its share of artistic talents from woodworking and leather work to painting and stained glass. To show off this rich culture, the Arts and Crafts Festival is held in mid-July at the Community Presbyterian Church. Call (303)944-2514 or the Chamber of Commerce for information on the festival or the individual artists.

Mountineer Theatre—on 8th St., it provides an interesting slide show about the town all summer long, *In the Shadow of Uncompahgre: A Lake City Portrait.* Starts at 8pm, contact Chamber of Commerce for days.

The Black Crooke Theatre—at 3rd and Silver St., it features fun for all with vaudeville, singing and melodramas presented by the Black Crooke Gang, famed for their local performances in music and acting. Hours: June to August, for daily schedule contact the Chamber of Commerce.

Jeep Rentals—a popular sport during the summer, it takes you to those little-known fishin' holes and that perfect picture-takin' spot atop the Continental Divide. Call these three agencies for details on rental 4 wheel drive vehicles. High Country Tours (303)944-2679, The Skinners (303)944-2262, Rocky Top Rentals (303)944-2780.

Lake City Scenic Drive—starting at Lake City, take Route 149 north to US 50 and go east through Gunnison to State Road 114 (Note: you can continue on 50 and go north at Parlin to see the famous Alpine Tunnel, for map see Pitkin). At 114, go southeast to Saguache, then south on US 285 to Monte Vista. There, take US 160 to South Fork, get on 149 and head northwest to Creede. About 6 miles past Creede, take the Forest Road south to the ghost town of Spar City (see Spar City for information). After you have explored the ghost town, go back to 149 and head west. You will go over

Slumgullion Pass, near the site where Al Packer did his dirty deeds. Return to Lake City.

Hiking—and snowmobiling on local trails provide that well-needed look at nature at any time of the year. Obtain the Recreation Map from the Chamber of Commerce and go for it!

Where to Eat and Sleep

The Crystal Lodge—2 miles south of town on 149, serving all your favorites, daily specials and homemade baked goods. Reservations requested for dinner. (303)944-2201.

Katy's Saloon—downtown across from Town Park. Your favorite Mexican foods, sandwiches, libations and, as they put it, lots of miscellaneous fun. (303)944-2719.

Lake City Cafe—near 3rd and Gunnison, home-style American and Italian meals with good service is their specialty. (303)944-2733.

Lake Fork Restaurant—5 miles north, it reminds the visitor of the big city and its around-the-world restaurants, with French cuisine, well-rounded wine list and a Champagne Brunch on Sunday. (303)944-2612.

Strawberry Patch—next to the theatre on 3rd and Silver, it serves all kinds of munchies from nachos, hot dogs and popcorn to frozen yogurt and ice cream. (303)944-2541.

Alpine Village—right off of 149, find log cabins complete with sitting areas, color TV, kitchenettes and one or two bedrooms. Price: $36.00 and up. (303)944-2266, in winter (817)429-2865.

Matterhorn Motel—above town on the mountainside, country cabins with kitchenettes and more. Price: $30.00 and up. Write for reservations: Box 603, Lake City, CO 81235. (30)944-2210 MC,V.

Oxyoke Resort—within walking distance of town you will find 1 and 2 bedroom cabins on the river with lots of relaxation. Price: $30.00 and up. (303)944-2252, in winter (806)362-4564.

Silver Spur Motel & Spa—year round and downtown, color TV, kitchenettes, jacuzzi and steam rooms. Snowmobile packages available. Price: $36.00 and up. (303)944-2231.

The Texan Resort—all year accommodations in modern cabins and RV sites on the river bank south of town. Price: $24.00 and up for cabins, $5.25 and up for RV's. (303)944-2246.

Town Square Cabins & Mini Mart—cabins on Gunnison Ave., with color TV, kitchenettes, and all the supplies you need in their own country store. Open from May to November. Price: $25.00 and up. (303)944-2236.

Westwood Resort—south of town on 149, has single, small and large double cabins with kitchenettes, TV's, and every seventh night is *FREE*. Price: $35.00 and up. (303)944-2205.

Lake City Chamber of Commerce, PO Box 405, Lake City, CO 81235 (303)944-2527. Visitor Information Center on Silver Street between 3rd and 4th.

MESA VERDE NATIONAL PARK—located in the high plateau country of southwestern Colorado, between the cities of Cortez and Mancos off of US 160. Park headquarters are located 21 miles from the entrance. This is not inconvenient as the whole road is a scenic drive, but be careful to obey road signs and do not park on any roadway. For your safety, also be aware that climbing to the ruins is strenuous work, especially at over 6,000 feet. Aside from regular National Park rules, Mesa Verde also enforces some others.

To protect fragile ruins, hiking is restricted to 5 trails within the park.

Hikers must register with the ranger's office before attempting the Spruce Canyon trails.

Some Recreational Vehicles and trailors may be restricted because of road conditions, parking is at the park entrance.

Cliff dwellings may only be entered when accompanied by a ranger.

The entrance station to the park can provide the visitor with all additional information, maps, and schedules for tours and lectures. Price: $2.00 per vehicle, .50¢ for bus passengers.

Where to Eat and Sleep

Far View Lodge Dining Room—traditional meals as well as Indian and Southwestern cuisine. Try a special Margarita, happy hour 4:30 to 6:30. Hours: 4:30 to 9:30 pm.

Far View Terrace—serves all three meals from 7:00 am to 9:00

pm with live Indian craft demonstrations during lunch hours.

Far View Lodge—15 miles into the park, accommodations are available from May to October. Rates: $46.00 to $57.00, $2.00 per extra person. Address: ARA Mesa Verde CO., PO Box 277, Mancos, CO. 81328, or phone: (303)529-4421 or (303)533-7731 in Winter for reservations.

Morefield Campground and Village—located 4 miles south of park entrance, it has over 450 sites with no hookups or reservations, open from May to October. It does have showers, store, and dumping station. Rates: $5.00 daily per site, 14 day limit. Arrive in early afternoon to choose best site.

For additional information, write the park at: Mesa Verde National Park, Colorado 81330, or phone: (303)529-4461.

MONTROSE—in the center of a thousand things to do, this town is indeed a sightseer's paradise. But if you prefer to relax among the trees and mountains, that's also fine with Montrose.

Things to See and Do

Black Canyon of the Gunnison—one of the deepest, steepest, wildest, scenic canyons in the world. It became a National Monument in 1933. Its visitor center is east 15.2 miles from Montrose on Colorado Road 347. There are scenic drives, hiking, climbing (for professionals only), picnicing, and camping.

Fishing/Boating/Float Trips—in the Black Canyon, guided tours that guarantee you to catch the big ones. Contact Double Haul Float Trips Inc., 719 S. 6th St., Montrose, CO. 81401. (303)249-3323. Or: Elk Creek marina, 46 Apache Rd., Gunnison, CO. 81230. (303)641-0402.

Biking—Montrose has provided its citizens and visitors with bike paths that will eventually connect all schools (except Morgan), parks, recreation facilities, and business districts. A map of the paths may be obtained from the Chamber of Commerce.

Scenic Drives—this area is so full of scenic areas that the Gunnison Chamber of Commerce provides a list and map of the 20 most popular routes. This includes drives through high country passes, National Monuments, historic mining towns, and breathtaking landscapes. For the pamphlet, stop by any of the local chambers or write:

PO Box 36, Gunnison, CO. 81230. (303)641-1501.

Balloon Affaire—during the week of July 4th, this festival features more than 50 hot air balloons which fill the sky with color.

Depot Museum—features artifacts of pioneer life, including a homesteader's cabin, a country store, instruments, clothing, toys, and Montrose newspapers dating from 1896 to 1940. Price: *Free.* Hours: 10:00 am to 5:00 pm Monday to Saturday and 1:00 to 5:00 pm on Sunday. Open May to September. Located at Main St. and Rio Grande.

Ute Indian Museum—focuses on the people and artifacts, as well as their daily activities. Many items belonged to Ouray, the famous chief, and his wife Chipeta, the only squaw permitted to attend tribal Council meetings. Her grave is on the museum grounds. The museum also holds a Native American Lifeways cultural fair each year. Price: adults—$2.00, students—$1.00, seniors and under—*Free.* Hours: 10:00 am to 5:00 pm Monday to Saturday and 1:00 to 5:00 pm on Sunday. Located at 17253 Chipeta Dr. in Montrose.

Where to Eat and Sleep

Glenn Eyrie Restaurant—located at 2351 S. Townsend, it features Colorado beef, seafood, American and European cuisine, and Champagne Brunch on Holidays. Hours: 11:00 am to 2:00 pm and 5:30 pm to 9:00 pm, Monday to Saturday. Price: lunch $4.00 to $8.00, dinner $8.00 to $17.00. (303)249-9263.

Backwoods Inn—located at 103 Rose Lane, it serves burgers, steaks, seafood, and presents live entertainment nightly. Hours: 4:00 pm to midnight Tuesday to Thursday, 4:00 pm to 2:00 am Friday and Saturday. Closed Sunday. Price: $4.95 to $15.95. (303)249-1961

The Root Cellar—at 44 S. Grand Ave., it serves steak, ribs, seafood, crepes, fresh baked goods which can all be eaten inside or on the patio. Price: $3.50 to $15.50. (303)249-7800.

Lazy IG Motel—located at 1624 E. Main, has kitchen units, cable TV, king size beds in some rooms, microwaves. Price: $26.00 to $60.00, $3.00 each extra person. (303)249-4567.

San Juan Inn—located at 1480 S. Townsend, it has kitchenettes, cable TV, restaurant, indoor pool and a jacuzzi. Price: $34.00 to $40.00, $3.00 each extra person. (303)249-6644.

Hofmann Ranch Retreat—on the Big Cimarron east of town, find a cabin in the woods with two trout ponds a short walk away. Cabins are equipped with kitchen facilities and all the modern conveniences. Get your family back to nature. Price: $50.00 a night, $250.00 a week. Reservations required. (303)249-9551 or (303)249-2363.

Montrose KOA—E. Main St. and Cedar Ave., it has full hookups, showers, flush toilets, and much more. Price: $8.00 for 2 people. (303)249-9177.

South Rim Campground—in the Black Canyon National Monument 8 miles east of Montrose by Highway 50 to Monument turnoff. No hookups, pit toilets, campfire program nightly in season. Price: $3.00 nightly.

Montrose Chamber of Commerce, 550 N. Townsend, Montrose, CO. 81401. (303)249-5515.

OURAY—this city and its county are named for the famous Ute Indian chief, Ouray, who strove for unity between his race and the whites. Today the town is an attractive Victorian style place, the perfect one to relax in. Perhaps it is best described by one of its residents, Mr. Gary Kunz, owner of The Kunz House bed and breakfast. "To the folks that live here, Ouray is a very special place that really can't be described with mere words but must be experienced.

"I discovered Ouray in 1978. I was retired from the Navy, my family and I were just passing through and we fell in love with the area. I traveled a lot in the Navy and although I mostly saw ocean water I was always looking for a home. As soon as we saw the Uncompahgre Valley, I knew I was home. We sold our house in San Diego where we had lived for five years and barely knew our neighbors and moved out of the fast lane to Ouray.

"Here we found a people who smile and warmly say 'hello', people who are so proud of their past that their history is always mentioned as reference in conversation... The majority of Ouray's 6-700 citizens have migrated here from elsewhere like myself. They fell in love with the beauty, serenity, simplicity of life, absence of crime and alpine charm of our village."

Mr. Kunz has indicated that he is willing to talk to anyone about the Ouray area and anyone interested may contact him in writing (Box 235) or stop by The Kunz House at 723 4th St.

COURTESY OF OURAY CHAMBER OF COMMERCE.

Awesome view of the city of Ouray and the surrounding mountains.

Things to See and Do

Hot Springs—there are geothermally heated springs throughout the county. The city of Ouray has a large pool filled by hot springs. Hours: May to September daily from 9 am to 9 pm (9 am to 7 pm Sundays). Winter hours: Thursday to Saturday 1 pm to 9 pm and Sunday from 1 pm to 7 pm. (303)325-4638.

The Ampitheatre—is to the east of town, an enormous natural bowl cut into the mountains by Ice-age glaciers. It is spotted with abandoned mines and campgrounds and is used for hiking and cross-country skiing.

Historic Walking Tour of Ouray—provided by the Chamber of Commerce, it winds through the National Historic District with its Victorian architecture, past Box Canyon Falls, and the Hot Springs Pool, as well as many other points of interest.

Cascade Falls—this beautiful waterfall is an easy walk from town. Take the trail at the east end of 8th Ave. It should take less than 30 minutes to reach the falls from the trailhead. There is no parking at the trail entrance (take a picnic lunch and remember to take all refuse out with you).

Scenic Drives—1. one mile south on Highway 550, the famous "Million Dollar Highway", then turn off east to the Ampitheatre Campground. This road gives spectacular views and is open from Memorial to Labor Day. 2. to get to Camp Bird Mine, take 550 south of Ouray to Camp Bird Road (just past the first switchback). Turn right at the sign for Box Canyon Falls but continue left at the junction on the other side of the Uncompahgre Bridge (the sign reads Yankee Boy Basin) and drive upward for five miles to the mine. 3. The scenic San Juan Triangle is an easy drive a half or full day adventure. From Ouray go south on 550 through Silverton to Durango. From Durango go west on Colorado 160 to Cortez, then north on Colorado 145 through Telluride to Placerville. Here turn east on Colorado 62 to Ridgway then south on 550 back to Ouray.

Gold Panning—any of the streams around the town should give "color".

Ore Samples—the easy way to get some precious metal for free. Watch for mining roads where the ore trucks bounce a lot. They are so full of ore that many of the rocks "jump" off. Walk along these roads (especially at corners) and look carefully for granite like rocks which are usually white and gray. If the sun is shining, the metals in the rocks will sparkle. Important: do not get so involved that you forget about the trucks which hurtle past at great speed. To test for deposits of pure gold, hold the sample next to some gold jewelry. If it is not the color of the jewelry, it is a combination of precious metals known as fool's gold.

Fishing—try your luck at East Dallas River and Willow Swamps southeast of Ridgway, the San Miguel River near Placerville, the Uncompahgre River, and Miramonte, Trout, and Molas Lakes.

Hiking—there are many trails around Ouray which vary in length from ½ mile to 20 miles. To best travel these trails, take along a copy of the *Ouray County Trail Guide* which can be purchased for $2.50 at many stores around town.

Snow Skiing—cross-country skiing is a favorite sport and there are many areas around the town to use for it. Tow rope skiing is free for everyone at the ski hill at the south end of town but is used primarily by children.

Sledding—the city of Ouray sets aside the street called Vinegar

Hill for this sport.

Cabin Fever Days & Winter Carnival—held in Ouray and Ridgway in mid-February, it features ski races and jumping, broom hockey, snow sculpting, sledding, a chili contest and supper, and lots more.

Colorfest & Jeep Givaway—highlight of the fall from mid October to mid-September, features a Victorian house tour, a Culinary Art Show and Champagne Brunch, food, dance, contests, and prize drawings.

Bachelor-Syracuse Mine Tour—see a real mine in operation. A working mine since 1884, it offers a unique look at mining both past and present. Hours: May 24th to September 30th from 10 am to 4 pm tours every hour on the hour. (303)325-4550.

Where to Eat and Sleep

The Alpine Cafe—at Main St. and 6th Ave., family style all day long. Has a lounge, coffee shop, and dining rooms. Hours: 6:30 am to 8:30 pm. (303)325-4474.

Coachlight Restaurant—118 W. 7th Ave. is the site of this restaurant which was originally a hotel in 1887, its Victorian atmosphere is truly authentic with stained glass and period oil paintings. Menu includes: steak, lamb, seafood, chicken, lasagna, soup and salad bar, and house specialties like spinach fandango and chocolate French silk pie! Children's menu and full bar also. Hours: late April to mid October from 5 pm daily. (303)325-4361 MC, V, AE.

Corner Nugget Cafe—at 740 Main St., this former saloon and brothel is over 100 years old. It commands a spectacular view of Cascade Falls through its huge dining room windows. Fresh pastry and home style food is prepared daily and served by folks who gladly answer questions about the area. Daily specials and big portions. Price: average $3.00 to $6.50. (303)325-4100 MC, V.

True Grit Cafe—in Ridgway north of Ouray, featuring sandwiches like **The Duke** and **Paramount 1969**, salads, pastries and Sunday Brunch. Reservations suggested for Friday and Saturday nights. Price: $2.50 to $5.00 (303)626-5915.

The Kunz House—723 4th St., built in 1896 this Victorian Bed and Breakfast Guest Home is on the National Historic Register. Its bedrooms are filled with beautiful antiques and there is a common living room, dining room, porch and garden where guests can visit with each other and relax as they watch the clouds go by and the stars at night. The breakfast is just as magnificent. Price: winter $29.50 to $32.00, summer $34.50 to $37.00. (303)325-4220.

St. Elmo Hotel & Bon Ton Restaurant—at 426 Main St., the restaurant serves unusual appeteasers with names like Melon Mt. Abrams and Roman Trilogy (a pasta delight) and Italian cuisine in the best old style tradition. Price: entree $8.25 to $15.00. The inn includes a continental style breakfast with lodging. Some rooms have private baths, all have comfortable beds. Price: $36.00 to $68.00 (303)325-4951.

House of Yesteryear—516 Oak St., overlooks the town and river, room includes a delicious continental breakfast, parlor contains piano for your playing pleasure. Some rooms have private bath. Price: $25.00 to $45.00 (303)325-4277.

Baker's Manor Guest House—317 2nd St., enjoy Victorian accommodations and a delicious continental breakfast. Rooms share common bath and separate shower. Price: $30.00 to $35.00. (303)325-4574.

Wiesbaden Hot Springs Spa & Lodgings—2½ blocks east of Highway 550 in Ouray, this small lodge was built in 1879 over a natural hot spring cave. Rooms include the use of the spa and exercise equipment. Guests also receive discounts on massages, facials, etc. Rooms vary from small to an apartment and a cottage on the hill behind the lodge. Some are available with fireplaces. The inn also has ski packages. Price: $57.00 to $66.00, apartments extra. Reservations recommended. (303)325-4347, 4845.

Alpenglow Condominums—2nd St. and 5th Ave., for those who wish to stay in larger accommodations, try a 2 or 3 bedroom condo with kitchen, fireplace, deck, jacuzzi and grill. Price: nightly $61.00 to $68.00, extra persons $9.00 each. Weekly $395.00 to $595.00, monthly $1000,00 to $1675.00. Write them at PO Box 1855, Ouray, CO. 81427 or phone (303)325-4664. Ask about the Champagne ski tour.

Ouray Chamber of Commerce, PO Box 145, Ouray, CO. 81427, (303)325-4746.

PAGOSA SPRINGS—this town invites you to have the time of your life! Easy to get to, it sits at the spot where Highway 84 meets Highway 160.

Things to See and Do

Pagosa Mountain Man Rendezvous—the third weekend of June literally explodes with black powder rifle contests, arts and crafts, and more.

Winterfest—weeklong party the first week of February, it features snow sculptures, sled and snowmobile races, hot air balloons, and other winter sports.

Chimney Rock Indian Ruins—20 miles west on 160 to where it meets 151. Bring your own water, good walking shoes and a camera. Tours of early Indian dwellings given on Wednesday and Friday, or any day by contacting the U.S. Forest Service at (303)264-2268.

Indians living atop Chimney Rock had a commanding view of the land for miles around.

Treasure Mountain—5 million in gold bars is said to be buried in the area, having been left by miners in 1790 because of necessity (they would rather have been alive and poor than dead and rich). Go 20 miles west to the top of beautiful Wolf Creek Pass. Just east of the summit, follow the signs which mark where the Continental Divide Trail goes south and meets the Treasure Mountain Trail.

Treasure Falls—this water fall is 100 feet of magic. 16 miles northeast on Highway 160 at the foot of Wolf Creek Pass.

Great Hot Springs—geothermally heated waters of the springs gave the town its name and are said to be medicinally beneficial. They can be tested in the town or the water can be purchased from many businesses.

Wolf Creek Ski Area—20 miles northeast via 160 will bring the skier to 435 inches of annual snowfall and excellent powder skiing. That's more than any other ski area in Colorado!

Williams Creek—4 National Forest campgrounds and great fishing make this the perfect place to relax, just take 160 west to Piedra Rd/631 and go north. The lake and most campgrounds are located at the junction of 631 and 640.

Upper San Juan Historical Museum—at the corner of Highway 160 and 1st St. It is open June to August, Monday to Saturday, 10 am to 5 pm.

Where to Eat and Sleep

The Eagle & The Owl—gourmet dining, live Maine lobster, vegitarian specials, and lots of other good food and drink. Across the street from Gambles, open daily from 11:30 am to 2 pm and 5 to 9 pm. Price: $1.75 to $18.95. (303)264-5882.

Wild Rose Bakery—breakfast and lunch served in a deli/cafe in the homemade style. On Lewis St. next to the Post Office. Open Monday to Friday 7 am to 3 pm and Saturday 9 am to 2 pm. Price: $1.85 to $4.00. (303)264-5642.

The Malt Shoppe—big, hearty meals all day; soft ice cream and the best burgers in town. At the River Center, open from 6:30 am to 10 pm. Price: $.89 to $3.49. (303)264-2784.

Oak Ridge Motor Inn—*the restaurant:* family dining with class and variety. Sandwiches, steaks, seafood, Mexican entrees, Sunday Champagne Brunch, lounge, and live entertainment. Across the bridge at Light Plant Road, open from 6:30 am to 2:00 pm and 5 to 10 pm. Price: $4.00 to $13.00. *The Inn:* Best Western, has sauna, hot tubs, cable TV, downtown area. Price: $45.00 to $53.00, additional person $5.00. (303)264-4173.

Davidson's Country Inn—2 miles east of town on Highway 160, bed and breakfast in 10 units on thirty acres of the Rocky Mountains, watch for elk and deer grazing nearby and enjoy the hiking trails, library, solarium, and fire pit while the kids play in the giant sandbox and toy chest. There is a great little steakhouse just down the road for your dinner enjoyment. Price: $42.00 to $48.00, additional person $6.00. (303)264-5863 (15% off with stay of more than 4 days).

Bruce Spruce Ranch—14 cabins with kitchens, and 32 trailer and tent sites. Price: tent sites $9.50 a night, cabins $25.00 to $45.00, additional person $3.00, kids under 6 free. 16 miles north on 160. (303)264-5374.

Pagosa Springs Chamber of Commerce, PO Box 787, Pagosa Springs, CO. 81147, (303)264-2360.

RICO—one of the smallest towns in Colorado, it boasts as much history as most. Its elevation is 8,827 feet which makes it a cool mountain retreat in the midst of the fabulous San Juan National Forest. Access is by Highway 145 between McPhee Reservoir and Telluride.

Things to See and Do

San Juan National Forest—make Rico your base camp and go out each day to the trails for a hike or to the streams to fish or pan for a little gold. Try the Dolores River.

Rico Scenic Circle—the drive takes you through some of the beautiful San Juan National Forest. Take 145 north to Placerville, 62 east to Ridgway, 550 south through Ouray and Silverton. Continue south to Durango, go west on 160 toward Cortez. Before Cortez, go north on 145 through Dolores and back to Rico. On the way, think about the fact that this area was frequented by outlaws like Butch Cassidy, miners in search of treasure, and good people seeking the promised land. Watch for ghost towns and abandoned mines, stop and explore the trails around the various campgrounds you pass, or just stop at the designated pull-offs to admire the view.

Cross-Country Skiing—everyone in town does it! The national Forest provides perfect trails to follow and explore. The town itself is at an elevation of 8,827 feet, so finding the powder should be quite easy.

Snowmobiling—nine miles to the north on Highway 145 is magestic Lizard Pass. At the top of the pass, locals and visitors alike enjoy this fun sport.

Mountains—Rico is surrounded by seven peaks which are all easily seen from town. They are Expectation, Sandstone, Johnny Bull, Elliot, Papoose, Telescope, and Wilson Mountains.

Fishing—try the beautiful Dolores River which flows right by the town. It's also not a bad idea to try your luck panning for a little gold.

Ghost Towns—Bear Creek, on railroad 12 miles southwest. Kings, on railroad 7.5 miles southwest. Montelores, on railroad 5 miles southwest.

Where to Eat and Sleep

Enterprise Cafe & Lounge—on Highway 145, the last of 27 original lounges. (303)967-2124.

Galloping Goose Cafe & Lounge—on Highway 145, breakfast, lunch, dinner, libation all the year round. (303)967-2851.

Rico Hotel—on Highway 145, a real, historic miner's bunk house remodeled to accomodate those with more refined taste. (303)967-2882.

Rico Chamber of Commerce, Box 176, Rico, CO. 81332.

RIDGWAY—typical rowdy western town. It has 5 saloons and Saturday nights are often said to be "rip-roaring". The local cowboys and ranch hands often have fun by racing horses down Main St. on these nights. Perhaps this is why such movies as True Grit and How the West was Won were filmed here.

Things to See and Do

Scenic Drives—1. west of town on Colorado 62, take the turn-off south on East Dallas Creek Road about 7 miles to Willow Swamps (a good fishing spot). 2. 2 miles north of town is Owl Creek Pass Road, a gorgeous drive past Chimney Peak and the Silverjack Reservoir. 3. At the edge of Ridgway are roads which lead to various scenic areas like Elk Meadows, Pleasant Valley, and Loghill Village. 4. San Juan Triangle is an easy drive for a half or full day adventure. From Ridgway go south on 550 through Ouray and Silverton to Durango. From Durango go west on Colorado 160 to Cortez, then north on Colorado 145 through Telluride to Placerville. Here turn east on Colorado 62 back to Ridgway.

Gold Panning—any of the streams around the town should give "color".

Ore Samples—the easy way to get some precious metal for free. Watch for mining roads where the ore trucks bounce a lot. They are so full of ore that many of the rocks "jump" off. Walk along these roads (especially at corners) and look carefully for granite like rocks which are usually white and gray. If the sun is shining the metals in the rocks will sparkle. Important: do not get so involved that you forget about the trucks which hurtle past at great speed. To test for deposits of pure gold, hold the sample next to some gold jewelry. If it is not the color of the jewelry, it is a combination of precious metals known as fool's gold.

Fishing—try your luck at East Dallas River and Willow Swamps southeast of Ridgway, the San Miguel River near Placerville, the Uncompahgre River, and Miramonte, Trout, and Molas Lakes.

Hiking—there are many trails around Ridgway which vary in length from ½ mile to 20 miles. To best travel these trails, take along a copy of the Ouray County Trail Guide (available at local book stores and the Chamber of Commerce for $2.50).

Snow Skiing—cross-country skiing is a favorite sport and there are many areas around the town to use for it.

Ice Skating—*Free* at the outdoor rink.

Cabin Fever Days & Winter Carnival—held in Ouray and Ridgway in mid-February, it features ski races and jumping, broom hockey, snow sculpting, and lots more.

Where to Eat and Sleep

True Grit Cafe—serving sandwiches (try The Duke), soup, and salads daily from 10 am to 10 pm. Brunch on Sunday, reservations suggested for Friday and Saturday nights. price: $2.50 to $5.00. (303)626-5915.

The Pueblo Hostel & Cantina—west of the river and south of Highway 62, a bed and breakfast with unique atmosphere and low prices. Member of the American Youth Hostels, it welcomes members and non-members both. The restaurant features great Mexican food! Price: average meal $6.00, for kids $2.75. Price: includes breakfast, dorm $12.00, room $16.00 to $24.00. Reservations recommended. Address: PO Box 346, Ridgway, CO. 81432. (303)626-5939.

COURTESY OF COLORADO TOURISM BOARD

San Juan Range as seen from near Ridgway.

MacTiernan's San Juan Guest Ranch—the American Plan is in effect at this ranch at 2882 Highway 23 (half way between Ridgway and Ouray). It includes all meals, lodging, horseback riding, jeeping, shooting, trail rides, and many other activities. For reservations write the ranch at: 2882 Highway 23, Ridgway, CO. 81432. (303)626-5360.

Ouray County Chamber of Commerce, Box 145, Ouray, CO. 81427. (303)325-4746.

SAN JUAN NATIONAL FOREST—this forest is absolutely gorgeous with its scenery and history. Many ghost towns dot its landscape of almost 2 million acres. They all have a story to tell, as do the old mines, alpine lakes and wildlife.

There are camping sites throughout the forest, many activities and it even is called home by the Bald Eagle and the peregrine falcon.

The many mountains, canyons and scenic drives through the forest are worth at least a day of your time. Take lunch and drive the famous "Million Dollar Highway" between Ouray and Durango. Other ways of getting around are also popular in the San Juan National Forest. Hiking trails are almost numberless, but remember that the high altitudes can slow you down tremendously and only the physically fit should attempt the more difficult ones. Jeeping is also popular and there are some very fun trails to drive in your 4 wheeler. Remember to be careful and if you plan an overnight trip into the wilderness, let someone know so they can watch for your safe return.

There are also quite a few Indian ruins in and around the forest (see Dolores and Cortez). The Anasazi left these for us to wonder about around 900 AD and no one knows where they went or why.

The campgrounds are mostly primitive, but do have toilets and tables. There are 32 camping areas ranging in price from $4.00 to $6.00 a night.

Forest Supervisor, 701 Camino del Rio, Durango, CO. 81301.

SILVERTON—silver by the ton was pulled from this unique high mountain town. The beauty of this village is unsurpassed and is immediately apparent as one sees it nestled in its valley from Highway 550. Its heritage has caused the whole town of Silverton to be declared a National Historic Landmark.

Things to See and Do

Silverton—the town itself is something to do, there are countless gift shops and curios. If you don't want to spend money, the town offers Victorian age buildings to admire like the old jailhouse, the courthouse, and most of the hotels and houses. The hotels are often famous for having been bordellos and saloons, especially along Blair St. A walking tour pamphlet is available from the Chamber of Commerce, the courthouse, the depot, or various stores. Silverton was named the county seat in 1876 after an all-night blow-out in Howardsville (then the county seat) caused the disappearance of county records. They turned up in Silverton and have been there ever since. Take the time to explore thoroughly part of your American heritage.

Durango - Silverton Narrow Gauge Railroad—this famous rail

Author and little brother on Greene Street in Silverton. Notice the classic Victorian architecture.

road connects the two towns in its name by 45 miles of track weaving through the awe inspiring San Juan mountains to a height of 9,318 feet. The views along the way are spectacular, of white water rapids and water falls, high mountain chalets and ghost towns, snow capped peaks in July, and Quaking aspens everywhere. The only round trips can be taken from Durango, but a bus takes visitors to Durango for a return ride to Silverton on the 9 am train. Backpackers can purchase tickets to Elk Park and Needleton from Silverton. Allow the whole day for a round trip. Hours: May to October. Times of departure vary with season, but average 7, 8, 9, and 10 am from Durango. Tickets must be purchased in advance, the farther the better, because seating and choice of seat are limited. Price: adults $28.10 ($48.30 in parlor car where only adults over 21 are allowed), children $14.10. Address: 479 Main Ave., Durango, CO. 81301. (303)247-2733.

Ore Samples—luckily for the rock hound, a mining road is located just above Silverton and runs within a short walk from town. Just take Greene St. north toward the courthouse and straight out of town. At the crossroad take the left branch and start hunting for the metal rich rocks which have bounced from the trucks. Be extremely careful to keep out of the way as the trucks go past, they are way too full of tons of ore to stop for people in the middle of the dirt road.

Jeeping—because of the rugged nature of many roads around Silverton, 4 wheel drive is the only motorized way to get to some of the ghost towns and old mines. For $.50, the Chamber of Commerce has a map with a wonderful circle tour available at their office and around town. Jeeps may be rented from the Silverton Lakes Campground (303)387-5721, the Triangle Motel on Greene St. (303)387-5780, and other establishments.

Christ of the Mines Shrine—the caboose on Blair St. can give directions on how to get to this shrine which overlooks the town from Anvil Mountain. Directions to other day-hike trails also may be obtained at the Caboose. Backpacking from Silverton into the mountains is also possible.

Cross-Country Skiing—after the last train has departed for the year, Silverton gets down to the serious business of being a small town. Skiers have long known that this makes it the perfect place to ski the back country along maintained trails, jeep roads, and hiking trails. Rental equipment is available in town and at St. Paul Ski Lodge at the top of Red Mountain Pass. Packages are available also.

Colorfest—held in mid-September, this festival celebrates the turning of the Aspen leaves throughout southwest Colorado. The events held in Silverton are a classical guitar concert, merchant 'n music fest, tennis tournament and a Tahiti raffle party. Contact the Chamber of Commerce for additional events and exact dates.

Great Snowscape Weekend—mid-February explodes with broomball, a fashion show, parade, ice-skating, sledding events, and an art show. All of this is repeated the next weekend also.

Silverton Victorian Days—at the end of July, the town pulls together and depicts the way things were in the Victorian Age.

Where to Eat and Sleep

Zhivago's Restaurant—at 1260 Blair St., features hot lunches, sandwiches, homemade soups, hamburgers, desserts, and a full bar. Has Silverton's only outdoor dining deck. Turn right on Blair from the train.

Romero's Restaurante y Cantina—at 1151 Greene, featuring

Lucy's homestyle Mexican food like Chilli Relleno, Burritos, and George's famous Mexican Margarita. Go left on Main from the train. (303)387-9934.

Teller House & French Bakery—at 1250 Greene, the bakery is a full service restaurant with bar, serving breakfast, lunch, and dinner. The motel offers a European style bed and breakfast service and is American Youth Hostel affiliated. Price: hostel dorm $6.75 to $9.50. Rooms: 1 person $20.00, 2 $26.50, 3 $33.00, 4 $37.50, 5 $40.00, 6 $42.50. All include breakfast. (303)387-5423.

Smedleys Bed & Breakfast—at 1314 Greene, has one bedroom units with living room, kitchen, bathroom, TV with HBO. Each unit sleeps up to 4 adults. Rates include breakfast at the Pickle Barrel next door. Price: single $29.00, double $39.00, extra person $8.00. 15% discount for 4 days or more. (303)387-5713, 5710, 5839. MC, V, AE.

Grand Imperial Hotel—on Greene St., it was built in 1882, it promises luxurious rooms in Victorian fashion, restaurant and bar on ground floor with limited menu. Price: $35.00 to $45.00 from March 1 to October 1. (303)387-5527.

Alma House—at 220 E. 10th, it is a restored European style hotel for non-smokers only. No kids or pets, but the rooms have one big bed and quiet, the perfect place to sleep in undisturbed. Open June 25 to labor Day. Price: 2 people $28.00. (303)387-5336.

Silverton lakes Campground—through town and right on 110. A full service facility with hookups, tent sites, hot showers, fireplaces, jeep rentals, and more. Weekly and monthly rates available, reservations essential in July and August. Open from May to October. Price: $10.00 for 2 camper facility with full service. Address: PO Box 126, Silverton, CO. 81433. (303)387-5721.

Silverton Chamber of Commerce, P.O. Box 565, Silverton, CO. 81433 (303)387-5654.

SPAR CITY—south of Creede by rural roads, it was once a boomtown. Spar City is mostly a ghost town itself which was known as Fisher City.

The route between Spar City and Creede was a favorite ambush site for many outlaws and is called Robber's Hill to this day. Countless wagons, stagecoaches, and travelers were pillaged and much of their wealth is believed to be buried nearby by the thieves who intended to retrieve it when the law was off their backs.

Stay at the Marshall Park Campground of the Rio Grande National Forest on Highway 149 6.5 miles southwest of Creede and north of Spar City. Has trailer spaces, no hookups, tables, toilets and fishing. price: $6.00. (303)658-2556.

TELLURIDE—has long been visited by famous folk, in fact Robert LeRoy Parker decided to *withdraw* a little cash from the bank here in June 24, 1889. Visitors will perhaps remember him better as Butch Cassidy, leader of the Wild Bunch. It is also in the middle of one of the richest deposits of precious metals in the world so panning for a little gold can turn out to be a worthwhile past-time for anyone. Winter brings ever increasing numbers of skiers each year, proving it to be an excellent place to get out on the slopes, maybe even try a little helicopter skiing.

Things to See and Do

Snow Skiing—Telluride has put together some very special packages for the skier. Christmas Special: 12/20-12/26, have a white Christmas in the Rockies. Includes 7 nights lodging and 6 days of lift tickets. Price: $301.00 to $441.00 per person. Telluride Ski Week: (all season, starts each Monday) designed for those who wish to perfect skills and have fun. Includes 6 nights lodging, 5 half day classes, and 5 full day lift tickets. Price: $297.00 to $381.00 per person. January White Sale: 1/4-2/11, after the rush, enjoy great snow, no crowds, and bargain prices. Includes 4 nights lodging and 3 full day lift tickets. Price: $141.00 to $184.00. March Madness: 2/12-3/29, the best snow conditions combined with spring break, it includes 7 nights lodging and 6 full day lift tickets. Price: $246.00 to $388.00. Contact Telluride Central Reservations for information and reservations. Address: Box 1009, Telluride, CO. 81435, or phone: nationwide 1-800-525-3455, in Colorado (303)728-4431. Also write the Chamber of Commerce for general information.

Helicopter Skiing—Helitrax introduces the new Rocky Mountain High with this different sport. Expensive but an experience well worth it to enthusiasts. Price: high alpine tours with gourmet lunch,

$165.00. Gourmet lunch and 4 runs, $265.00. Address: PO Box 1560, Telluride, CO. 81435, or phone (303)728-4904.

Trail Riding—tour famous ghost towns, old mines, and wilderness areas on horseback. Bring your camera. Price: 2 hour ride $15.00 per person, ½ day with snack $25.00 per person, full day with lunch $55.00. ½ day and full day leave at 8:00 am. 2 day packtrip $125.00 per person, Friday night cookout ride $35.00, Sunday breakfast ride $25.00. Write: D & E Outfitters, 805 Pacific, PO Box 516, Telluride, CO. 81435, or phone: (303)728-3200.

Gold Panning—take a trip to one of the nearby gold-rich streams by yourself or with a guide. Guide provides pans, shovels, screens, tweezers and vials as well as take you to several locations to try your luck. Price: adults $15.00, children $10.00, under 6 free. Write: Far Flung Adventures, PO Box 685, 224 E. Colorado Ave., Telluride, CO. 81435, or phone: (303)728-3895.

Mineral Collecting/Ore Samples—visitors will notice ore trucks trundling along the roads. They are packed so full for their trips to the foundery that ore inevitably jumps out along the roadside. Make a point to notice where many travel, especially along the dirt roads closest to the mines and walk carefully along the side. The samples mostly look like striped granite, but the metals shine brightly and attract the eye. To test for pure gold and to distinguish between it and fool's gold, simply hold it up to some gold jewelry and you will immediately see the difference. These samples usually contain many precious metals that are separated during smelting.

Bridal Veil Falls—the highest waterfall in the state, its beauty is uncompared. Located south of town, 2.54 miles off of Highway 145.

Wine Festival—early June, it features gourmet lunches, cooking with wine demonstrations, seminars, and world-renowned experts. For information, write Box 798 , Telluride, CO. 81435.

Music Festivals—Bluegrass & Country, mid-June, write Box 908. Jazz, late July, write Box 25. Chamber Music, early to mid-August, write Box 1040.

Festivals—Mushroom festival, late August, write Box 5503, Denver, CO. 80217. Hanggliding festival, mid-September, write Box 456.

Hiking—1. take Bear Creek Road at the end of S. Pine St., it ends at Bear Creek Falls about 2 miles away. 2. Wasatch Trail, take the Bear Creek Road and take the trail to the right just before the Falls (it crosses other trails and many old mines). 3. Cornet Creek, go north on Aspen St., continue on the trail 30 minutes to waterfall. 4. Savage Basin/Tomboy Ruins, north on Oak St. and follow the road to the ruins (2½ hours one way, take lunch and drinks).

Where to Eat and Sleep

Colorado O'Willy's—at 114 E. Colorado it is an 1890's style bar and restaurant featuring full menu, lunch and dinner. Try their goodies from stuffed potatoes to prime rib, they even have buffalo burgers. (303)728-4969. MC, V, AE.

The Excelsior Cafe—at 200 W. Colorado it is a European style cafe offering fondues, pastries, vegitarian specials, and expressos. **The** place for lunch. (303)728-4250. MC, V.

Oak Street Tavern—at 134 N. Oak (under the Oak St. Inn and behind the Opera House) they have buffet breakfast 7:00 am to 11:00 am. They then open at 4:00 pm with pizza and steak sandwiches, dinner specials, and drinks to take away the cold from the slopes. Entertainment is cable TV, pool, foosball, video games, and darts. (303)728-3678. MC, V.

The Coonskin Inn—500 feet from base lift, bed and breakfast, cable TV, spa, and located at 333 S. Davis. Price: summer $22.00 to $35.00, winter $47.00 to $57.00 (rates slightly higher during festivals and holidays). Address: Box 1890, Telluride, CO. 81435, or phone: (303)728-3181.

Victorian Inn—401 W. Pacific, whirlpool, sauna, no phones, no A/C, special events, nearby cafe. Price: $47.00 to $59.00. (303)728-3684.

Sunshine Campground—8 miles southwest on Highway 145, it is run by the Uncompahgre National Forest and has 15 sites, no hookups, 3 pull-thrus, toilets and tables. Price: $5.00.

Telluride Chamber of Commerce, PO Box 653, Telluride, CO. 81435, or phone: (303)728-3041.

UNCOMPAHGRE NATIONAL FOREST—can be reached by US Highway 550 and State Route 145. It features picnicking, hiking, backpacking, hunting, fishing, horseback riding, and camping. One attraction is the Mt. Sneffels Wilderness, a 16,500 acre area ranging in height from 9,600 feet to 14,150 feet. This high, alpine wilderness is crossed by trails for hiking and backpacking. Hikers should bring warm clothing and water. The Big Blue Wilderness is also impressive, its elevations all above 8,400 feet. It has 75 miles of trails for hiking and horseback riding. Visitors are likely to see a variety of wildlife, including elk, deer, Big Horn sheep, bear, bobcat, mountain lion, coyote, and even Golden Eagle. The fishing enthusiast should try Lake Hope, on a 2 mile trail off of Forest Road, 626 east of Lizard Head Pass. Camping fees range from free to $7.00.

Uncompahgre Forest Supervisor, 2250 Highway 50, Delta, CO. 81416.

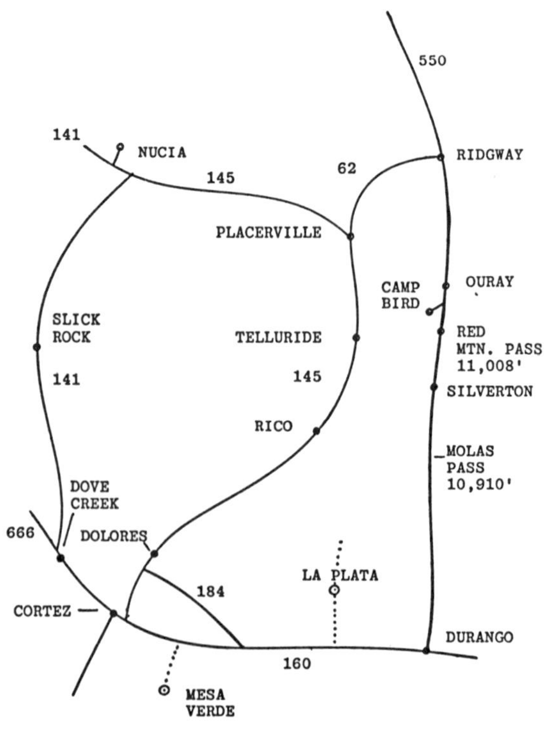

AREA FOUR

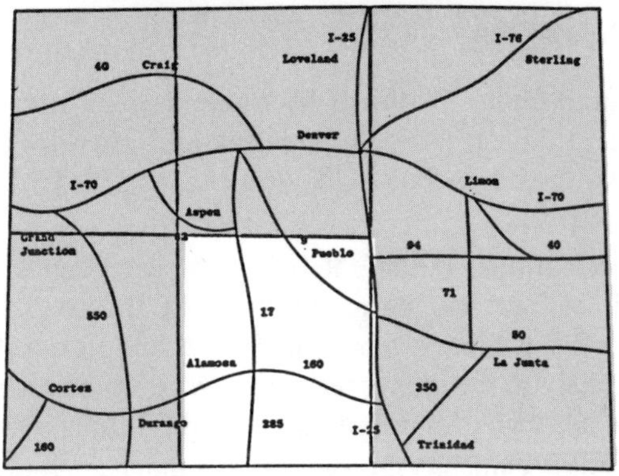

ALAMOSA—is home to many unique land features that cannot be found anywhere else in the country.

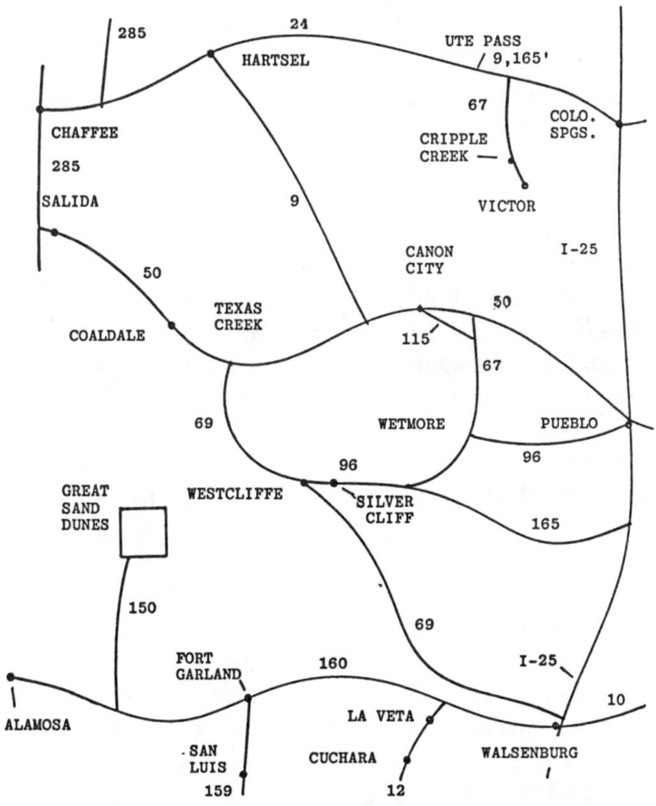

Things to Do and See

Great Sand Dunes National Monument—this area is home to the tallest sand dunes in North America and provides a refuge to many unusual creatures. Take U.S. 160 east to 150. Go north until you reach the park.

Alamosa National Wildlife Refuge—The Rio Grande River flows through this refuge and although most of the roads are rather primitive, viewing wildlife can be done from the Bluff Overlook. From here, one is likely to see cranes, eagles, hawks, waterfowl, and shore birds. There are trails for hiking around the refuge also.

Adams State College Observatory—to make an appointment to look through the telescope call (303)589-7616. Price: Free. There are also museums and galleries to view.

Where to Eat and Sleep

Bauer's Campus Pancake House & Restaurant—located at 435 Poncha, 1 block north of 160, has breakfast all day, homemade breads and pastries, and lunch specials. Hours: 6:00 am to 2 pm daily. Phone: (303)589-4202.

Sands Restaurant & Lounge—at 801 Main, it offers all three meals home-cooked. Specializes in Mexican and Italian fare. Hours: 7:00 am to 9:00 pm Monday to Saturday, closed Sunday. Phone: (303)589-2242.

Navajo Trails Campground—1 mile west of town on 160, has full hookups, hot showers, and pool. Write: Navajo Trails Campground, 7655 West US 160, Alamosa, CO. 81101, or phone: (303)589-9460.

Walsh Hotel—in downtown Alamosa, if offers a Mexican-American restaurant and a lounge. It is a registered youth hostel and sleeping rooms start at $9.00 a night. Write: Walsh Hotel, 617 Sixth Ave., Alamosa, CO. 81101, or phone: (303)589-6641.

Econo Lodge—425 Main St., cable TV, pool, sauna, some oversize beds. Price: $26.50 to $48.50. (303)589-6636.

Great Sand Dunes Oasis Campground—16 miles north of junction of US 160 and Highway 150, great view of the dunes, full hookups, separate tent area, store, firewood, showers. Price: $6.00 and up. (303)378-2222.

Alamosa County Chamber of Commerce, Cole Park, CO. 81101. (303)589-6531.

ANTONITO—Antonito is located in the San Luis Valley in the Colorado Rockies. It is in the south central part of Conejos County, six miles north of the New Mexico border. The town's elevation is 7,888 feet above sea level and it was founded in 1880. The tourist can enjoy many activities here.

Things to See and Do

Oldest Church in Colorado—Our Lady of Guadalupe was built in 1858 and was established on June 10th of that year. It is located at Conejos, Colorado, one mile north of Antonito.

Cumbres and Toltec Scenic Railroad—It is the longest and highest narrow-gauge railroad in North America, being 64 miles long and 10,015 feet high. It runs between the towns of Chama and Antonito and has many different travel packages, including a ride to and from the town Osier, a half-way point. There is even an overnight package that includes hotel accommodations and meals, as well as the return aboard the train. Reservations and pre-payment are required and run between $27.00 for adults, $10.00 for children on the half-way ride to Osier to $131.00 for adults and $55.00 for children on the overnight special. Reservations should be made as far in advance as possible. Reservations can be made in person at the Chama or Antonito depots or by mail or phone. For a free brochure and reservation order form, write to: The Cumbres and Toltec Scenic Railroad, Box 668, Antonito, Colorado 81120. (303)376-5483.

Fishing—Fishing is available in many of the lakes and streams surrounding Antonito, some of which are in the Rio Grande National Forest. For a free map of these, write to the Chamber of Commerce.

Special Events—Bathtub Races - third Saturday in July, 4-H Rodeo - Labor Day.

Where to Sleep

Narrow Gauge Railroad Inn—Located next to the railroad depot on the corner of Highway 285 and 17, has rooms and campground, summer rates are between $26.00 for one person in queen bed to $48.00 for four people in two queen beds. The phone number is (303)376-5441.

KOA Conejos River—13 miles west on Highway 17, sites for tents and RVs, full hookups, firewood, all the extras. Price: $8.00 and up. (303)376-2255.

Josey's Cottages & RV Park—5 miles west on Highway 17, sites for tents and RVs, some cabins for rent. Price: $6.00 and up. (303)376-5774.

Antonito Chamber of Commerce, Box 427, Antonito, Colorado 81120, (303)376-5443.

BUENA VISTA—once a silver mining boom town, this high mountain town has settled down to the business of being a community of fun and relaxation.

Things to See and Do

Collegiate Peaks Rodeo—mid-July celebration bringing three days of fun, food (all you can eat pancake breakfast for $2.50 the first day) and excitement to town. In fact, it is the second largest amateur Colorado State Rodeo Association sanctioned event in the state.

Gold Rush Days—mid-August celebration of the old west brings the Collegiate Peaks Burro Race to town as well as a parade and gem show.

Colorfest—the changing of the aspens brings the Colorfest Poker Run to town in early September. Motorcyclists from around the country participate in the all day ride through the mountains, passing checkpoints. Prizes are awarded for various categories.

Fishing—Cottonwood Lake west of town on CR 306 is the perfect place to try your luck angling. There are also picnic areas with barbeques and facilities for canoeing. Camping is also permitted. Another good fishing spot would be anywhere along the Arkansas River.

Ghost Towns—there is a multitude of these little abandoned villages among the valleys and peaks near Buena Vista. They are fun to explore and yield some interesting pictures and souveniers (see sections on rockhounding and ghost towns). A walk down any railroad bed should lead to an old mine or town.

COURTESY OF SOUTH PARK CHAMBER OF COMMERCE

This is an example of what is left of many ghost towns, an abandoned miner's cabin.

Where to Eat and Sleep

Delaney's Depot—559 Highway 24, it features a Sunday smorgasborg for only $6.95. They serve breakfast, soup, salad, sandwiches, and dinner specials like fresh pan fried trout, all prepared with that homemade goodness. Price: average $7.50. (303)395-8854.

Delaney's Caboose—on south Highway 24, it serves the same good homemade fare as that of the Depot, barbeque specials with family size portions of pork, beef and chicken available. Price: $4.25 to $8.00. (303)395-8059.

Woodland Brook Cabins—at S. San Juan and Pine, 1 and 2 bedroom cabins with kitchenettes, fireplaces (and wood) only $37.00 to $49.00 a night. One room efficiency cabins with kitchenettes, $30.00 a night. For reservations, write them at PO Box 418, Buena Vista, CO. 81211 or phone (303)395-2922 MC, V.

Blue Sky Inn—719 Arizona, this bed and breakfast inn is on the bank of the Arkansas River and has beautiful gardens to relax in as well as information on nearby attractions. Rates not available at time of printing. (303)395-8861.

Fishermans Bridge Campground—from US 24, 3 miles south on US 285 . Full hookups, separate tent sites, toilets, showers, tables and ice. Price: $6.75 and up. (303)395-8207.

Heart of the Rockies Chamber of Commerce, 406 W. Rainbow Blvd., Salida, CO. 81201, (303)539-2068.

CANON CITY—is set in Central Colorado, and like most other cities it has untold numbers of activities for visitors.

Things to See and Do

Scenic Drives—almost any road will take you to paradise, but here are 4 local favorites. Along their routes, you will see rich ranch land, oil fields, old and abandoned mining towns, canyons, National Forest, and grasslands. Watch also for the wildlife along the way, even Big Horn Sheep.

Wet Mountain Valley—104 miles long, take Highway 50 west to Highway 69 and turn south. Reach Highway 96 and go east to Highway 67. Take 67 north to Florence and take Highway 115 west to Canon City.

Collegiate Mountains—170 miles long, take Highway 50 to Highway 9 and travel northwest. At Hartsel, turn southwest on Highway 24 to Chaffee and take 285 south to Highway 50. Go east back to Canon City.

Cripple Creek or Bust—take Highway 50 west to Highway 9 and go north. Take Highway 24 northeast from Hartsel and then take 67 south to Victor, one of the best preserved western gold towns. Travel back on 67 to Cripple Creek where you are likely to find turquoise stones in the dirt streets after a good rain. From here take Teller County Road 1, then turn south on High Park Road which returns to Highway 9. Take 9 back to 50 and back to Canon City.

San Isabel—east on 115 to Florence, and take 67 south to Wetmore. Go west on Highway 96 to the junction with 165 and drive southeast through the Forest. When you get to Interstate 25, go south to Walsenburg. Take 69 north to Texas Creek and then 50 to Canon City.

Royal Gorge Park—the gorge is spanned by the world's highest

COURTESY OF ROYAL GORGE BRIDGE COMPANY

The world's highest suspension bridge is a truly awesome sight.

suspension bridge, 1,055 feet high. Take Highway 50 west and follow the signs.

Royal Gorge Bridge—the wire in each 2,100 strand cable weighs over 300 tons! A true engineering wonder, at Royal Gorge just west of Canon City on Highway 50. Price: includes one ride, adults $5.00, kids $3.00, under 7 *Free.* (303)275-7507.

Royal Gorge Scenic Railway—30 minute train ride gives visitors a spectacular view of the bridge as well as glimpses of animal life like jack rabbits and deer. Price: includes train and museum, adults $5.00, kids $3.50. *Ladies Free* to museum. (303)275-5485.

Buckskin Joe—in Royal Gorge Park, this unique part of history was used in countless movies with stars like John Wayne and Tom Selleck. There are saloons and restaurants, stagecoaches, mock street fights, and bank robberies. Take Highway 50 west of Canon City to Royal Gorge Road. Price: adults $4.50, kids $3.50, under 5 *Free.* Horseback riding, $9.00 an hour. (303)275-5485.

Canon City Municipal Museum—612 Royal Gorge Blvd., features artifact of the Indians, pioneer historical items and railroad memorabilia. Behind the museum are the Rudd Cabin and Stone House, constructed in 1860 and 1881. They are full of Victorian age antiques. Price: *Free.* (303)275-2368.

Temple Canon Park—on Temple Canon Rd., it contains a natural temple used by Indians and drives through canyons and rugged scenery. Price: *Free.*

Red Canyon Park—on Red Canyon Rd., features a natural ampitheatre, hiking trails with scenic vistas and interesting rock formations. Price: *Free.*

Where to Eat and Sleep

Merlino's Belvedere—1330 Elm Ave., *four star* family restaurant. Started in 1946, it has expanded many times over the years and has gotten better each time with Italian specialties, steaks, sandwiches, and seafood. Open at 5 pm daily and 12:30 pm on Sundays. Price: $2.00 to $23.95, average meal is $7.95. (303)275-5558.

Bavarian Inn—on Highway 50 at the Royal Gorge turnoff, serving German specialties, American favorites, seafood and kid's menu. Price: $1.75 to $10.50. (303)269-3594.

Janey's Chili Wagon—840 1st St., cocktails, light meals and lunch specials. (303)275-4885.

Super 8 Motel—209 N. 19th St., cable TV, 24 hour cafe next door. Price: $23.88 to $65.00. (303)275-5504.

KOA Kampground & Loma Linda Motel—in Cotopaxi west of Canon City at 21435 US Highway 50. Campground has separate tent area and full hookups for $10.00 and up. Motel has kitchenettes in some units. Price: $30.00 and up. (303)275-9308, 275-2249.

Canon City Chamber of Commerce, PO Bin 749, Canon City, CO. 81212. (303)275-2331.

COALDALE—at the edge of the awe inspiring Sangre De Cristo Range, it gives you the perfect excuse to stay the night just so you can see the sunrise on the mountains.

Rainbow Trail—this trail runs for more than 80 miles in the beautiful mountains and has various trailheads. One of these is in Coaldale at the Hayden Creek Campground, 5 miles southwest on Forest Road 249. Another nearby access point is at Big Cottonwood Creek. The trail is open to hikers, bicyclers, and motor vehicles not more than 40 inches in width. All motorized vehicles must stay on the trail.

Fishing—try Big Cottonwood Creek for Rainbow trout. The Arkansas River is another good bet.

Rafting—whitewater excitement can be yours for reasonable prices. The Lazy J Resort & Rafting CO., Inc. can provide all you need for rafting as well as cabins, a motel, a campground and cafe. Rafting rates start at $9.95 per person for a short trip. Camping rates average around $8.00 with full hookup. Motel rates unavailable. Write to: PO Box 85, Coaldale, CO. 81222 or phone (303)942-4274.

Heart of the Rockies Chamber of Commerce, 406 W. Rainbow Blvd., Salida, CO. 81201, (303)539-2068.

COLORADO SPRINGS—nestled at the foot of Pike's Peak, this busy city receives an average of 300 sun-filled days a year. All through the summer and winter, there is a multitude of things to do for the whole family.

Things to See and Do

Air Force Academy—10 miles north on I-25, see where young officers are trained to fly. Open all year. Graduation in May is cause for much celebration. Price: *Free.*

High Point & Camera Obscura—for an excellent view of the Garden of the Gods and some breathtaking shots. Visit this attraction at Garden of the Gods, Ridge Road, Colorado Springs, CO. 80829, or phone: (303)623-9768. MC, V, AE. Price: adults $.35, children *Free.*

Garden of the Gods—3 miles northwest on US 24 then right at 30th St., this Registered Natural Landmark is a 940 acre city park that contains some of the most unusual and breathtaking rock formations in the world, including the red sandstone Cathedral Spires. Open early June to October, the visitors center and guided walking tours are all *Free.* (303)578-6933.

Manitou & Pikes Peak Railway Company—the world's highest cog railway to the summit of Pikes Peak (elevation: 14,110 ft.) the round trip takes 3 to 4 hours and is open May to October. Address: PO Box 1329, Colorado Springs, CO. 80901. (303)685-5401.

Pikes Peak Ghost Town—authentic buildings, furniture and clothing bring back the wild days of early Colorado and its gold rush. Open May to October. Highway 24 W. at S. 21st St. Price: adults $2.50, children under 12 $1.25, under 5 free. (303)634-0696.

Pikes Peak Vineyards Ltd.—see how the wine is made and fermented. Open Thursday to Saturday or by appointment at 3901 Janitell Rd. (303)576-0075.

River Runners, Ltd.—will take you on a trip you will never forget, guaranteed! White water in beautiful Brown's Canyon. ¼ day to 3 day trips. Price: $9.75 to $159.75. Address: 11150 Highway 50, Salida, CO. 81201, or phone: nationwide 1-800-525-2081, in state 1-800-332-9100.

McAllister House Museum—tours of homes constructed in 1873 which belonged to Major Henry McAllister. Learn about life in early Colorado Springs. Hours: May to August open on Wednesday through Sunday at 10:00 am to 4:00 pm. September to April open on Thursday through Saturday at 10:00 am to 4:00 pm. Address: 423 N. Cascade Ave., Colorado Springs, CO. 80903. (303)635-7925.

Pioneers' Museum—exhibits from early life in the West and Colorado Springs. Hours: Tuesday to Saturday from 10:00 am to 5:00 pm, Sunday from 2:00 pm to 5:00 pm (closed Mondays and holidays). Price: *Free.* Address: 215 Tejon St., Colorado Springs, CO. 80903.

(303)578-6650.

ProRodeo Hall of Champions and Museum of the American Cowboy—learn more about this truly American sport and the men and women who made it and the West famous. Tours are self-guided with sound effects, music, and theatres along the way. It is a great educational opportunity for all. Hours: 9 am to 5 pm daily, noon to 4:30 Sundays, closed Mondays. Price: adults $2.50, students $1.00, under 5 *Free.* Address: 101 ProRodeo Dr., Colorado Springs, CO. 80919. (303)593-8840, MC, V.

COURTESY OF PRO RODEO HALL OF CHAMPIONS

Prorodeo Hall of Champions and Museum of the American Cowboy, Colorado Springs—Situated on a parklike five-acre site set against the Colorado Rockies, this attractive facility features two theaters, three exhibit halls, and outdoor exhibit garden.

Where to Eat and Sleep

House of Yakitori Restaurant—4 locations where you can enjoy barbequed chicken, sushi bars, and lounge. Address: 2431 N. Union Blvd., (303)630-7507; 5975 N. Academy Blvd., (303)593-7004; 16 E. Bijou St., (303)578-0915, and 2036 S. Academy Blvd., (303)574-9937.

King's Table Buffet—2 locations for great salads, desserts, hot meals and seconds at no extra charge on food and beverage. Open for lunch and dinner and Sunday breakfast. Price: only $4.15 to $5.50. Address: 3015 N. Nevada Ave., (303)473-8471, and 3020 E. Platte Ave., (303)634-5182.

Sunbird Restaurant—a truly magnificent view of the city from inside or in the spring and summer from any of the 4 patios. Steaks, seafood, full bar, wine list, try the Fettucini Pacifica or the Baked Baby Veal Chop. Price: lunch $4.50 and up, dinner $6.95 to $21.95. Address: 230 Point of the Pines Dr. (303)599-8550.

Drury Inn—bed and breakfast, pool, cable TV, Denny's next door. Price: $35.00 to $51.00. Address: 8155 N. Academy Blvd., Colorado Springs, CO. 80918. (303)598-2500. MC, V, AE.

Crown & Rose Motor Inn—in-house movies, pool, hot tubs, restaurant, and more. Price: $28.00 to $38.00. Address: 1703 S. Nevada Ave., Colorado Springs, CO. 80906. (303)632-2663. MC, V, AE.

Bed & Breakfast-Rocky Mountains—over 100 participating homes and inns in the area, from modest cabins to elegant mansions. If you plan an extended stay, this could be for you. Price: $23.00 to $95.00, for a descriptive directory, send $3.00 to PO Box 804, Colorado Springs, CO. 80901 or call: (303)630-3433.

Hearthstone Inn—stay in a beautifully restored Victorian mansion, all rooms are furnished with antiques, some with fireplaces, balconies, the perfect honeymoon hideaway. Gourmet breakfast included. Price: $58.00 to $95.00. Address: 506 N. Cascade Ave., Colorado Springs, CO. 80903. (303)473-4413.

Colorado Springs Chamber of Commerce, 104 S. Cascade Ave., Suite 104, Colorado Springs, Colorado 80903, (303)635-7506.

CRIPPLE CREEK—a near ghost town now, Cripple Creek boasted over 800 businesses (and 91 lawyers) in the 1890's. It no longer produces mega amounts of riches, but visitors can find a few samples and souveniers to satisfy themselves. In fact, after heavy rains, the dirt streets sometimes yield turquoise. The town holds many mysteries also, for instance, who was responsible for the skeleton with the bullet hole in the skull. It was found in what once was the safe in the courthouse.

Things to See and Do

Cripple Creek District Museum—on Highway 67, features relics and exhibits from the early days of this rowdy mining town. Price: *Free* in summer. (303)689-2634

Cripple Creek/Victor Narrow Gauge Railroad—this train used to carry miners and their riches, now it carries visitors through the beautiful mountains. It travels past many old mines and ghost towns which wait to be investigated. The ride only takes an hour. Price: adults $4.50, kids $2.50, under 3 *Free.* (303)689-2640.

Fishing—try Skagwuay Reservoir which is stocked and controlled by the state, there also are boating and camping facilities. Try also Eleven Mile and Wright's Reservoirs and any of the rushing streams of Pike National Forest.

Where to Eat and Sleep

Imperial Hotel & Dining Room—at 123 N. 3rd St., the restaurant features trout fresh from the streams, salad bar and a buffet/show combination with the best entertainment in the mountains. Price: $2.50 to $20.00. The hotel has a lounge, some oversize beds and Victorian atmosphere which is hardly surprising because it's been around since 1896. Price: $24.00 to $60.00. Restaurant and hotel are closed from October to May. (303)689-2713. **For additional accommodations and restaurants, see Victor.**

CUCHARA—ski resort of southeast Colorado, it resides in the beautiful mountains of the San Isabel National Forest.

Things to See and Do

Cordova Pass—go south on 12 from Cuchara, just before Cuchara Pass take the road to the left. This will take you to Cordova Pass and the trail to the top of West Spanish Peak. There are camping and picnicking facilities.

Bear Lake & Blue Lake—from Cuchara, go south on 12 then west on FR 413. Enjoy hiking, fishing, skiing, and more in this beautiful countryside.

San Isabel National Forest—only 6 miles west of Weston on Route 12, it offers beautiful scenery, high mountain passes, fishing, hunting, and awesome views from the roadside as well as a large elk herd that winters here.

Fishing—the big sport of the area both in winter and summer.

Try Monument Lake, North Lake, Blue Lake, Bear Lake, the Purgatoire River and any promising stream.

Snow Skiing—at the Cuchara Valley Resort, turn west on US 160 to Highway 12 and south to the resort. Ski passes are priced: whole season $87.00, full day $17.00, age 7 to 12 $7.00, under 6 *Free.* (303)742-3163, nationwide 1-800-227-4436.

Where to Eat and Sleep

Vietti's Streamside Restaurant—Italian food at its finest, chef's specials and the ever popular pepper steak all by the Cuchara River. Lounge opens at 3 pm with cocktails and hors d'oeuvres. Restaurant hours: Monday to Saturday 5 to 9 pm, reservations recommended. (303)742-3434.

Cuchara Valley Resort—open for snow skiing from December to April, it is perfect for the family who wishes to ski together. Prices for skiing are listed above. Lodging price: for one night and four people $110.00 to $240.00, prices decrease with length of stay. (303)742-3163, nationwide 1-800-227-4436.

Picketwire Lodge & Store—on Route 1, cabins are complete with kitchen and all utensils, a nearby restaurant, a beautiful view of the Purgatoire River which flows through the property, and great rates. Price: $28.00, add $3.00 for each extra person. Write them at: Route 1, box 32, Weston, CO. 81091 or call (303)868-2265.

Spanish Peaks Campground—3 miles south on Highway 12, it has full hookups, separate tenting area, store, showers, toilets, tables and more. Price: $10.00 and up. (303)742-3392.

Cuchara Chamber of Commerce, PO Box 32, E. Field, Forest Service Building, La Veta, CO. 81055, (303)742-3676.

DEL NORTE—often called the Gateway to the San Juans, is located on the Rio Grande River at the west edge of the San Luis Valley halfway between Monte Vista and South Fork. It offers easy access to ghost towns, big game hunting grounds, gold medal fishing streams and lakes, and the surrounding mountains, yet is not quite in them. It is sheltered by them and therefore receives a mild climate year round. Del Norte is over 100 years old and still retains the atmosphere of the old West.

Things to See and Do

Wolf Creek Ski Area—35 miles southwest of Del Norte on highway 160, this area offers skiers a day of fun *without long lines on the slopes.*

Covered Wagon Days—festival held on the first weekend of August, it celebrates the pioneers and their way of life. Events include a parade, pancake breakfast, barbeque, logging skills, black powder shooting, and a music festival.

Indian Head Peak—just outside of Del Norte, this and a natural stone arch in the National Forest near Twin Mountain mark the spots where visitors may find arrowheads and other Indian artifacts. Please see section on rockhounding for laws regarding artifacts.

Ghost Towns—*Granger* is on an old railroad track 7 miles west and *Haywood* is on the track 7 miles southeast.

Rio Grande national Forest—to the north, west and south of Del Norte, it contains many abandoned mines and towns to explore as well as streams and rivers to fish and pan and animals to watch and photograph. Make Del Norte your base camp and discover the forest and its beauty.

Where to Eat and Sleep

The Brass Lantern—located in downtown Del Norte, this establishment serves all three meals, cocktails, and has live entertainment on Friday and Saturday nights. Hours: 6:00 am to 9:00 pm Monday to Thursday, 6:00 am to 10:00 pm on Friday and Saturday, and from 9:00 am to 2:00 pm on Sunday. Phone: (303)657-3618.

The Tin Cup—216 Oak on Colorado 112, it has a complete menu of down home country favorites to *homemade cinnamon rolls and pies.* Hours:, 7:30 am to 7:30 pm Monday to Saturday, closed Sunday. Phone: (303)657-3973.

KOA Kampground—east of South Fork on the river, has 100 sites (32 with full hookups). Rates: on river, $11.50 for two people. Write: KOA Kampground, 26359 West US 160, Del Norte, CO. 81132, or phone: (303)873-5500.

El Rancho Motel—located on US 160 east of town, it includes cable TV, phone, and excellent rates. Price: $25.00 to $28.00 for one person, $30.00 to $35.00 for two, and $3.00 for each additional person. Write: El Rancho Motel, Box 225, Del Norte, CO. 81132, or phone (303)657-3332.

GARFIELD—this area is full of ghost towns and abandoned mines just waiting to be explored. It is also rumored that outlaws buried and hid much of their loot in the area to escape the long arm of the law, only it caught up and they never came back. The wilderness around the town makes it the perfect place to stay and from which to investigate its mysteries.

The Stable, Grog & Grain—22753 Highway 50, this interesting restaurant invites you to come and enjoy their comfortable and relaxing atmosphere. Excellent sandwiches and Mexican specialties. Price: $3.00 to $6.95. (303)539-7143.

Monarch Lodge & Ski Resort—on Highway 50 in Garfield, fine dining, lounge, spa, pool, whitewater rafting, hiking and fishing. Special package rates in summer. For example, for $18.88 per person you get two nights lodging and ½ day whitewater rafting. Call for information and reservations 1-800-332-3668.

GREEN MOUNTAIN FALLS—outside the big city of Colorado Springs, yet in the middle of the Pike National Forest, this town is a strategic point from which to explore many aspects of the state.

Things to See and Do

Bronc Day—in early August, this rodeo event is sponsored by the Ute Pass Triangle Chamber of Commerce.

Yule Festival—in early December, come celebrate the Christmas season with all the fabulous events.

Pike National Forest—this beauty filled wilderness is easily explored from Green Mountain Falls. Any back road will take you to a new world.

Scenic Drive—past ghost towns, abandoned mines and gorgeous wilderness. Take US 24 north to Woodland Park, then take State Road 67 north. Look for the ghost town of Torrington 7 miles north of Woodland Park. As you head into Deckers watch for Devil's Head Mountain on the right. This mountain was a favorite hideout spot for outlaws who were rumored to have left much of their loot in the canyons, caves and guiches of the area. At Deckers, take Colorado 126 through Buffalo Creek to US 285 and go west. You will travel over Kenosha Pass (10,001 feet), Red Hill Pass (9,993 feet) and into Fairplay. Just past Fairplay, take State Road 9 southeast and watch for the elk herds which graze here. At US 24, go east over Wilkerson Pass (9,525 feet) and back to Green Mountain Falls.

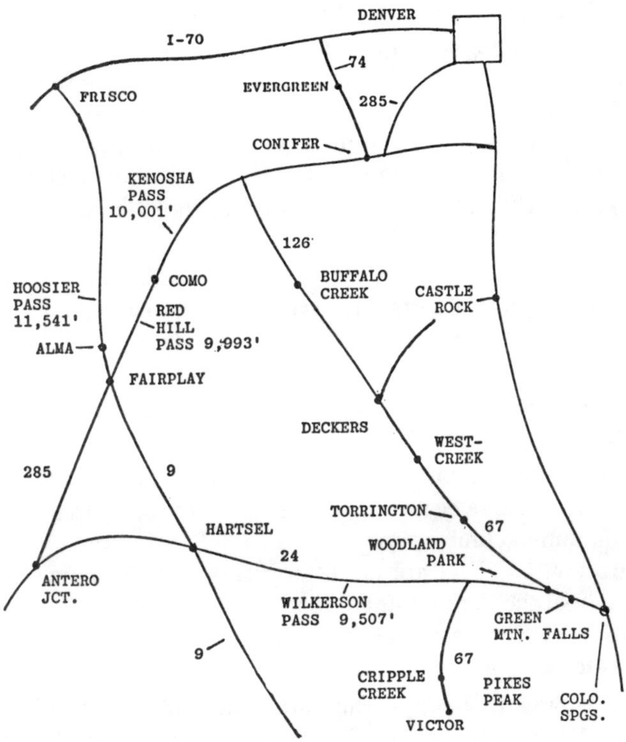

Where to Eat and Sleep

Rocking X Motel & Hi Vu Campground—at 10090 Highway 24 W. (Box 215, Green Mountain Falls, CO. 80819). Motel has rooms and kitchenettes. Campground has full hookups, game room, and pool (open May to October). Price: motel $25.90 and up, campground $7.00 and up. (303)684-9044.

LA VETA—at an altitude of 7,000 feet, this town is the gateway into beautiful Cuchara Valley.

Things to See and Do

Snow Skiing—at the Cuchara Valley Resort, turn west on US 160 to Highway 12 and south to the resort. Ski passes are priced: whole season $87.00, full day $17.00, age 7 to 12 $7.00, under 6 *Free.* (303)742-3163, nationwide 1-800-227-4436.

Horse Racing—held in La Mesa Park, New Mexico, the route is scenic and a nice day trip. Take State Road 12 south from La Veta to I-25 and go south to Raton. The races feature both thoroughbred and quarter horse events. Hours: late April to late September Friday to Sunday and holidays. Price: $3.00 grandstand boxes, $1.50 general and $1.00 parking. Children admitted with adult, limited playground available.

Fort Garland—take US 160 west over La Veta Pass to this little town famous for its fort which was once commanded by the legendary Kit Carson. Hours: Memorial to Labor Day daily. Labor Day weekend it hosts Mountain Men Rendesvous.

San Luis—the oldest town in Colorado is just south of Fort Garland on Colorado 159.

San Isabel National Forest—just south of La Veta on Colorado 12, it offers unique beauty to visitors. There are many trails for hikers and mountain climbers, and lots of wildlife for photographers and nature lovers. There are lakes for fishing and camping facilities throughout the Forest. Other branches of the Forest are north of La Veta, take US 160 east to I-25 and go north to 165 which you take east into the Forest.

Highway 12 Loop—scenic drive, take 12 west to Walsenburg then I-25 south to Trinidad. There, take 12 northwest back to La Veta. It is a complete loop through National Forest, high mountain passes, and wilderness beyond compare.

Hiking—there are many trails in the National Forests. Here are a few. *Huajatolla Road Trail*—at the south end of town, take this road to the left which leads to the Bullseye Mine at the end. *Cuchara Campground*—is the beginning of quite a few trails. Take 12 south past the ski resort then right on Forest Service Road 413 to the campground. *Chaparral Trail*—south on Highway 12, the trail starts on the left, just after the Devil's Stairsteps rock formation. Bring water on these treks.

COURTESY OF LA VETA CHAMBER OF COMMERCE

Devil's Stairstep south of La Veta on Highway 12.

Great Sand Dunes National Monument—take US 160 west to Highway 150. Go north to the Monument's visitor center. These dunes were formed a millennia ago and are beautiful in their almost moon-like appearance.

Fort Francisco Museum—at the center of La Veta, it is on the original Francisco Plaza built of adobe in 1862. Hours: opens Memorial Day, 9 to 5 daily. Price: adults $1.50.

Ski Packages—sponsored by the 1899 Inn Adobe Arch Trading Post, includes rentals, trail lunches, guided tours, all levels of wilderness trails. Price: $25.00 per person double occupancy. Address: 314 S. Main, La Veta, CO. 81055. (303)742-3576.

Where to Eat and Sleep

Covered Wagon Steak House & Lounge—on Main St. in La Veta, look for the covered wagon on the roof, it offers lunch and dinner with specials daily. Enjoy a cocktail beside the fireplace in an Old West atmosphere. Hours: 11 am to 9 pm daily. Price: $3.50 to $11.95. (303)742-3679. MC, V.

Sundown Saloon—912 S. Oak, western atmosphere serving beef nuggets, Rocky Mountain Oysters, pizza, ham & beans. Weekends bring live entertainment and dancing. Open at noon daily. Price: $1.75 to $4.50. (303)742-3093.

Triple G Cafe—on Highway 160 just west of town, open 24 hours serving home cooked American and Mexican food and breakfast anytime. Price: $2.25 to $10.00.. (303)742-9987. MC, V.

The La Veta Lodge & Restaurant—in downtown La Veta close to the slopes. The restaurant opens daily at 6:30 am (lounge opens at noon) and its specialties include a full array of Mexican and American food. Price: $4.00 and up. The lodge offers rooms and kitchenettes. (303)742-3700.

1899 Inn—bed and breakfast with special packages for such activities as cross-country and downhill skiing, horseback riding, hiking, fishing, and relaxing. Price: packages $25.00 and up, per person double occupancy. Address: 314 S. Main, La Veta, CO. 81055. (303)742-3576.

La Veta Mall Motel—in La Veta, close to everything with twin and queen size beds, cable TV, and more. Price: $25.00 to $30.00. (303)742-9990. MC, V, AE.

La Veta Chamber of Commerce, 103 E. Field, Forest Service Building, La Veta, CO. 81055. (303)742-3676.

MANASSA—located in south central Colorado.

Things to Do and See

Mormon Pioneer Days—held the weekend closest to July 24th, this celebration includes a rodeo, parade, Bar-B-Q, and a carnival.

Jack Dempsey Museum—for those boxing fans, this museum is open from June to September. Price: *Free.*

Ghost Towns—*Espinoza* is 2 miles south; *Los Cerritos* is 2.5 miles southeast.

Scenic Drive—take State Road 142 east to Road 159 and go north to US 160. At 160, go east to State Road 12. This road goes through the beautiful Cuchara Valley and the San Isabel National Forest. Take 12 to Trinidad, then I-25 south into New Mexico. There, take US 64 west through the Santa Fe National Forest and northwest at Taos. Join US 285 at Tusas and go north back into Colorado to Romeo. Turn right onto 142 and head back to Manassa.

Town of Manassa, PO Box 130, Manassa, CO. 81141.

MANITOU SPRINGS—full of mineral springs used by the Indians who believed the waters could give the power of the great spirit of Manitou, thus the town's interesting name.

Things to See and Do

Manitou Cliff Dwellings—east of town you can see some of the best preserved examples of artifacts and homes of cliff dwelling Indians. The museum there provides a look into America's past with buildings, pottery, urns, tools, and native dancing June to August. Open May to October; call for hours. Price: adults $2.50, kids $1.25, under 6 *Free.* (303)685-5242.

Miramont Castle—off of Ruxton Ave., this castle is being restored by the Manitou Springs Historical Society and is open from 10 am to 5 pm Memorial Day to Labor Day. Price: adults $2.00, kids $1.00. (303)685-1011.

Mt. Manitou Incline—on Ruxton Ave. across from Railway depot. Climb over 2,000 feet in 1 mile. Evening tours provide a spectacular view of the valleys and the towns nestled in them. During the day, you may stay at the top as long as you like and hike the trails, take pictures, picnic and relax. Ride leaves every 30 minutes. Price:

adults $5.00, kids 5 to 11 $2.50, under 5 *Free.* (303)685-9086.

The Iron Springs Chateau Melodrama—at 444 Ruxton Ave., it was declared the official Colorado Centennial Bicentennial Melodrama with productions like "Yo Ho Ho and a Barrel of Fun". There is also a restaurant with complete bar to enjoy before the show if you like. Price: dinner and show, adults $15.50, kids $9.00, seniors $14.50. (303)685-5104 or 685-5572.

Florissant Fossil Beds National Monument—take US 24 west to Florissant and take County Road 1 south 2 miles. This unique monument contains 6,000 acres of what was once a lake. It was covered by lava flow 35 million years ago. Today, the visitor can see the life that was present in those bygone days. A self-guided tour leads you through the fossils. Price: *Free.* (303)685-748-3253.

Where to Eat and Sleep

Million Bell Inn—178 Crystal Park Rd., Mexican specialties, home made in a family style setting. Children's menu. Price: $7.00 to $10.00. (303)685-5089. MC, V.

Stagecoach Inn—702 Manitou Ave., fresh steak, seafood, and you have to try their homemade cherry preserves and baked goods. All this and setting too because it just happens to be an 1880's stage station. Price: $5.25 to $15.95. (303)685-9335. MC, V, AE.

Red Wing Motel—at Beckers Lane and El Paso Blvd., free continental breakfast, cable TV, pool, some refrigerators and oversize beds. Price: $29.00 to $41.00. (303)685-9547.

Crystal Kangaroo Campground—1 block west on Manitou Ave., then 1.5 miles south on Crystal Park Road. Full hookups, pull-thrus, showers, store, ice tables, and fishing nearby. Price: $10.00 and up. (303)685-5010.

Manitou Springs Chamber of Commerce, 354 Manitou Ave., Manitou Springs, CO. 80829, (303)685-5089.

MONTE VISTA—located in the Great San Luis Valley, this town is endowed with some unique and beautiful landscapes.

Things to Do and See

Ski-Hi Stampede—the last week in July brings a rodeo, parade, carnival, barbeque and dancing to the Ski-Hi park in this western town.

Monte Vista National Wildlife Refuge—features a self-guiding loop drive open sunrise to sunset during winter, spring, and summer. This is an area of wetland situated in a dry desert. Its residents include the rare and elegant Whooping Crane, the sandhill crane, bald and golden eagles, and many waterfowl and shore birds. Located 6 miles south on Highway 15.

Great Sand Dunes National Monument—take US 160 to 150 and go north to the park. It is home to the biggest sand dunes in North America, and its unique environment is home to many rare creatures.

Earnest's Taxidermy, Crafts & Tours—learn self-help skills at their Primitive Skills Camp during July, take guided fishing and hunting tours, or just examine the buffalo heads and hides in the shop. For information, write: Earnest's Taxidermy, 3596 W. US 160, Monte Vista, CO. 81144, or phone: (303)852-3277.

Where to Eat and Sleep

Kelloff's Restaurant & Lounge—2½ miles west of town on US 160 (next to the Best Western). Diners can enjoy an array of steaks and seafood in the Academy Award Dining Room or sip cocktails in the Fireside Den. It opens for breakfast at 7:00 am and serves until 2:00 pm. Dinner is from 5:00 to 9:00 pm. Open every day. Phone: (303)852-3626.

Mountain View Restaurant—located at 2099 Sherman at the east edge of town, it serves its full menu with a family style flare. Hours: 6:00 am to 9:00 pm every day. Phone: (303)852-9919.

High Country Steakhouse—at 819 1st Ave., the steaks can't be beat, Pirate's Cave upstairs, open evenings. Price: $4.95 and up. (303)852-5866.

Valley Farmer Restaurant—on north Highway 285, it features local favorites, and down home cooking just the way you like it. Price: $4.95 and up. (303)852-4977.

Monte Villa Inn—in downtown Monte Vista, it offers rooms, a coffee shop, a cocktail lounge, antique dining room, and live entertainment on Tuesday nights. Price: $29.00 to $40.00 for rooms. Restaurant prices are $4.95 and up. Address: 925 1st St., Monte Vista, CO. 81144, (303)852-5166.

Movie Manor Motel and Trailer Park—Best Western with restaurant and lounge. Something interesting about the rooms is that they all contain speakers. When you look out the window and see the drive-in move screen you'll know what to do. Price of meals $3.50 to $9.00. Price of RV space $8.00 to $9.00. Price of motel rooms $36.00 to $58.00. Address: 2830 W. Highway 160. (303)852-5921.

Monte Vista Chamber of Commerce, 1125 Park Ave., Monte Vista, CO. 81144. (303)852-2731.

NATHROP—this region is known for its riches in history and metals. Try some panning in any stream or go exploring in a ghost town.

Things to See and Do

Ghost Town Auto Trip—there are many abandoned villages in the mountains around Nathrop. It you have a sturdy car with high ground clearance or a rented four-wheel drive, this will make a fun and interesitng side trip into the past. Head west out of town on Chaffee County Road 162 which goes up a steep incline. At the top of the hill, the road follows the old Denver and South Park Railroad bed then curves around before reaching the ghost town of *St. Elmo.* About 5 miles south of *St. Elmo* on CR 295 there is an old log building in a meadow. It is believed that this is the sight of the town of *Hancock.* Halfway to *Hancock,* you should see the Forest Service sign for the ghost town of *Romley.* You can return to Nathrop or continue on and explore on your own. A good map of the area, its ghost towns, landmarks, and attractions is available in the *Fun in the Home of the Fourteeners* newspaper put out with the cooperation of many county businesses and individuals.

Where to Eat and Sleep

Chalk Creek Junction Bed & Breakfast—at 16370 County Road 162, your room includes a gigantic country breakfast, the backyard, view of Chalk Creek and some rest and relaxation like you've never had it before. (303)395-2712.

Brown's Campground—in town just east of US 285 on CR 197, hookups, separate tent sites, toilets, showers, tables and store. Price: $7.00. (303)395-8301.

Heart of the Rockies Chamber of Commerce, 406 W. Rainbow Blvd., Salida, CO. 81201. (303)539-2068.

COURTESY OF MINERAL COUNTY MINER

This is what's left of the old Creede jail. It illustrates the need for caution around such structures.

PITKIN—a former ghost town first incorporated in 1879, 28 miles northeast of Gunnison. Roads are open all year round, take Highway 50 to Parlin then go northeast through Ohio City to Pitkin. The town is in the heart of the beautiful Gunnison National Forest at an elevation of 9,241 feet. The village was not without its famous visitors; Teddy Roosevelt stayed here in 1912 and a mine nearby was named after him in his honor.

Things to See and do

Gunnison National Forest—Pitkin is the perfect place from which to explore the beauty of the forest. Stay in town, but venture into the wilds during the day.

Hiking—is excellent all the year round via cross-country skiing or snowmobile during the winter.

Jeeping—renting a four wheel drive is a fun way to get onto the back roads. Explore the near ghost town of Tincup, the Continental Divide, and the historic Alpine Tunnel.

Fishing—anglers should try these. Mirror Lake and Taylor Reservoir. Also, any local stream should yield a few fish.

Ghost Towns:there are many abandoned mines and towns throughout the area which can be reached by backroads or on foot. The nearby town of *Tincup* is a near ghost town which has its own visitor center. To learn more about ghost towns, especially *Tincup,* stop by the center at 500 E. Tomichi Ave. and pick up a few maps. Open Monday to Friday 8 am to 5 pm.

Alpine Tunnel—take Forest Road 765 north through Pitkin and watch for the right turn marked Alpine Tunnel 2.4 miles out of town. Follow the road carefully. Only cars with good ground clearance should be used. The tunnel was a masterpiece of engineering but also a death trap! Several workmen died in its construction because of of carbon monoxide poisoning, rock slides and cave-ins. It is said to be *haunted* by their spirits.

City Hall Melodrama—the last weekend in July and the first in August bring good, old timey fun to Pitkin. You are invited to come boo the villian and cheer the hero who perform on stage in the 84 year old City Hall, right next door to the Pitkin Hotel.

Where to Eat and Sleep

The Pitkin Hotel & Restaurant—built in 1904, this hotel has a long and colorful past with sad times, like when it was boarded up and abandoned, as well as happy, like when it was touted as "the most modern and best equipped mountain hotel in Colorado". It has been most lovingly restored and when it is completely as splendid as in its heyday, the owners hope to have it listed as a Colorado Historical Building. All rooms are upstairs with no elevator and the bathrooms are down the hall; the dorm has its own bathrooms. There are no TV's or phones in the rooms, but they are equipped with comfortable beds topped with electric blankets. The restaurant serves homemade, country style meals. Guests are invited to bring musical instruments or play the piano in the lobby, and if you bring games or cards, the popcorn is free. Child care is available and pets are OK. Prices: dormatory (can be rented for groups of 20 to 25 at group rates) $7.00 or $5.00 for youth hostel members. Private rooms: $15.00 to $20.00. You will have to call or write for reservations. The Pitkin Hotel, PO Box 53, Ohio City, CO. 81237. (303)641-2757.

PONCHA SPRINGS—right down the road from the South Arkansas River, it is a great place to stay if you favor fishing, actually if you favor anything having to do with relaxation and fun.

Things to See and Do

Fishing—try O'Haver Lake, south on US 285 to the Marshall Pass turnoff and up that road a mile or so. There are a few campsites around the lake.

Angel of Shavano—picnic area 6 miles west of town on US 50 to Maysville, then 4 miles north on County Road 240. Run by US Forest Service, small fee. Bring your camera.

Hiking—there are many trails nearby and a visit to the Chamber of Commerce will help in their location. Here is one to try on your own. *Little Cochetopa Creek*—take US 50 2 miles west of town to CR 210. Follow it carefully as the last three miles are very rough. The trailhead is at the parking lot on CR 210. The 4 mile long trail is moderate in difficulty so go easy and bring water.

Where to Eat and Sleep

Grimo's—146 S. Main, lounge, fine Italian cusine, kids menu.

Price: $5.75 to $12.95. (303)539-2903.

Poncha Truck Stop Cafe—in Poncha Springs, open 24 hours with family meals and their famous Alaskan burger. Price: $1.50 to $8.95. (303)539-3330.

Jackson Hotel—Highway 285 one block south of Highway 50, this bed and breakfast inn has been serving the west since 1878, they have steak, seafood, light menu, burgers and sandwiches. Price: $2.50 to $15.95. Room rates unavailable. (303)539-3122.

Heart of the Rockies Chamber of Commerce, 406 W. Rainbow Blvd., Salida, CO. 81201, (303)539-2068.

RIO GRANDE NATIONAL FOREST—the major access routes to this beautiful forest are Highways 160 and 285 and State Route 149. This south central land of the state is rightly a National Forest because it boasts a variety of attractions which are unique to its area. The Wheeler Geological Area, 10 miles northwest of Creede, is full of unusual rock formations, a few of which are called the Temple, Milk Bottles, Beehives, Cyclops, Dante's Lost Souls, Pipe organ, and Finger Rocks. Most of the formations are extremely fragile so climbing on or around them is strictly forbidden. The Forest also features many of the gorgeous features present in other Forests around the state like alpine meadows and streams, high mountain peaks, miles of hiking trails, water falls, the Continental Divide, abandoned gold mines and ghost towns, and abundant wildlife (hunting and fishing are permitted with valid Colorado licenses). Most hiking and backpacking trails are well marked and easy to follow. However, there are also trails which are not marked by signs and are not maintained. These trails should only be taken by experienced hikers and backpackers. Warm clothing (and rain gear) should be worn or at hand because nights (and days in the high country) are always cool, sometimes dipping into the 40's and there is always the chance of a summer shower. Camping permits are not required and generally there are no fire restrictions enforced (except when extreme fire danger is possible). One wilderness area in the Rio Grande is the Weminuche Wilderness, signed into existence on January 4, 1975 by President Jerry Ford. Its average elevation is 10,000 feet and it has three peaks over 14,000 with most others averaging 13,000 or more. It is the joy of area hikers and backpackers with *over 400 miles of trails!* There are some restrictions here though to preserve the forest in its natural state. These are: **1.** no camping within ¼ mile of Emerald or Little

Emerald Lakes and saddle or pack stock are not allowed to graze or remain overnight within ¼ mile of the lakes. **2.** There are similar restrictions concerning Flint Lake but the distance is 300 yards. Camping in the Rio Grande National Forest is truly convenient with 41 campgrounds and 691 sites. Price: $6.00 with some available at no cost.

Scenic Drives—there are three tours which are briefly given here in map form. For a complete account of the sights along the way, write the Forest or stop by one of the Ranger Stations. *Great Sand Dunes National Monument* - adjoining the Forest, it presents a unique opportunity for visitors to observe a desert and its habitat. The dunes, which were formed during the Ice Age, at times present an almost eerie moonscape of shifting sands. To reach the Monument, take Highway 160 west from Walsenburg or east from Alamosa and then take 150 north to the Visitor Center. Price: $1.00 per vehicle, hikers, bicyclists and bus passangers pay $.50. For information write the Monument at Mosca, CO. 81146.

Rio Grande National Forest, 1803 W. Highway 160, Monte Vista, CO. 81144. (303)852-5941.

SALIDA—this city was well traveled by miners and outlaws in its early days and much treasure is believed to be hidden in the area and its ghost towns. Today, the town becomes crowded with visitors who come to enjoy the weather, scenery and relaxation.

Things to See and Do

Tenderfoot Mountain & Spiral Drive—to get the best view of Salida and the surrounding area, take Route 175 out of town to the north to 173 and go right. This changes into 176, follow it to the top of the mountain where there is a pavilion. Bring lunch and a camera or binoculars to observe the countryside.

Duke's Monument—once upon a time, in Salida, there lived a stray dog. This dog became a friend and companion to the railroad workers and visitors who climbed the Tenderfoot Mountain. He met every train as if looking for his long lost master, and once even saved a little girl who had fallen into the path of an oncoming train by pulling her off the tracks. Sadly, Duke never found his master and died in 1902. The Manager of the Monte Cristo Hotel, C.F. Catlin, decided the little dog deserved to be remembered for all the joy he had brought the town. He erected a monument on the rise known as Little Tenderfoot and you can see it there today on the way up the Spiral Drive.

Five Pass Loop—143 mile trip over the highest passes around, it takes about six hours, so pack lunch and drinks for a mid-day stop. To start, go west from Salida on US 50 about 22 miles to Chaffee County Road 237 and go right to the 11,386 foot high Old Monarch Pass. The road slopes down on the west side of the Continential Divide, at the first intersection with a good dirt road, a sharp right turn leads 1.5 miles up the valley to Gunnison County Road 887. Turn left and climb to the summit of Black Sage Pass, 9,745 feet. At the junction with US Forest Road 765, turn right onto 765 and go over 10,303 foot Waunita Pass (watch for the cabin half way up which marks the ghost town of *Bowerman.* The road will take you through Pitkin (watch for the right turn marked Alpine Tunnel, it makes a good side trip) and over 12,200 foot Cumberland Pass which is the second highest in the state. Go through Tincup and take the Cottonwood Pass turnoff marked as Gunnison National Forest Road 209, which leads up the 12,126 summit and then 36 miles to Buena Vista where you take a right at the US 24 signal. Meet up with 285 to the south and head back to Salida.

Ghost Towns—there are many small ghost towns around Salida, one is given here but contacting the Chamber of Commerce can get you directions to more. *Turret* - take Colorado Road 291 northwest and go right on Chaffee County Road 175 (Ute Trail). Follow it for 10 miles to a Y where you take CR 184 to the left. Take the right branch of the next Y which is CR 185 which goes over a narrow bridge. At the summit rest and have a snack and enjoy the view of Turret. Remember that careful driving is a must on these small back roads.

Trail Rides—the Ponderosa Guest Ranch at 9010 CR 240 in Salida specializes in horseback trail riding, pack trips, and chuckwagon meals. Rental price for a horse: 1 hour $7.50, 4 hours $22.50, and 1 hour ride with chuckwagon meal $20.00. Group rates available. (303)539-2730.

Mt. Shavano State Trout Hatchery—this rearing unit is just 2 miles north of Salida on Highway 291. It produces 345,000 pounds of fish a year and is an educational side trip well worth the time.

Salida Hot Springs Pool—the healing powers of hot springs have long been touted as miracles (or could it be the relaxing 96 degree mineral rich water), so here is your chance to test the theory. Price: adults $3.00, students $1.50, under 5 $.50. Seniors and infants Free. Hours: summer 1:30 to 9 pm, winter 5 to 9 pm Wednesday to Friday and 1:30 to 9 pm on the weekend. At 410 W. Rainbow Blvd. in Salida. (303)539-6738.

Hiking—there are many trails around the county so check with the Forest Service and the Chamber of Commerce for specific directions. Ask about Denny Creek Trail, Denny Gulch, North Cottonwood Creek, Clear Creek Drainage Trail.

Fishing—try these creeks, lakes and reservoirs for some of the best angling in the state. Silver Creek, Poncha Creek, Little Cochetopa Creek, Pass Creek, Arkansas River, O'Haver Lake, North Fork Reservoir, and Clear Creek Reservoir. Information on these and other fishing spots may be obtained at the Chamber of Commerce and any old timer who is crazy enough to give away his secrets.

Rafting and Jeeping—River Runners Ltd. at 11150 Highway 50 in Salida offers good rates of fun ways to explore the wilderness. Price for rafting ½ day for adults $19.75, children $14.75. Price for jeep tours ½ day for adults $19.75, children $13.75. In Colorado 1-800-332-9100, nationwide 1-800-525-2081.

Fourth of July—probably *the biggest celebration in central Colorado,* here are just a few of the events. Potluck supper, sports from volleyball to swimming and horseshoes, pie and watermelon eating contest, pickle and whistle contest *(the one who whistles soonest after eating a pickle wins),* Down by the River Chili Cookoff, kid's parade, kids trout fishing derby, fireworks and more.

Where to Eat and Sleep

The Windmill—720 E. Rainbow, nightly specials, salads, sandwiches, Mexican combos, seafood, steaks, and kids menu. Salad bar special only $3.45, lunch buffet $3.95 all you care to eat. (303)539-3594.

Country Bounty—Highway 50 in Salida, Mexican, light menu, grandburgers, breakfast specials and country favorites. Price: $3.50 to $12.95. (303)539-3546.

Salida Inn—Highway 50 and Hunt St., snacks, burgers, light menu, steaks, Italian specialties and Rocky Mountain Oysters. Price:

$3.00 to $12.95. (303)539-4561.

El Placido—1015 E. Highway 50, Mexican everything and American favorites too. Price: $15.90 for a family special which feeds four hungry people. Average prices: $3.00 to $7.00. (303)539-9951.

Salida Sweet Shop—130 W. 1st St., ice cream, breakfast served all day, burgers. Price: $1.00 to $3.45. (303)539-9931.

Sweet Adeline's—949 F St., this bed and breakfast inn gives you the delux treatment right down to the country breakfast in the restored turn-of-the-century Queen Anne building. Price: $28.00 and up, no smoking please. (303)539-4100.

Budget Lodge—1146 E. Highway 50, cable TV, free coffee, free swimming at Salida Hot Springs Pool, free continental breakfast. Price: single $21.50, double $26.50, suite (up to 8 people) $50.00. (303)539-6695.

The Poor Farm Country Inn—8495 County Road 160, a National Historic Place, this inn on the Arkansas River has been in business for a hundred years and features a gigantic, homemade, country breakfast free with your room. Price: single $29.00, double $39.00, with private bath $49.00. (303)539-3818.

Heart of the Rockies Chamber of Commerce, 406 W. Rainbow Blvd., Salida, CO. 81201. (303)539-2068.

SAN ISABEL NATIONAL FOREST—this forest stretches from central Colorado to near the New Mexico border in bits and pieces totaling over a million acres. There are campgrounds, attractions, wildlife and many activities to be enjoyed here.

The highest mountain in Colorado, Mt. Elbert, is located in this forest, making it a paradise for mountain climbers. There are many other mountains over 14,000 feet also and their beauty is uncompared.

One area of special interest is the Collegiate Peaks Wilderness, which contains many of the fourteeners (mountains over 14,000 feet). The visitor's center is located at Monarch Pass where you can obtain information on the mountains and the forest.

Some other attractions of this forest are fishing lakes and streams, water falls, caves, ghost towns, mines and the wildlife which includes the bighorn sheep, mountain goat and mountain lion.

Camping is permitted throughout the forest and it does maintain quite a few campgrounds. These are usually primitive with a few

COURTESY OF COLORADO TOURISM BOARD

A grand view of Mt. Elbert (Colorado's highest at 14,433 feet) from Half Moon Creek.

disposal facilities. There are 32 camping areas which range in price from $5.00 to $7.00 a night.

Forest Supervisor, 1920 Valley Dr., Pueblo, CO. 81008.

SILVER CLIFF—the whole town is a ski resort with the San Isabel national Forest to the east and west just waiting to be explored.

Things to See and Do

Snow Skiing—at the Conquistador Ski Area five miles west of Silver Cliff. Beginner to advanced, it is family oriented and friendly. Open from December to April. Full day lift ticket: $15.00. Cross-country skiing is available at the base area and there are Forest

Service trails in the vicinity. Contact the resort at P.O. Box 347, Westcliffe, CO. 81252, 1-800-821-0642 or (303)783-9206.

Winter Festivals—Light up the New Year, December 31. 4-H Winter Carnival, Valentines Day. Fiesta Daze, around the 20th of February. St. Patty's Day Celebration, March 17.

San Isabel National Forest—make Silver Cliff your base and go out to the Forest to explore the trails, streams, ghost towns, or just relax.

SOUTH FORK—a great place to stay while you explore the southwest part of the state and its National Forests. Of course, for a complete listing of local events, one should pick up a complimentary copy of *The Mineral County Miner/The South Fork Tines (yes, tines).*

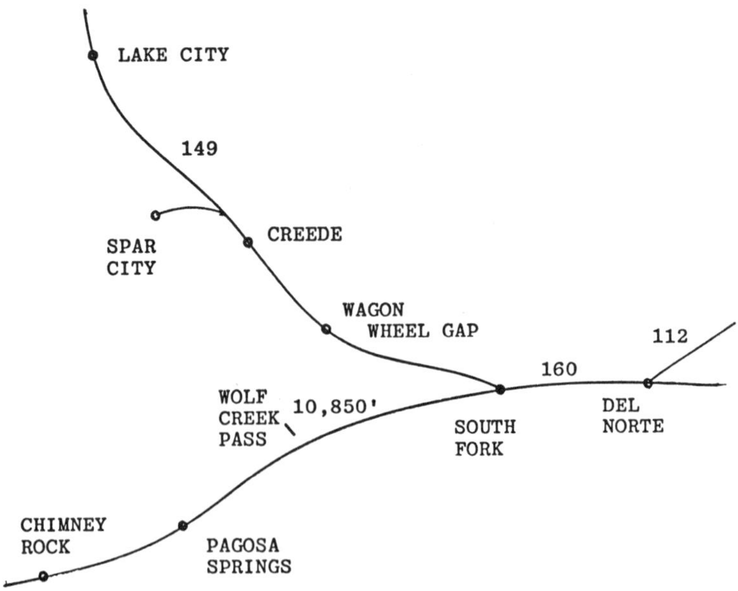

Things to See and Do

Rio Grande River Raft Races—early June, on the river between South Fork and Creede, with both amateur and professional races down the roaring Rio Grande. Top prize is $1000.00! Sponsored by South Fork Chamber of Commerce, Box 116, South Fork, CO. 81154 or (303)873-5512.

Lumberjack Days—woodsmen from around the area show their skills with chainsaw, axe, and heavy logging equipment. Held at the Rickel Arena in South Fork in early July.

Little Britches Rodeo—early to mid-July, held at the Rickel Arena. Contact Chamber of Commerce for exact dates.

Big Game and Wild Game Dinners—first Wednesday in July and August. Held at the South Fork Community Building, these special meals give visitors a chance to try such culinary delights as deer, elk and even bear.

Old Timer's Rodeo—early August in the Rickel Arena.

Rio Grande National Forest—make South Fork your base camp and explore the forest by day. Fish, camp, hike, picnic and relax in the mountains of the sunny west.

Where to Eat and Sleep

Brown's—east on US 160, this restaurant provides barbeque and sandwiches (29 varieties) at their finest. Housed in an old sawmill commissary, antique tools and equipment are on display. Summer hours are 8:00 am to 9:00 pm. Phone: (303)873-5582.

Rio Quinta Restaurant—located at the bridge on 149, they specialize in homemade Mexican and American food. Customers can eat and watch the Rio Grande River flow by from their tables. Hours are 11:00 am to 9:00 pm on weekdays and noon to 9:00 pm on Sunday. Closed Thursdays. Phone: (303)873-5849.

Chinook Motel—on east US 160, has cabins with fireplaces, trailer and tent spaces, and a grocery store. Rates: cabins start at $25.00 a night, spaces at $9.00 a night. Write: Chinook Motel, Box 530, South Fork, CO. 81154, or phone: (303)873-9993.

G-Bar Guest Ranch—located 6 miles west of town on US 160, it has outfitters, guides, and a tackle store. It has 6 modern cabins and 20 trailer spaces with hookups. Price: cabins $38.00 per couple, each additional person $3.00, hookups $8.00 a night. Write: G-Bar Guest Ranch, Box 309, South Fork, CO. 81154, or phone: (303)873-5827.

Lucky Lodge—north on the "Y" on US 149, has cabins with kitchenettes and trailer spaces. Price: cabins start at $26.00 a night, spaces $10.00 a night, $70.00 a week, $170.00 a month. Write: Lucky Lodge, Star Route, South Fork, CO. 81154. (303)873-5921.

Rainbow Motel—offers cable TV, cabins with fireplaces, and motel units. Price: $20.00 a night and up. Write: Rainbow Motel, 30359 West US 160, South Fork, CO. 81154, or phone: (303)873-5571.

South Fork Chamber of Commerce, P.O. Box 12, South Fork, CO. 81154. (303)658-2374.

VICTOR—this town was founded in 1893 and was a gold boom town. Over 800 million dollars worth of the precious metal was mined there between 1891 and 1961. In fact, panning in any of the nearby streams will usually yield a little "color".

Things to See and Do

Gold Coin Mine—a rich deposit of ore was discovered while digging the foundation of a hotel. The remains of the mine can still be seen on Diamond Ave.

Fishing—try Skagwuay Reservoir which is stocked and controlled by the state, there are also boating and camping facilities. Try also Eleven Mile and Wright's Reservoirs and any of the rushing streams of Pike National Forest.

Scenic Drives—1. *Phantom Canyon,* US 50 to Victor, County Road 44-67 south. This was known as Phantom Canyon because of the flash floods and railroad cars that jumped their tracks, causing death and destruction.

2. *Gold Camp Road,* County Road 4, Pike National Forest Road 470/336.

3. *Rangeview Road,* for an awesome view of the Continental Divide, take County Road 45.

Mountains—Victor offers clear and unobstructed views of Pike's Peak, the Sangre de Cristo range, the San Juan range, and the Collegiate range.

Lowell Thomas Museum—exhibits of mining and local memorabilia. Price: adults $1.00, under 12 Free. Located at the corner of Victor Ave. and 3rd St.

Gold Rush Days—held the third weekend in July, this celebration includes parades, dances, mining contests, a breakfast, crafts, and activities for all ages.

Cripple Creek and Victor Narrow Gauge Railroad—see the mountains from the view of your ancestors, by rail. Price: adults $4.50, children $2.50, under 3 *Free.*

Where to Eat and Sleep

Amber Inn—homecooked food with outstanding breakfasts and full bar. Price: $2.00 to $10.00.

Drift Inn—country cooking, great morning meals and dinners. Price: $2.00 to $10.00.

Sugarplums—lunch and dinner in fine setting. Price: $3.00 to $7.00.

Gold Coin Bar & Cafe— home style breakfasts and delicious dinners, bar. Price: $2.00 to $15.00. (303)689-7775.

Zeke's Place–burgers, sandwiches, home cooked chili, bar. Price: average meal $4.00. (303)689-7794.

Victor Park—at Victor Ave. and 2nd St., camping area with tables, water, grills, rest rooms. Campers are also welcome at the Gold Bowl ball park across the street.

Bed and Breakfast Inns—no specific information at the time of printing, contact the Chamber of Commerce. Average price: $25.00 to $30.00.

Victor Chamber of Commerce, P.O. Box 83, Victor, CO. 80860. (303)689-2102.

WALSENBURG—originally settled by the Spanish who farmed and mined the region, it is now a prosperous cattle raising, farming and mining town.

Things to See and Do

Lathrop State Park—2 miles west of Walsenburg on Highway 160. Features water sports, fishing, hiking, horseback riding, and camping (some with hookups).

Wildlife Museum & Taxidermy Service—at exit 34 off of I-25, this unique gift shop offers real animals preserved in all their wild beauty. Tour the shop and the taxidermy studio. Hunters may obtain a price list and have their catches stuffed. (303)941-4041.

Highway 12 Loop—take Highway 12 west and south through La Veta and into the beautiful San Isabel National Forest where there are many mines, mountains and ghost towns. When you reach Trinidad, go north on I-25 back to Walsenburg.

Francisco Museum—12 miles west on US 160 then south on Highway 12 to La Veta, it has historical artifacts and antiques from the early settlers. It is unique in that it also has some old stores like the barber shop and grocery store. Price: *Free.*

Where to Eat and Sleep

The Rio Cucharas Inn—on Highway 160, serving breakfast, lunch and dinner, daily specials, continental fare, Mexican specialties, and all in a southwestern atmosphere. (303)738-1282.

The Inn features fireplaces in each room, ski packages in season and health club. (303)742-3191.

Rambler Best Western—1 mile north of Walsenburg on I-25 at Exit 52, restaurant and lounge featuring fine American food, family dining and nightly specials, color TV, direct dial phones. Price: $38.00 to $58.00. (303)738-1121.

Huerfano County Chamber of Commerce, 500 Main, Walsenburg, CO. 81089. (303)738-1065.

WESTCLIFFE—the whole town is a ski resort with the San Isabel National Forest to the east and west just waiting to be explored.

COURTESY OF CONQUISTADOR HALENDA - KING PHOTOGRAPHY

Powder!

Things to See and Do

Snow Skiing—at the Conquistador Ski Area five miles west of Westcliffe. Beginner to advanced, it is family oriented and friendly. Open from December to April. Full day lift ticket: $15.00. Childcare for those 3 to 7: $14.00 a day. Children's ski school with lessons, lunch and snowplay: $28.00 a day. Cross-country skiing is available at the base area and there are Forest Service trails in the vicinity. Contact the resort at P.O. Box 347, Westcliffe, CO. 81252, 1-800-821-0642 or (303)783-9206.

Winter Festivals—Light up the New Year, December 31. 4-H Winter Carnival, Valentines Day. Fiesta Daze, around the 20th of February. St. Patty's Day Celebration, March 17. Caribbean Fest celebrates spring in early April.

San Isabel National Forest—make Westcliffe your base and go out to the Forest to explore the trails, streams, ghost towns, or just relax.

Ghost Towns—once the 3rd biggest town in the state, Silver Cliff

COURTESY OF CONQUISTADOR HALENDA - KING PHOTOGRAPHY

Ordinary day school becomes an adventure.

now has only 100 residents, but the original streets remain, it is 2 miles east of Westcliffe. The ghost town of *Rosita* is 10 miles southeast of Westcliffe and *Ula* is 5 miles northeast.

Where to Eat and Sleep

LeSage Building—located at the ski base area, its facilities range from hot meals to nutritious snacks and there is an outdoor barbeque when the weather permits.

The Castile Lodge—within easy walking distance of the slopes, complimentary continental breakfast by the fireplace, hot tub, sauna, all rooms come with color TV, phone, kitchenettes, queen size bed and sleeper sofa. Price: $45.00 to $70.00, children under 12 free with parent. In state (303)783-9701, nationwide 1-800-325-4682.

Alvarado Campground— in the San Isabel National Forest, take Highway 69 south 3.5 miles, then County Road 302 west 5 miles and Forest Road 302 southwest 1.25 miles. There are 44 sites, RV sites but no hookups, toilets and tables. Price: $5.00.

Conquistador Ski Resort, P.O. Box 347, Westcliffe, CO. 81252 (303)783-9206.

WESTON—the perfect small town to use as your base camp to one of the most unique and beautiful forests around, the San Isabel.

Things to See and Do

San Isabel National Forest—only 65 miles west of Weston on Route 12, it offers beautiful scenery, high mountain passes, fishing, hunting, and awesome views from the roadside as well as a large elk herd that winters here.

Fishing—the big sport of the area both in winter and summer. Try Monument Lake, North Lake, Blue Lake, Bear Lake, the Purgatoire River and any promising stream.

Hiking—the Forest Service has marked off several trails for your walking pleasure. Contact them in regard to location and difficulty.

Where to Eat and Sleep

Picketwire Lodge & Store—on Route 1, cabins are complete with kitchen and all utensils, a nearby restaurant, a beautiful view of the Purgatoire River which flows through the property, and great rates. Price: $28.00, add $3.00 for each extra person. Write them at: Route 1, Box 32, Weston, CO. 81091 or call (303)868-2265.

Trinidad Lake Campground—go east on 12 about 6.5 miles. Has tent and trailor sites, hookups, tables, toilets and showers. Fish and swim in the lake. Price: $5.00 and up. (303)846-6951.

WOODLAND PARK—known as "the city above the clouds", it is almost impossible to find a spot in town where you cannot see fabulous Pikes Peak. In fact, the view so inspired Katherine Lee Bates in 1893 that she wrote "America the Beautiful".

Things to See and Do

Pikes Peak Highway—to get there, take Highway 24 east to Cascade, and follow the signs to the toll road. The drive gives spectacular views and an easy way to the summit. Hours: May 1 to June 7 and Labor Day to close 9 am to 3 pm. June 10 to Labor Day 7 am to 6:30 pm. Price: adults $4.00, kids under 12 $1.00. (303)684-9383.

Chin-Qua-Pin Pow Wow—held in late June at the Bergstom Arena it celebrates the customs of the Indians. It is sponsored by the Lone Feathered Indian Council. Events include traditional dancing and contests, a parade, native American arts and crafts and more. All proceeds go to a scholarship fund for native American college students.

Rodeos—the Ute Trail Stampede Rodeo with a View is held in Bergstom Arena the 5th of July. The Ute Pass Little Britches Rodeo is held in Bergstom Arena around July 20th.

Fishing—world-renowned for its trout, Woodland Park invites you to breathe the mountain air, camp out, and reel in a few of the big ones. Try any of the nearby streams or lakes, especially Manitou Lake which is a few miles north of town on Colorado Highway 67.

Skiing—US Route 24 is the most direct route to the ski resorts of Breckenridge, Dillon, Copper Mountain, and Vail.

Where to Eat and Sleep

The Melting Pot Cafe—at the Midland Depot next to the People's Natural Gas. Specializes in homemade soup and delicious entrees. Price: $2.00 to $5.00. Hours: 11 am to 7:30 pm. (303)687-3144.

Horse Creek Cafe—19 miles north of Woodland Park on Highway 67. It serves breakfast, lunch and dinner. Saturday night features a Chuck Wagon Barbeque and Sunday night presents hot dogs in the beer garden. Price: average meal, $3.25. Hours: 7 am to

9 pm. (303)647-2329.

The Settlement House Restaurant—in east Woodland Park on Highway 24, it serves all three meals. Fabulous Sunday Brunch! Price: lunch - $2.75 to $4.75, dinner - $5.50 to $12.95. Hours: Monday to Saturday 7 am to 9 pm (opens at 11 am on Sunday). (303)687-6870.

The Lofthouse—at 222 E. Henrietta (Box 67, Woodland Park, CO. 80866), has rooms, efficiencies, 1 and 2 bedroom apts. Price: $30.00 to $48.00, $4.00 each extra person and kids under 13 free. (303)687-9187.

Wishing Well Motel & Campground—at 425 County Road 21 (Woodland Park, CO. 80863) south of town off of US 24 on 16½ acres with hiking trails. Motel has clean rooms, 1 and 2 bedroom apartments, and kitchenettes. Campground has electrical hookups only, hot showers, and picnic tables and is open May to October. Price: motel $28.00 to $42.00, extra person $2.00. Campgrounds $8.00 and up. (303)687-9697.

Woodland Park KOA—off of N. Highway 67 on W. Bowman Ave. (Box 725, Woodland Park, CO. 80863). Open May to October. Wooded with 107 sites for tents and RVs. All the pluses, including church services, store, LP gas and more. Camper cabins available for $19.00 per night. Price: $12.00 and up for tents, $15.50 and up for RVs. (303)687-3535.

Woodland Park Chamber of Commerce, P.O. Box W, Woodland Park, CO. 80863. (303)687-9885. (Office is located at the junction of Highways 24 and 67).

Notes.

AREA FIVE

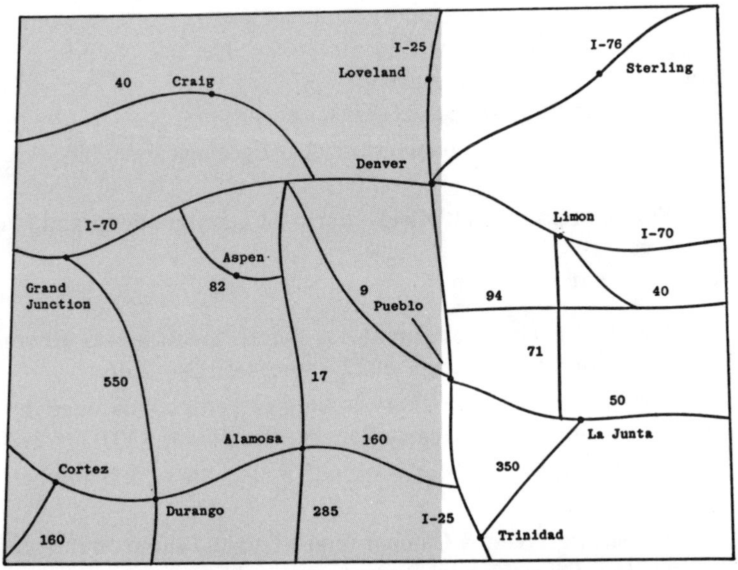
I-25
Loveland
40
Craig
I-76
Sterling
Denver
I-70
Limon
I-70
Aspen
82
Grand
Junction
9
Pueblo
94
40
71
550
17
50
Alamosa
160
La Junta
Cortez
350
Durango
285
I-25
Trinidad
160

AKRON—on the beautiful, wide open plains of eastern Colorado.

Things to See and Do

Washington County Fair and Round Up—the fair is held in mid-August in the best of country tradition with all the contests, exhibits, carnivals, and games you could ever hope to see.

Fort Wicked—north of Akron on Highway 63, it was once a stage station which operated in the 1860's. The site should be fun to explore and hunt for souvenirs.

Overland Trail Museum—north of Akron on US 6 in Sterling. It holds artifacts and regional historical and geological exhibits. Price: *Free.*

Summit Springs Battlefield—north off of Highway 63 and I-76.

Where to Eat and Sleep

Hearty Rancher Restaurant—at 901 E. 1st, it serves all your country favorites and much, much more. (303)345-2616.

4-B's Motel—at 60 Hickory, it features 36 air conditioned units and is just south of the Hearty Rancher Restaurant. (303)345-2028.

Crestwood Manor Motel—at 625 E. 1st, the phone number is (303)345-2231.

Prewitt Reservoir & Campground—fish and camp on the reservoir for free. Primitive sites for tents only, tables, boat launch, bring your own water. To get there, take 63 north from Akron to US 6 and go west to the access road, which leads one mile east to the lake.

Akron Chamber of Commerce, Akron, CO. 80720 or phone the city clerk at (303)345-2624.

ARRIBA—this town is located on the plains of Eastern Colorado in Lincoln County. It is easily accessible, being directly off I-70.

Things to See and Do

Tarado Mansion—Built in 1917, this building has become a unique treasure. It began as a hotel, but is now a showplace for items from around the world as well as for local historical pieces. It has a "Back When" museum with old stores, a cemetery and a farmyard.

The mansion is also known for its Christmas Walk, held from the first Saturday in December to December 23rd. It is open daily from 10:00 am to 5:00 pm. Location: just south of Exit 383 of I-70, just watch for the brown and white "Point of Interest" signs. Price: adults: $3.50, children under 12: Free. Write to: Tarado Mansion, Rt. 1, Box 53, Arriba, CO. 80804, or phone (303)768-3468.

"Tarado"

COURTESY OF TOWN OF ARRIBA

Scenic Drive—from the sparse plains to the mountains and back. Take I-70 west to Interchange 352 and take State Road 86 through Kiowa to Castle Rock. Go north along I-25 to State Road 67 and go west. You will travel through Deckers and Westcreek to Woodland Park. As you go through these towns, watch on your left for Devil's Head Mountain which was a favorite hideout for outlaws. In Woodland Park, take US 24 east through Colorado Springs and north-east through the small towns of Peyton, Calhan, Ramah, and Matheson to Interchange 359 of I-70. Go east back to Arriba.

Ghost Town—Saugus, on railroad and east county line 6 miles east of town.

Where to Sleep

Tarado Mansion—bed and breakfast are also available at the historic museum described above.

Town of Arriba, Arriba, CO. 80804.

BURLINGTON—This town's main claim to fame, besides the fact that it is the fastest growing city on the eastern plains of Colorado, is the Horned Jack Rabbit *(Lepus Texianus)* which is only found in this region.

What to See and Do

Special Events—*Little Britches Rodeo* - middle of June. *Kit Carson County Fair* - early August.

Old Town—See what life was like for the pioneers. Old Town contains a real red barn, a blacksmith shop, windmill, a one-room school and many other old time buildings. There is also a *free* melodrama which starts at 7:00 each night except Monday. It is open every day from 2:00 pm until dark and has *free* guided tours. To get there, take the Lincoln St. exit on I-70 and go north to Rose Ave. Go east on Rose Ave. to 14th St. Take a right on 14th and follow it to Old Town.

Kit Carson County Carousel—Built in 1905, this carousel is the only one in the nation which still has its original paint. It was therefore proclaimed a national Historic Sight in 1979. On it are forty-six hand-carved animals, forty-five oil paintings, and a Monster Military Band Organ. The carousel is open from 6:00 to 8:00 pm on summer weekends and during the county fair in early August. Tours at other times can be arranged by writing the Kit Carson County Carousel Association, P.O. Box 28, Stratton, Colorado 80836.

Bonny State Recreation Area—20 miles north of Burlington on Highway 385, the lake is over three miles long and covers over 2,000 acres. Visitors can enjoy fishing, water skiing, swimming, boating etc. Rentals available. Admission fees are: annual pass, $20.00, daily pass, $2.00. Additional fees for overnight camping.

Where to Sleep

Chaparrell Inn—I-70 and US 385, Best Western with cable TV, 24 hour cafe, pool, etc. Price: $32.00 to $40.00. (303)346-5361.

Bonny State Recreation Area—no electrical hookups, 200 campsites in four campgrounds. Fees: $4.00 per night ($5.00 when showers are open in Wagon Wheel campground). All four offer vault toilets. Location: 20 miles north of Burlington on Highway 385.

Burlington Chamber of Commerce, 480 15th St., Box 62, Burlington, CO. 80807.

CHEYENNE WELLS—this town, situated out on the plains, knows how to have fun. Their many interesting pastimes attract people from around the state, especially for the hunting and the softball tournament.

Things to See and Do

Softball Marathon Tournament—held in the last weekend of July, it attracts teams from around the state including those from Denver and Colorado Springs. The tournament usually starts on a Saturday morning and lasts all day and all night as the teams battle for first place. The winners are crowned Sunday evening, tired but happy.

Hunting—Cheyenne Wells is the favorite spot for small game hunting for many hunters in and around the state. The most common game found are pheasant, rabbit, antelope, and deer.

Cheyenne County Jail Museum—created by the Eastern Colorado Historical Society, the old jail houses the memoribilia of the town and the surrounding area.

Cheyenne County Fair & Rodeo—the best of country traditions is the county fair and this one, held around the first week in August, is no exception. Fair grounds are south of town on Highway 40, so come and enjoy a day of old-fashioned family fun.

Scenery—any road will take you by golden wheat fields and pumping oil wells. Take time to stop and observe two of America's products being made. Do not touch the wells as they are pieces of sophisticated machinery.

Where to Eat and Sleep

Starlite Lounge—on Highway 40, serves chicken and steak
Tigers Den, on Highway 40, serves burgers, breakfast, daily specials, ice cream and chicken.

Phoenix Restaurant—on Highway 40, serves breakfast, chicken,

Pumping black gold!

steaks, popular appetizers like breaded mushrooms and zucchini, and sandwich and burger plates. Price: $2.00 to $11.25, (303)767-5966.

Trail In Motel—on Highway 40, features 12 modern units with TV, refrigerator, AC, and more. (303)767-5425.

Town of Cheyenne Wells, P.O. Box 125, 151 S. 1st, Cheyenne Wells, CO. 80810 , (303)767-5865.

DEER TRAIL—44 miles east of Denver.

Things to See and Do

September—Rodeo held annually to celebrate the world's first rodeo ever, which was held in Deer Trail on July 4, 1869.

July—Pioneer Chuckwagon Supper and Fireworks Display, held on the Fourth.

Turkey Shoot—Held in April, July, and October/November. Historic marker—4 miles east of town, marker tells the story of the first rodeo and how it was *"Begun On A Bet".*

Benham—this site 9 miles southwest of town was once a station on the Smokey Hill North stage route. Some interesting souvenirs

COURTESY OF PRO RODEO HALL OF CHAMPIONS

A real rodeo clown kids around and talks about the sport of rodeo with visitors.

might be found here.

Peoria—a ghost town 5 miles northwest of Deer Trail.

Scenic Drive—from the sparse plains to the mountains and back. Take I-70 west to Interchange 305 and go south to Kiowa. In Kiowa, take State Road 86 west to Castle Rock. Go north along I-25 to State Road 67 and go west. You will travel through Deckers and Westcreek to Woodland Park. As you go through these towns, watch on your left for Devil's Head Mountain which was a favorite hideout for outlaws. In Woodland Park, take US 24 east through Colorado

Springs and northeast through the small towns of Peyton, Calhan, Ramah, and Matheson to Interchange 359 of I-70. Go northwest back to Deer Trail.

Town of Deer Trail, P.O. Box 217, Deer Trail, CO. 80105.

FORT MORGAN—the plains of Colorado have riches. Fort Morgan sits east of a stretch of land that is known for its diamonds. Take a walk along the country roads 20 miles west of town and maybe you'll get lucky.

Things to See and Do

Fort Morgan—after the fort was abandoned by the army, it was mostly dismantled by the local pioneers for their own use. To see what remains, however, find the park which is at the corner of Riverview Ave. and Prospect St.

Jackson State Recreation Park—off Highway 144, 16 miles northwest of town. It features fishing, skiing, boating and swimming. Picnicing and camping are permitted and a small store provides groceries. (303)645-2551.

Where to Sleep

Central Motel—at 201 W. Platte Ave., has TV, free coffee, and some oversize beds. Price: $36.00 to $41.00, (303)867-2401, MC, V, AE.

Fort Morgan Chamber of Commerce, 617 Main St., P.O. Box 971, Fort Morgan, CO. 80701, (303)867-6702.

GREELEY—this northern Colorado town, made famous in James Michener's *Centennial,* is situated in an area where the visitor has access to almost all the activities the state can offer. It is also only 54 miles from Denver.

Things to See and Do

Rocky Mountain National Park—begins only a few minutes west on Highway 34. It offers picture-perfect rivers, valleys, cliffs, and forests. Enter and take a guided tour or explore on your own.

Fort Vasquez—to get the feel of the old days, visit Fort Vasquez. It is an authentic reconstruction of a fur trading post 20 miles south on Highway 85. Hours: 10:00 am to 5:00 pm Monday to Saturday, 1:00 pm to 5:00 pm on Sunday. Price: adults $2.00, and children $1.00.

A Walk Through History—if you enjoy the architectural style of buildings constructed from 1870 to 1900, this is a stroll you will truly enjoy. Hosted and presented by the IntraWest Bank, this tour can be self-guided or shown by a trained guide. Going on a guided group tour is advantageous because the group will be able to enter at least 4 of the buildings (possibly more). For information or a guide map, write the bank at 1025 9th Ave., Greeley, CO. 80631, or phone (303)352-1651, Ext. 272.

Centennial Village—to celebrate the 200th birthday of America and the 100th of Colorado, the spirit of our history is preserved in this group of buildings comprised of settler homes built when the town was first founded. These buildings have been brought together and restored so that the public may enjoy them. Tours are conducted every hour. The Village is open from mid-April to Memorial Day, Monday to Friday 12:00 to 5:00 pm, and 1:00 to 6:00 pm on weekends and holidays. Located at 14th Ave. and A St., adjacent to Island Grove Park. Phone: (303)353-6123, Ext. 396.

UNC Jazz Festival—held in May, it features major musicians as well as local participants. Write: Performing Arts Box Office, Frasier 115, Greeley, CO. 80329, or phone: (303)351-2200.

Semana Latina & Cinco De Mayo—held the first week in May, this festival is a week long party filled with Hispanic heritage and culture shown through film, theatre, art, music, poetry, dance, and much more. Write: Carlos Alers, Cultural Affairs Office, 919 7th St., Greeley, CO. 80631, or phone: (303)353-6123, Ext. 417.

Independence Stampede—features the worlds largest 4th of July rodeo, this celebration includes parades, night shows, barbeques, flapjack feeds, and a fun run. The six day party ends in fireworks and the rodeo. Write: Greeley Independence Stampede, Island Grove, Greeley, CO. 80631, or phone: (303)356-2855.

Greeley/Weld County Agri-tours—visit nurseries, feed lots, horse breeding farms, and dairy farms. For a free list of all tours, write to, or stop by, the Greeley Chamber of Commerce and ask for the Agri-tours pamphlet.

Where to Eat and Sleep

The Eat'n Place/Oval Office—6 miles north of Greeley on Highway 85, it features Continental and American cuisine, seafoods, steaks, and gourmet entrees. Most prices are under $10.00 for a whole meal. In the Oval Office, customers may grill their own steaks. This restaurant is the winner of the 1985 American Gourmet Society Silver Spoon Award. (303)454-3136.

State Armory—good food, including 6 oz. burgers (try the "singing the blues" burger), steak sandwiches, and chicken. Perhaps the most fun you've had in a long time, the decor contains a B-17 bomber, weapons, carriages, movie props; there is a live D.J. who takes requests Wednesday to Saturday, and free hors d'oeuvres during happy hour (4 to 7 pm, Monday to Friday). Located at 614 8th St. or phone (303)352-7424.

Golden Corral—at 3502 W. 10th St., it serves steaks and a huge salad bar (with 43 items!), also a stuffed potatoe bar with sour cream, melted cheese (with and without broccoli), and chili to name a few. Opens at 11:00 am, call (303)353-8212.

Holiday Inn—609 8th Ave., Greeley, CO. 80631, in the downtown area. It contains every luxury, restaurant, lounge, heated pool, color TV, AC, in-room saunas, in-room movies, free local calls, and 100 rooms to choose from. (303)356-3000.

Greeley Area Chamber of Commerce, P.O. Box CC, 1407 8th Avenue, Greeley, CO. 80631. (303)352-3566.

JULESBURG—this city in the northeastern corner of the state is appropriately known as the *"Gateway to Colorado".* Here, the visitor will find the history of the wild west. And he will find a city busy, happy and friendly. Common activities include fishing, hunting, arrowhead collecting, boating, golf and much more.

Things to See and Do

Sedgwick County Fair & Rodeo—held at the fair grounds east of town in the last week of August, it brings a lot of excitement to the town with a carnival, contests, shows, music and food, not to mention the great entertainment that is rodeo. Come and have a grand ole time!

Drag Racing—fans of this sport will want to gather at the airport runway on Sundays, April through October. The airport is just west of town off of Highway 138/385.

Sedgwick Historical Museum & Tour—learn about the cowboy and Indian days through the artifacts and antiques housed in this museum. Also observe the collection of arrowheads and fossils. The audio tour is on cassette tape and can be obtained at area restaurants and stores. A local historical expert takes you through the county, reliving the Indian invasion of Fort Sedgwick, famous gun battles and the old west.

Arrowheads—hunting for these artifacts and others is a favorite pastime for many local residents. Please refer to rules regarding this practice under Rockhounding. The recommended spots for this activity are along the South Platte River and any of the Indian battlegrounds or village sites. Several such sites can be found by taking Highway 385 south to the county road just past Lyons park. Take this road to the right and you will pass old town sites, battlegrounds, the Italian Caves, the Pony Express route, Fort Sedgwick and the old cemetery. This makes a wonderful scenic and educational tour because there are numerous historic markers and sites to explore.

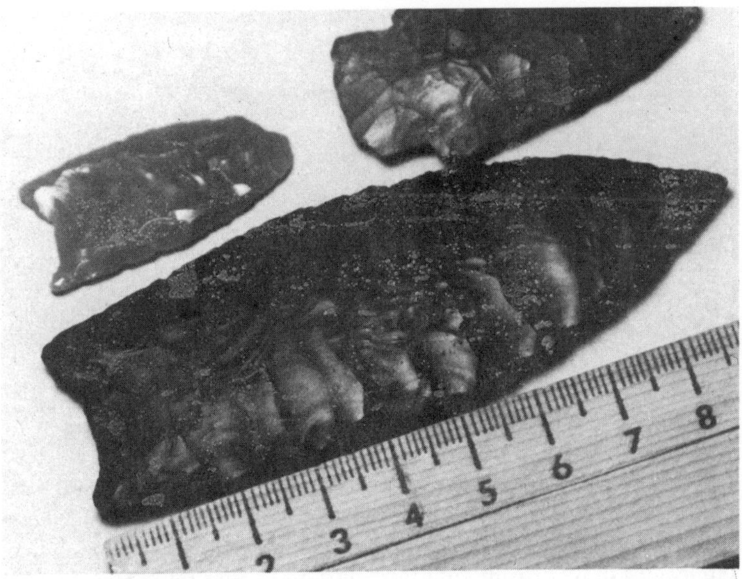

COURTESY OF S.C.O.R.E.

Ruler shows size of some arrowheads found in this region.

Hunting—whether you hunt with a camera, binoculars or a gun, you will be likely to capture antelope, deer, Canadian geese, pheasant, quail and many other species. There is also a herd of buffalo in the area.

Julesburg Reservoir—west of town, off of US 138, you will find the perfect place to go boating, hunting and fishing.

Pony Express—Julesburg was the only Colorado stop of this famous corps of young brave men. They even included Buffalo Bill, who was the youngest rider (age 16) at the station. Around the town, one can see reminders of the Pony Express.

Buffalo—there is a herd of these huge animals which grazes the prairie south of Julesburg and Sedgwick. This animal does so represent the west and all its glory that a view of these majestic creatures is a must for the Colorado traveler.

COURTESY OF S.C.O.R.E.

Buffalo on the move south of Julesburg.

Thad Sowder Memorial—in the Ovid cemetery north of that town, one can see the last resting place of one member of the Cowboy Hall of Fame. He was a great rodeo champion and horseman. Take Highway 138 west from Julesburg and go north on the county road just before Ovid.

Italian Caves—originally constructed in the 1920's by a Sicilian who wished to produce wine there, these cavernous ruins are shrouded by rumors of treasure and riches. The caves are represented by a marker on the county road west of Highway 385. Take 385 south and then a right on the county road just past Lyons Park.

Old Julesburg—also on the above county road, you will find three previous Julesburgs. One was burned by Indians, one abandoned for a better site on the railroad, and Jules Trading Post. There is also Julesburg number 3, known as Weir. Its marker is west of town on Highway 385. Here you will also find the Boothill Cemetery and the Lodgepole Lookout. These old sites make for some interesting exploring.

Where to Eat and Sleep

Wagon Wheel Cafe—at 14989 Highway 385, serving a smorgasbord of lunches and delicious dinners. Price: average meal $5.00. Open 5 am to 9 pm in summer, 6 am to 9 pm in winter. (303)474-2615.

Old Jules Restaurant—on Highway 385, specializing in Mexican food, also the best fried chicken in the west. Lunch specials. Price: average meal $3.50 to $7.00. Open May to September, 8 am to 10 pm. (303)474-3757.

Platte Valley Inn & Restaurant—on Highway 385, the restaurant and lounge serve your favorites in food and libation. Price: average meal $7.00. Open 6 am to 10 pm in summer, 7 am to 2 pm and 4 to 9 pm in winter. The inn has 59 rooms, outdoor pool and more. Price: average $35.00. (303)474-3336.

Holiday Motel—on Highway 138/385, 11 units available with cable TV and telephones. Price: average $25.00. (303)474-3371.

Grand Motel—located at 220 Pine, its 29 units offer relaxation and good service and prices. Price: average $25.00. (303)474-3302.

Sedgwick County Organization to Revitalize the Economy, 123 Cedar, Julesburg, CO. 80737. (303)474-3504.

KIT CARSON—named after the famous guide and soldier, Christopher "Kit" Carson, who was known for his courage in fighting Indians throughout the West.

Things to See and Do

Arrowhead Hunting—east and north of town, watch for rolling hills. At the top and sides, walk slowly and watch for flint chips. This indicates a village or campsite and by digging up each chip you see, you should be able to find some arrowheads, cutting tools, and other artifacts. Avoid trespassing please. Dirt storms may have covered some sites, so it is best to contact the Chamber of Commerce or a helpful resident in regard to location. Also, it is a state law that artifacts may not be removed from public land under the penalty of fines and imprisonment, you may remove arrowheads only from private land and then only with the permission of the owner. The Chamber or a resident may help you contact the owner.

Kit Carson Museum—on Highway 287/40, it features early homesteading memorabilia like clothing, tools, machines, and furniture. Hours: Memorial to Labor Day daily from 9 am to 5 pm. Price: *Free,* but a donation is requested. (303)962-3306.

Oregon Trail—a historical marker 10 miles north on Highway 59 marks this famous road to the west. There is also another marker about the trails 20 miles east of town on Highway 40.

Oil Wells—these pumping machines can be seen along the highway all around Kit Carson and throughout the region. Take time to inspect one up close if you find one near the road. Be careful to not touch the machinery.

Kit Carson Day—the Saturday before Labor Day, the whole town gets out to enjoy the parade, games, *free* barbeque, and the big dance afterwards.

Where to Eat and Sleep

Wagon Wheel Motel & Chuckwagon Cafe—great food in a country atmosphere and rooms at a super rate. Price: $16.00 and up. (303)962-3291.

Trading Post Motel & Restaurant—good food and good rates, the name indicates that Kit Carson had his trading post in this western town. Price: $20.00 and up. (303)962-3294.

Kit Carson Motel & Camper Park—one block east of Main on US 40, for self-contained units only, has hookups, tables, toilets and showers. Price: $6.50 and up. (303)962-3266.

Other motels and restaurants may be found in the neighboring towns of Eads 20 miles to the south, Cheyenne Wells 25 miles east, and Hugo 46 miles northwest.

Kit Carson Chamber of Commerce, Kit Carson, CO. 80825.

LA JUNTA—is located north of the Comanche National Grasslands and has many historical sights.

Things to Do and See

Early Settler's Day—2nd Saturday in September, it includes a parade, bed races, live entertainment, fiddler's contest, free seniors lunch, evening Bar-B-Q, and arts and crafts.

Mountain Man Rendezvous—is a four day reinactment of life in the mid-1880's which ends on Labor Day. It is held at Bent's Old Fort, 8 miles east of La Junta on Highway 194. Participants dress and live as they would have over a hundred years ago.

Bent's Old Fort National Historic Site—8 miles east of La Junta on Highway 194, it is open from 8:30 to 4:30 year round. It is a reconstructed fort built originally in 1833 and was the filming site for a number of major movies including *Centennial* and *Dreams West.* Visitors are able to tour all the rooms and to watch demonstrations of how our ancestors lived. Price: *Free.*

Bent's Old Fort National Historic Site.

Koshare Indian Kiva Museum—home of the Koshare Indian Dancers, who perform authentic dances around the U.S., this museum features a collection of Indian artifacts and art valued at over five million dollars. It is open daily from June to August from 9 to 5, and 1 to 4:30 the rest of the year. Price: *Free.*

Historic Homes of La Junta Walking/Driving Tour—A free brochure can be obtained at the Chamber of Commerce or by writing to them.

Comanche National Grassland—covers over a million acres, it is approximately 20 miles south of La Junta via Highway 50 and Highway 109. Recreational uses include hiking, hunting, fishing, watching and photography of wildlife, and rock hunting.

Scenic Drive—through the prairies and the mountains. Take US 350 southwest to Trinidad. you will go through the Comanche National Grasslands which harbor all the wildlife typical to the prairie. In Trinidad, take State Road 12 west and north through the awesome Cuchara Valley of the San Isabel National Forest. In La Veta, head to US 160 and go east to Walsenburg . Fill up your gas tank and take State Road 10 northeast back to La Junta.

Where to Sleep

Stagecoach Motor Inn—905 W. 3rd St., Best Western which includes cable TV, pool, some oversize beds. Price: $32.00 to $45.00. (303)384-5476.

KOA La Junta—1½ miles west from junction of US 50 and Highway 10, full hookups, separate tenting area, hot showers, store, ice, etc. Price: $9.00 and up. (303)384-9460.

La Junta Chamber of Commerce, 110 Santa Fe, La Junta, CO. 81050, (303)384-7411.

PUEBLO—a diversified city which offers unnumbered activities for everyone.

Things to See and Do

Pueblo Reservoir State Recreation Area—is the largest body of water in southern Colorado and offers boating, sailing, wind surfing, swimming, fishing, biking, hiking, and camping. It can be reached from Pueblo via Highway 96 and from West Pueblo via Highway 50.

Sangre De Cristo Arts & Conference Center—at 210 N. Sante Fe Ave., an extremely large collection of local, regional, and international art. Hours: 11 am to 4 pm. Price: *Free. (303)543-0130.*

El Pueblo Museum—at 905 S. Prairie Ave., it offers exhibitions ranging from Indian basketry and historic photographs to the history of steel and a full size reproduction of the early trading post that eventually became the Pueblo of today. Hours: Memorial to labor Day, Monday to Saturday 10 am to 5 pm, Sunday 1 to 5 pm. Other times throughout the year, hours are: Wednesday to Saturday 11 am to 3 pm. (303)564-5274.

Rosemont Victorian House Museum—at 419 W. 14th, it was built in 1891 and was given to the museum. The first two stories are originally decorated and the servant quarters contain the McClelland Collection of world curiosities. Hours: June 1st to September 1st Monday to Saturday 10 am to 4 pm, Sunday 2 to 4 pm, and September 2nd to May 31st Tuesday to Saturday 1 to 4 pm, Sunday 2 to 4 pm, closed Mondays and January. Price: adults $2.00, children and seniors $1.00, under 5 *Free.* (303)545-5290.

Walking Tour—the Historic District of Union Ave. is a beautiful and educational tour through the Old West. For a copy of the guide call, stop by, or write the Chamber of Commerce.

US Government Printing Office—over 900 best sellers can be found in the bookstore at 720 N. Main St. in the World Savings Building. Hours: Monday to Friday 9 am to 5 pm. (303)554-3142.

Fred E. Weisbrod Airplane Museum—at Pueblo Memorial Airport 6 miles east of the city on Highway 50. It houses over 20 aircraft including futuristic high speed and railroad engines. *Free.* (303)948-3355.

Colorado State Fair—late August brings the 10 day state fair to town with a parade, rodeo, live entertainment by international stars, All-American Horseshow, Jr. livestock sale and a gigantic carnival.

Where to Eat and Sleep

Don's Cafe—2921 N. Elizabeth, home cooked meals. (303)543-5814.

Fireside Restaurant—801 Highway 50 W, shrimp and barbeque ribs. (303)542-4557.

Gaetano's Restaurant—910 Highway 50 W., Italian all the way. (303)546-0949.

Pinon Truck Stop—4803 Interstate 25 N., 24 hours and daily specials. (303)545-6560.

The Mozart—1120 N. Main, steaks and prime rib. (303)542-9622.

Townhouse Restaurant—8th and Santa Fe Ave., daily specials 24 hours a day. (303)545-6993.

Quality Inn—800 Highway 50 W., rates start at $25.00. (303)543-6820.

Super 8 Motel—1100 Highway 50 W., rates start at $22.88. (303)545-4104.

Motel 6—at 4103 N. Elizabeth, rates start at $22.88. (303)543-8900.

KOA Pueblo—6½ miles north of junction of US 50 and I-25, take exit 108 and go north on W. Frontage Road, full hookups, separate tent area, store, showers. Price: $9.50. (303)542-2273.

Pueblo Chamber of Commerce, 302 N. Santa Fe, P.O. Box 697, Pueblo, CO. 81002, (303)542-1704.

ROCKY FORD—melon capitol of the world from watermelons to cantaloupes. It has a warm climate most of the year and lots of things to do.

Things to See and Do

Rocky Ford Wildlife Area—northeast of the city along the Arkansas River, it has many ponds which are stocked with trout, bass, and catfish for the angler. Hunters will find deer, quail, duck, geese, and small game. (licenses are required)

Holbrook Lake—only 10 miles northeast of town, it offers boating, water skiing, fishing, swimming, and overnight camping.

Arkansas Valley Fair and Exposition—held in mid-August, this is one of the oldest fairs around, being well past its 100th anniversary. It is famous for its "Watermelon Day" in which 50 tons of locally grown melons are given away. This ceremony is sometimes even opened by the Governor. The fairgrounds are on the north side of town.

Scenic Drive—through the mountains and the plains of the state.

Start by taking Highway 71 south to Highway 10 and head southwest. In Walsenburg, take US 160 southwest to La Veta and take Highway 12 south through the San Isabel National Forest with all its mountains, rivers, and hiking trails. At Trinidad, take US 350 northeast through the Comanche National Grasslands (watch for antelope and buffalo) to Highway 71 and go back to Rocky Ford to the north.

Where to Eat and Sleep

Casa Luz Restaurant—possibly one of the best Mexican restaurants in the state, it features all your favorites. Address: 1211 Elm Ave. (303)254-3557.

High Chaparral Restaurant and Motel—excellent food in the restaurant with morning and noon all you can eat buffets featuring the juicy, mouthwatering melon that made the town famous. Price of buffet $3.50. Motel is Best Western and features refrigerators in the rooms, cable TV, and an indoor pool. Price: $35.00 and up. (303)254-3616.

Rocky Ford Inn and Restaurant—a good place to stay and eat. 1710 Elm Ave. (303)254-9960.

KOA Crooked Arroya—east of Rocky Ford on US 50 (about 8 miles), has tent and RV sites, hookups, tables, toilets, showers and store. Price $8.50 and up. (303)384-9817.

Rocky Ford Chamber of Commerce, 908 Elm Ave., Rocky Ford, CO. 81067. (303)254-7483.

TRINIDAD—this little western town had many famous visitors and residents, including one-time sheriff, Bat Masterson, and Kit Carson, the well-known guide. The Santa Fe Trail made Trinidad one of its main stops on the way to the West.

Things to See and Do

Baca and Bloom Houses/Pioneer Museum—entrance is on Main St. across from the Post Office at 300 E. Main. The Baca house is adobe and two stories high built in 1869. The Bloom house is a masterpiece in Victorian architecture. It is three stories high and was built in 1882. The Pioneer Museum contains displays pertaining to the history of the West and Colorado. Hours: open from Memorial Day to Labor Day, Monday to Saturday 10 am to 4 pm, Sunday 1pm to 4 pm. (303)846-7217.

Highway 12 Loop—scenic drive, take 12 west to Walsenburg then I-25 south back to Trinidad. It is a complete loop through the San Isabel National Forest, high mountain passes, and wilderness beyond compare.

Simpson's Rest—is a sandstone bluff north of town where explorer George Simpson is buried. He allegedly saved Trinidad by leading attacking Indians away from the town to the bluff. There he hid in caves and escaped capture and death at their hands. Take Nevada or Arizona Ave. to North Ave. and turn left. Follow this to the summit, you might want to pack a picnic to enjoy while you admire the view.

A.R. Mitchell Museum of Western Art—131 W. Main St. It features work by Arthur Roy Mitchell and other nationally known artists. There is also western memoribilia, Indian artifacts, early Hispanic religious art, and more. Hours: 10 am to 4 pm, closed Sunday and holidays. Price: *Free. (303)846-4224.*

Santa Fe Trail Days—in June this art festival attracts many artists and patrons.

Labor Day Round-up—come and enjoy the rodeo, parade, barbeque, dances, fair, carnival, and food of this festival. Held Labor Day weekend.

Trinidad State Recreation Area—in the Purgatoire River Valley, travelers have been stopping here since the early Indian days according to archeologists. There is boating, water skiing, hiking trails, fishing and hunting. Campers may choose from 62 sites with modern facilities and hookups (campsites $7.00 to $10.00). Take Highway 12 from Trinidad 3 miles to the park. Price: $3.00 per car. (303)846-6951.

Wildlife Museum & Taxidermy Service—at I-25 exit 34 north of Trinidad, tour the taxidermy studio the gift shop where wildlife specimens are for sale. Hunters can have their kills stuffed here also. For a price list, write: P.O. Box 599, Aquilar, CO. 81020. (303)941-4041.

The Ludlow Monument—off of I-25 north of Trinidad, it marks the place where on April 20, 1914, 15 women and children were massacred by the Colorado State Militia and Company Men. The monument was placed by the UMWA in their memory.

Apishipa Wildlife Area—the Canyon/Desert habitat presents a unique opportunity to both hunter and nature lover. This land is full of deer, quail, Big Horn sheep and rabbits. Take US 350 to Tyrone. At Tyrone, go northwest 20 miles.

Where to Eat and Sleep

El Capitan Restaurant & Lounge—321 State St., excellent Mexican and Italian food and the best Margaritas in town. (303)846-4153.

Trinidad Donut Factory—at 130 Pine St., it serves not just breakfast of heavenly donuts, but excellent Italian dinners and pizza. Price: pizza large with cheese and two toppings $9.30. Dinners $4.95 and up, sandwiches $3.95. (303)846-9464.

Monument Lake Resort & Campground—36 miles west of Trinidad on Route 12 in the Sangre de Cristo Mountains. Good food in a wonderful atmosphere at the Kendall House Cafe, beautiful lakeside cabins, trailer and tent sites from primitive to group sites with hookups. (303)868-2226.

Trinidad/Las Animas County Chamber of Commerce, 309 Nevada, Trinidad, CO. 81082, (303)846-9285.

WILEY—is situated in southeast Colorado and though it is a small town, it is close to a series of reservoirs. For directional purposes, this book states US 50 as Wiley's location because everything in that direction uses 50. To get to US 50 from Wiley, take 287 south.

What to Do and See

Wiley Hay Day—held on the third Saturday in June, this celebration includes races and games for all ages, a parade and street dance. There are 10k, 5k, and 1 mile runs.

Reservoirs—North of Wiley are four reservoirs: Nee Grande, Nee So Pah, Nee Noshe, and Nee Shah. From Wiley go north on US 287.

Ghost Towns—Sugardale, on railroad 3 miles east of town. Sweetwater, 14 miles north. Keesee, on railroad 4 miles west of town.

Bent's Old Fort National Hstoric Site—8 miles east of La Junta on Highway 194, take US 50 west from Wiley to 194 and keep heading west, the fort will be on your left. It is open from 8:30 to 4:30 year round. It is a reconstructed fort built originally in 1833 and was the filming site for a number of major movies including *Centennial* and *Dreams West.* Visitors are able to tour all the rooms and to watch demonstrations of how our ancestors lived. Price: *Free.*

Comanche National Grasslands—take 287/385 south past Springfield and enter one part of this preserved prairie land. Or, take US 50 west and go southwest on US 350 at La Junta. Taking 350 to Trinidad will bring you to another scenic drive.

San Isabel National Forest—take US 50 to US 350 and go southwest to Trinidad. Here, take State Road 12 through the beautiful Cuchara Valley and northward to La Veta. Continue on to US 160 and go east to Walsenburg. Make sure your tank is full and take State Road 10 northeast to La Junta and back along US 50 to Wiley.

Town of Wiley, P.O. Box 128, Wiley, CO. 81092.

WRAY—come up to the friendly city in the heart of the plains of Colorado. Just 165 miles east of Denver, you can enjoy the rolling vistas and the roaming herds of buffalo.

Things to See and Do

Wray Daze—the last weekend of July brings to town a carnival extravaganza with a parade, sporting events and fun for kids both young and old.

Beecher Island Reunion—held during the third weekend of September, 16 miles southeast of Wray at the site of the Battle of Beecher Island. The party includes excellent entertainment, activities *(like the infamous Turtle Race)* for adults and children.

Wray Lions Ampitheater—1 mile southeast of town, this very scenic area offers natural beauty to observe as you get your exercise.

Stalker Pond—4 miles northwest of the city, you can camp around the stocked pond and fish to your heart's content.

Colorado State Fish Hatchery—.6 miles northwest of Wray, see how the state raises its own trout and other fish to stock its rivers and lakes. Tours are available upon request. (303)332-5382.

Where to Eat and Sleep

Goody's Gourmet Hamburgers—just next door to the Sandhiller, it features 10 different burger specialties, each guaranteed to make your mouth water.

Stalker Pond—*see above*

Sandhiller Motel & Restaurant—at the junction of US Highway

385 and Highway 34, rooms include 2 double beds, phone and color TV. Price: $30.70 for double occupancy. (303)332-4134.

Notes.

CUT ON DOTTED LINE

To receive your **FREE** Colorado State Map and other information, please check those catagories in which you are interested. Then mail this page to:

Colorado Tourism Board
1625 Broadway, Suite 1700
Denver, Colorado 80202

✓	State Map	________	Camping/Hiking
________	Hunting/Fishing	________	Dude Ranches
________	Lodging/Dining	________	Historic Districts
________	Gold Mining	________	Rodeos
________	Indians	________	Wildlife
________	Ski Areas	________	Ghost Towns

Please send information on the above subjects to:

Your Name ______________________________

Street Address ______________________________

City, State, Zip ______________________________

Signature ______________________________